The Regional Imagination

Books by Dewey W. Grantham

Hoke Smith and the Politics of the New South
The Democratic South
The United States since 1945: The Ordeal of Power
The Regional Imagination: The South and
Recent American History

Edited by Dewey W. Grantham

Following the Color Line: American Negro Citizenship in the
Progressive Era
(by Ray Stannard Baker)
The South and the Sectional Image: The Sectional Theme Since
Reconstruction
Theodore Roosevelt
(Great Lives Observed Series)
The Political Status of the Negro in the Age of FDR
(by Ralph J. Bunche)

The Regional Imagination

The South and Recent American History

Dewey W. Grantham

1979
Vanderbilt University Press
Nashville

Library of Congress Cataloging in Publication Data

Grantham, Dewey W.
  The regional imagination.

  Including bibliographical references and index.
  1. Southern States—History—1865—I. Title.
F215.G739   975'.04   78-26556
ISBN 0-8265-1207-0

To

Fletcher Melvin Green

(1895–1978)

IN MEMORIAM

Contents

Preface

The historian who seeks to describe the evolution of American society and politics in the twentieth century must do more than deal with national aggregates and political affairs in Washington. He must also examine smaller geographical units and such social categories as class, ethnic group, and race if he is to make sense of a society as large, diversified, and complex as that of the United States. The persistence of clearly identified regions in modern America, most notably the South, offers the scholar another classification for the analysis of American life. The region, when it can be used as a focus or concept, provides both a comprehensible division in its own right and a tool of analysis for the illumination of the national context.

The essays in this volume consider some of the important manifestations of regionalism in recent American history and the nature of what I have called "the regional imagination" as reflected in the experience of the American South. One of the major themes is the continuity of southern distinctiveness. The South has been and continues to be measurably different from other parts of the country. There is, moreover, an exotic quality about the region; its mystery and mystique make it, in David M. Potter's phrase, an enigma, "a kind of Sphinx on the American land." At least as early as the middle of the nineteenth century, non-Southerners began to think of the South as separate from the rest of the United States, as aberrant in attitude and defiant in mood, and as differentiated in some mysterious and irrational way from the national experience and ideals.

Nevertheless, Southerners have shared a common culture with other Americans and have responded to the cumulative effects of a national business system, powerful new transportation and communications media, migration into and out of the region, and the emergence of the modern welfare state centered in Washington. Indeed, changes in the South's economic, social, and political habits have done much to nationalize the region. The convergence in the thinking and behavior of Southerners and non-Southerners in the twentieth century constitutes a second important theme of this collection. There is a special irony in the fact that the Negro, whose proscription in the South was so long a principal source of sectional conflict, should have become in the middle of the twentieth century a dynamic force in the nationalization of all parts of the country. In any case, Southerners have become increasingly less distinguishable from other Americans, even though their historical experience has woven its own pattern into the fabric of the nation's past. Still, the gradual diminution of southern particularism has not obliterated the South's distinctiveness in our own day, although it has blurred the image in some respects.

Historically, southern sectionalism has been most conspicuous in the arena of politics, another concern of this book. The South has had its full measure of internal conflicts, and over the years the region has made concessions to the demands of national conformity. But sectional issues have frequently dominated political affairs below the Potomac. Once it became institutionalized, the one-party system was supported by the most potent economic and social interests in the section. It was skillfully defended by politicians who never failed to identify the Solid South with regional traditions and who were able to perpetuate the system by taking advantage of both local prejudices and national pressures. These essays discuss some of the revealing points of political interaction between South and North during the century since Reconstruction.

Far upstream in the course of southern sectionalism, at that juncture in our history represented by the Civil War, the South was given a psychological heritage which Robert Penn Warren has labeled "the Great Alibi," by which the region "explains, condones, and transmutes everything." The war also provided the North with a powerful myth, "the Treasury of Virtue," by which Northerners ever since have felt "redeemed by history, automatically redeemed . . . for all sins past, present, and future. . . ." Sectional unity was promoted, of course, as a means of protecting special regional interests, particularly those associated with the most affluent and influential Southerners. But the sectional theme may owe some of its vitality to the fact that many Americans have been able to externalize inner conflicts by focusing on the South as a convenient scapegoat. It should be noted that in the dialogue carried on between North and South since antebellum days, the Negro's place in American life has always assumed a position of central importance. One of this volume's themes is the interplay of Southernism, racism, and national behavior embodied in the treatment of black Americans.

Several of the chapters in this book are essays in contemporary history. They attempt to describe aspects of the recent past and to interpret them from a historical perspective. Despite its hazards and limitations, contemporary history is a field of growing vitality and usefulness in the interpretation of American society and culture. It can be especially helpful in the development of a historical consciousness that relates the present and the past. And the themes of region and race are particularly relevant to the reconstruction of our national experience since World War II, including such matters as the process of modernization, the pattern of cultural homogenization, the revival of ethnicity, the way consensus and conflict are intertwined in recent American history, and the relationship between politics and social change.

Finally, I hope these essays will provide an elaboration of "the regional imagination," not only by suggesting the role of traditional beliefs, popular imagery, and mythology in the thinking about the South, but also in demonstrating the reality that underlies southern distinctiveness, the functions of sectionalism in national politics, and how some interpreters have conceptualized the region and its significance in American history. I would also like to think that this book will contribute to an understanding and appreciation of the complexity of recent United States history as well as to the cultivation of what John Higham has described as "an integral view of human experience."

D.W.G.

Acknowledgments

I am grateful to my colleague Jacque Voegeli not only for helpful advice in the selection and organizing of the essays that comprise this book but also for his encouragement of the project. I want to thank John W. Poindexter, Director of the Vanderbilt University Press, for his continuing interest in and support of the undertaking. The essays in this volume were written over a period of two decades. They are published here substantially as they first appeared, with minor changes in capitalization, punctuation, and footnote form. I am indebted to the original publishers for permission to reprint the following essays:

"The South and the Politics of Sectionalism," in *The South and the Sectional Image: The Sectional Theme since Reconstruction,* ed. Dewey W. Grantham (New York: Harper and Row, 1967), pp. 37–55.

"The Southern Bourbons Revisited," *South Atlantic Quarterly* 60 (Summer 1961): 286–95. Copyright Duke University Press.

"Dinner at the White House: Theodore Roosevelt, Booker T. Washington, and the South," *Tennessee Historical Quarterly* 17 (June 1958): 112–30. Reprinted by permission of the Editor.

"Goebel, Gonzales, Carmack: Three Violent Scenes in Southern Politics," *Mississippi Quarterly* 11 (Winter 1958): 29–37. Reprinted by permission of the Editor.

"Black Patch War: The Story of the Kentucky and Tennessee Night Riders, 1905–1909," *South Atlantic Quarterly* 59 (Spring 1960): 215–25. Copyright Duke University Press.

"Introduction to the Torchbook Edition," in *Following the Color Line: American Negro Citizenship in the Progressive Era,* by Ray Stannard Baker (New York: Harper and Row , 1964), pp. v–xiv.

"Hoke Smith and the New Freedom, 1913–1917," in *Studies in Southern History,* ed. J. Carlyle Sitterson (Chapel Hill: University of North Carolina Press, 1957), pp. 139–51. An earlier version of this paper was presented at the annual meeting of the Southern Historical Association, Jacksonville, Florida, in November 1953.

xiii

"Editor's Introduction," in *The Political Status of the Negro in the Age of FDR*, by Ralph J. Bunche (Chicago: University of Chicago Press, 1973), pp. xi–xxx.

"The Regional Imagination: Social Scientists and the American South," *Journal of Southern History* 34 (February 1968): 3–32. Reprinted by permission of the Managing Editor.

"The South and the Reconstruction of American Politics," *Journal of American History* 53 (September 1966): 227–46. Reprinted by permission of the Managing Editor.

"Contemporary American History," in *Contemporary American History: The United States since 1945*, by Dewey W. Grantham (Washington, D.C.: American Historical Association, 1975), pp. 3–30. Copyright American Historical Association.

The publication of this volume affords me a welcome opportunity to express my admiration and affection for the distinguished historian Fletcher Melvin Green. As a mentor and friend for more than thirty years, he influenced my life far more than he could possibly have realized. Like all of his students at the University of North Carolina, I shall always be grateful for his guidance and his example. I also want to salute Mary Frances Green, a charming and valiant lady, who not only lighted a thousand candles in the life of Fletcher Green but also extended her extraordinary warmth and generosity to encompass the large circle of her husband's students and friends.

1

The South and the Politics
of Sectionalism

The publication of two remarkable books soon after
World War II—V. O. Key's *Southern Politics in State and Nation*
(1949) and C. Vann Woodward's *Origins of the New South,
1877–1913* (1951)—had a profound influence on the scholarly
investigation of the American South. The following essay,
although written many years after the appearance of the
volumes by Key and Woodward, was conceived, in some
measure at least, as a result of those two books. For
Woodward's brilliant portrayal of the late nineteenth-century
South and Key's compelling treatment of the region's politics
half a century later not only quickened my imagination and
reinforced my research interest in the modern experience of the
South; they also led me and other students to begin thinking
about the largely unexplored period that stretched from
Woodward's "origins" to Key's current "politics." The essay
reprinted here was an attempt to create an organizational
framework for the study of the South's political history since
Reconstruction. It owes a good deal to two of my earlier efforts
along the same line: "An American Politics for the South," in
The Southerner as American edited by Charles Grier Sellers, Jr.
(1960), and a series of lectures entitled *The Democratic South*
(1963). The article was originally published in *The South and the
Sectional Image* (1967).

The essay outlines the dimensions of the South's political
sectionalism since the 1870s. It describes the coalescence of the
Solid South, delineates the role of one-party politics both in the
region and in its response to national issues, and examines the
continuing clash between the forces making for southern unity

and those moving in the opposite direction. The major thesis is that despite internal conflicts and nationalizing pressures, sectionalism has been and remains a significant factor in southern politics. Once it became institutionalized, the one-party system was supported by the most powerful economic and social interests in the region. It was skillfully defended by politicians who ceaselessly identified the Democratic South with sectional traditions and who were able to perpetuate the system by taking advantage of local prejudices and national pressures.

The scholarly literature on the political history of the modern South and on contemporary southern politics has mushroomed in recent years, particularly during the last decade. This scholarship has filled in many of the gaps that existed when Key and Woodward published their seminal works. The process of documenting, analyzing, and interpreting the rise, perpetuation, and decline of the one-party South is now in full swing.

T H E Southerner, we are frequently reminded, is a peculiar man in a peculiar land. The extent of his peculiarity as an American has doubtless been exaggerated, but few people would deny that for well over a century now the South has provided the most striking example of particularism in our national experience. It was inevitable, of course, that sectional rivalries would develop in a country as large and internally diversified as the United States, and sectionalism has been a major theme of the nation's political history. "In domestic politics," wrote V. O. Key, "sectionalism represents a sort of sublimated foreign war in which one part of the country acts as a unit against the rest of the nation."[1] New England, the Middle Atlantic states, the South, the Old Northwest, the Great Plains, and other broad provinces west of the Mississippi River at one time or another have assumed a conspicuous character in the sectional typology of American politics. But the South is the great exemplar of modern sectionalism.

1. V. O. Key, Jr., with the assistance of Alexander Heard, *Southern Politics in State and Nation* (New York, 1949), p. 15.

Certain aspects of the South's political solidarity need to be noted at the outset. In the first place, southern sectionalism has seldom been incompatible with American nationalism. It is significant that the sectional rivalry engendered by economic and cultural differences was conducted, except for the great controversy of the 1850s and the resort to war in the 1860s, within the framework of a common nationalism. Southerners have always shared with other Americans the essential features of the national culture, and the seeming paradox of continuing sectionalism in a republic steadily growing in homogeneity is to be explained by the fact that acute conflicts of interest may be generated within an integrated culture.[2]

A second consideration is that historically southern sectionalism has been greatly influenced by the nature of the federal system on the one hand and by chronic threats of internal division on the other. If undesirable federal policies adopted at the behest of nonsouthern regions encouraged the political unification of the South, the federal structure of government and party politics also tempered sectional recalcitrance and promoted a degree of national involvement. It was the federal system that made possible alliances of southern spokesmen with conservatives from other regions, as well as the South's great influence in the Democratic party and its administrations in Washington. Moreover, the changing character of federalism has inevitably affected the politics of sectionalism. Whether the federal government represented intervention at the state and local levels or whether it became the source of appropriations and welfare legislation which state and local governments could not or would not provide, the growing authority of the central government relentlessly nationalized the politics of all regions, even though it frequently generated new waves of sectional dissent in the process.

At the same time, the South's political response has depended upon internal requirements for solidarity. These have not always been easily satisfied. Indeed, the contending groups spawned by the South's social structure and geography have been a continuing obstacle to the region's political unity. Recurrent social and economic cleavages have been present in virtually all southern political crises—in the interparty competition of the Old South, in the struggle over secession and southern independence, in the agrarian upheaval of the eighties and nineties, and in the factionalism of south-

2. David M. Potter, "The Historian's Use of Nationalism and Vice Versa," *American Historical Review* 67 (July 1962): 924–50.

ern politics in the twentieth century.[3] No matter how assiduously they played upon the themes of race and tradition, the advocates of sectional solidarity were never able to impose sufficient unity on the white majority to override its internal divisions for very long.

This suggests a third point that should be emphasized in an interpretation of modern southern sectionalism: the forging of the Solid South took much pulling and hauling and its completion required the better part of a generation after the Redemption of the seventies. For one thing, Republicanism did not disappear from the scene in 1877. Nor was Republicanism the only threat to the Bourbon Democrats and southern unity. Almost from the beginning Democratic leaders were faced with intraparty dissension and the emergence of independent movements that held out the dreaded possibility of a merger with the Republicans and a transfer of political control. The greatest challenge of all came in the agrarian revolt of the 1890s. This crisis was not unlike the secession crisis in that the black belts and their allies overcame their opponents and used the specter of insurgency as a means of suppressing future nonconformity. But the situation in the 1890s differed in several respects from that of the 1860s, and the outcome of the later crisis revealed the possibility of greater sectional cohesion. For one thing, most men of Whiggish persuasion had joined the Democratic party by the 1880s, giving that party overwhelming ascendancy among the most affluent and influential people of the region. In addition to their control of the black belts, the historic centers of southern wealth and power, Bourbon leaders found support in river towns and piedmont industrial centers, whose spokesmen represented the commercial and bourgeois elements associated with the "New South" movement. Moreover, the black-belt politicians strengthened their position through disproportionate representation in legislatures and party conventions and through astute use of Negro votes and alliances. Yeoman farmers and ordinary workingmen, usually supporters of the Democratic party, were unable to exert much political influence.

Furthermore, the economic privation and cultural neglect of the southern masses fostered a mood of hopelessness and political apathy. Writing in 1889, a critical and informed Virginian described the South as a backward land—a land of wretched poverty for "the six millions of Negroes who are in the depths of indigence," as well as 90 percent of the whites who had "nothing beyond the commonest

3. For an analysis of this factor and other "democratic" components of southern politics, see Dewey W. Grantham, *The Democratic South* (Athens, Ga., 1963).

necessaries of life," if that.[4] The commanding influence of the plantation element and the rising commercial interests in an environment
of minimum government and niggardly appropriations rendered the
small farmers and lower classes generally almost impotent. In such an
atmosphere political independence and experimentation were not
likely to flourish.

Meanwhile, the shining vision of the Old South, the romantic cult
of the Lost Cause, and the mythology growing up around Radical
Reconstruction were infusing the folklore of the southern whites and
erecting another support for the Solid South in politics. "We may
say," observes Robert Penn Warren, "that only at the moment when
Lee handed Grant his sword was the Confederacy born; or to state
matters another way, in the moment of death the Confederacy entered upon its immortality."[5] Southern white unity was also enormously strengthened by the Redeemers' version of Reconstruction, a
grim story of human suffering and of the southern battle for civilization. The folklore that helped sustain the Solid South was filled with
mystic overtones of white unity and heroic sacrifice in that earlier
time of trial and tribulation. The emotional attachment to the idea of
"the South," constantly reinforced by vague memories, family tales,
and endless rhetoric in public places, produced what was surely one
of the most remarkable loyalties in American history. Its rationale
that was to explain and justify "southern" politics was itself trans-
muted into a set of trusted political principles: state rights, economy
in government, southern unity, and distrust of active government,
especially in Washington.

Finally, there was the Negro. With the abolition of the Negro as
property, Wilbur J. Cash has noted, "the road stood all but wide
open to the ignoble hate and cruel itch to take him in hand which for
so long had been festering impotently in the poor whites."[6] The
temptation to draw the color line and to make the Negro the
scapegoat grew with every challenge to the precarious white solidarity of the post-Reconstruction years. Ironically, even when insurgent
movements such as the Readjusters in Virginia during the early
eighties and the fusionists in North Carolina during the nineties

4. Lewis H. Blair, *A Southern Prophecy: The Prosperity of the South Dependent Upon
the Elevation of the Negro (1889)*, ed. C. Vann Woodward (Boston and Toronto, 1964), p.
xxix.
5. Warren, *The Legacy of the Civil War: Meditations on the Centennial* (New York,
1961), p. 15.
6. Cash, *The Mind of the South* (New York, 1941), p. 113.

brought the Negro some gains, they served further to embitter the whites against him and to coerce white unity for the future.[7] And the Populists, who seemed on the verge of shattering the incipient solidarity of the region, constantly faced, in Professor Woodward's phrase, "the implacable dogmas of racism, white solidarity, white supremacy, and the bloody shirt."[8]

In withstanding the assaults of the Populists the Solid South had become institutionalized. Yet the significance of the Populist movement in the history of southern politics is not always appreciated. It invigorated the region's politics and brought into sharp relief longtime cleavages which the Redeemers had never been able to suppress completely. It brought to the surface for a moment a vigorous strain of radicalism long submerged in the stream of southern politics, led to a revival of Jeffersonian and Jacksonian principles, popularized the concept of positive government, and challenged the "New South" system and the mythology that helped uphold it. It left the region a constructive heritage, but it also contributed to the quickening pace of Negro disfranchisement and in the end served the needs of southern sectionalism.

The most distinctive attribute of political affairs in the South at the turn of the century was the overwhelming domination of the Democratic party. While in the upper South Republicanism remained strong enough to exert some influence on the practices of the majority party, the Democrats dominated state government in every commonwealth except Kentucky, which came closest of all southern states to having a genuine two-party system.[9] The structure of political solidarity created by war and Reconstruction and made more inflexible by the divisions of the 1890s proved impervious to the solvent of independent party action in this period.

The Solid South was patently real in terms of the region's Democratic loyalties. Yet the South soon entered upon an era of almost unparalleled intraparty competition. One thing that stimulated this factionalism was the continued agitation of agrarian reform groups. Populist principles survived to leaven the factional politics of the

7. Helen G. Edmonds, *The Negro and Fusion Politics in North Carolina, 1894–1901* (Chapel Hill, 1951); Charles E. Wynes, *Race Relations in Virginia, 1870–1902* (Charlottesville, 1961).

8. C. Vann Woodward, *The Burden of Southern History* (Baton Rouge, 1960). p. 150.

9. The only other southern state to elect a Republican governor between 1900 and 1918 was Tennessee, in 1910 and 1912, and that occurred only because of a bitter conflict within the Democratic party.

early twentieth-century South, while the leadership of William Jennings Bryan and the Populist program strengthened the liberal wing of the Democratic party in most southern states. Paradoxically, at the same time that constitutional changes and new election laws were disfranchising Negroes and making it more and more difficult for Republicans to offer any real opposition, the adoption of the direct primary and other democratic devices encouraged ambitious politicians who could see little hope of advancing in the established hierarchies to launch insurgent movements within the Democratic party.

Another invigorating ingredient in this era was the growing influence of southern cities and the activities of an increasing number of middle-class men and women interested in civic reforms, humanitarian causes, and "good government." In addition, the enhanced stakes of public policy at the state and municipal levels promoted the political involvement of numerous economic groups—corporations, shippers, farmers, and labor organizations—determined to protect or advance their interests through state action. Also significant was the movement, in which the South played a vital role, to nominate the Virginian Woodrow Wilson for the presidency. The Wilson movement served to give the liberal factions a kind of national base and temporarily to sharpen the bifactional politics that had been developing in the South. Wilson's election also gave new pride and satisfaction to millions of Southerners, and the South assumed an influence in Washington it had not enjoyed since the 1850s.

All of these forces contributed to the widespread and rather durable bifactionalism that characterized the politics of southern states during the first two decades of the twentieth century. In a vague and imperfect way these contending factions separated progressives from conservatives, advocates of change from champions of the status quo, and politicians who appealed to the white masses from those who were supported by the "machines" and vested interests. But if factional competition within the one-party system was vigorous and if the progressive currents ran stronger in the South than is sometimes realized, it was nevertheless true that southern sectionalism lost little of its vitality and for the most part managed to assimilate the threats to its integrity, whether they were internal or external in origin. Although an extraordinary amount of competition existed in intraparty politics during the progressive era, and this competition reflected the historic divisions and changing character of southern society, it should not be supposed that this condition approximated a two-party system. The extent and significance of such intraparty division varied from state to state and from time to time, always subject to the vagaries of the amorphous and highly personalized politics resulting from the dominance of a single party. In such politics there were no effective means to recruit and train leaders and no reliable restraints to preserve factional discipline and program coherence for any length of time.

The war years diluted the bifactionalism of the earlier period, swept many of the old leaders from the scene, and brought other changes in state and local government. But the old factionalism did not entirely disappear. Toward the end of the 1920s the latent class conflict in Louisiana provided the setting for Huey P. Long, whose leadership brought a durable and well-disciplined bifactional system into existence. At about the same time the emergence of powerful new leaders in several other states, including Edward H. Crump in Tennessee, Harry Flood Byrd in Virginia, and Eugene Talmadge in Georgia, created fresh intraparty patterns that were to survive for decades. But whatever the politics in individual states, the passing years brought no real threat to the one-party system. The danger of outside intervention was virtually nonexistent, though it was a note often heard in campaign rhetoric. Meanwhile, one-party politics provided an outlet, however vicarious, for the lowliest white Southerner as well as his most influential neighbor.

The democratization of the white South around the turn of the century may have energized one-party politics, but it also contributed to the orchestration of sectional themes under the direction of demagogues and charlatans. The excesses and irrelevancies of such leaders were perhaps evidence of the difficulties they faced in attempting to break the political domination of the vested interests, especially in the lower South. While these "men of the people" helped give politics in the South whatever form and coherence it possessed, while they evoked a fierce loyalty from their supporters and doubtless acted as a "safety valve for discontent," they tended to bring forth, as Cash said of Coleman L. Blease, "the whole tradition of extravagance, of sectionalism and Negrophobia in Southern politics." [10]

The demagogues received much of their support from the rural South, which by the 1920s was assuming a more negative role in the region's politics than during the Populist and progressive periods. The political and social influence of the county-seat governing class

10. Cash, *The Mind of the South*, p. 248.

(there were more than a thousand counties in the South in 1900) remained extraordinarily great; in most southern states no statewide political campaign and no important legislation could succeed without approval from these citadels of power. On the other hand, the widening rural-urban cleavage reflected the mounting fears and suspicions of the southern farmer, and men like Tom Watson, in V. O. Key's words, "turned the towns into whipping boys." [11] It was the rise of the city and the farmer's relative decline that caused many rural inhabitants to concentrate their reform energies on prohibition, religious fundamentalism, and cultural conformity. And it was these issues that precipitated the sharpest sectional conflict in the era of normalcy. The political outlines of this conflict were evident in the protracted struggle in the Democratic National Convention of 1924.

While the rural Deep South rebelled against the growing influence of the urban, Catholic, and "wet" East in the Democratic party, the Republican victories that disrupted the Solid South in 1928 occurred in the rim states of Virginia, North Carolina, Kentucky, Tennessee, Florida, Texas, and Oklahoma. The black belts and the areas of strongest rural, prohibition, and Protestant sentiment generally tended to support Alfred E. Smith in spite of their fears of his religion and leadership. Republican successes in 1928 came in those states with relatively few Negroes, traditional Republican strength, and economic interests that pulled them toward national integration. [12] In general these states were undergoing the most rapid economic and social change in the region. The "business progressivism" of the twenties manifested in many state capitols and the moderate increase in southern Republicanism in presidential elections reflected these economic and demographic developments. [13] But the onset of the Great Depression, the election of Franklin D. Roosevelt in 1932, and the popularity of the New Deal destroyed any hopes the Republicans had of building on the southern defections of

11. Key, *Southern Politics*, p. 118.

12. Ibid., pp. 317–29. In his perceptive analysis of this election in the South, Key observes that "the whites of the black-belt counties were bound in loyalty to the Democracy by a common tradition and anxiety about the Negro. Whites elsewhere could afford the luxury of voting their convictions on the religious and prohibition issues." But he also notes that "a complex of factors—ruralism, cotton-growing, plantation organization, intense Reconstruction memories—as well as anxieties about the racial equilibrium characterized the Democratic areas." Ibid., pp. 319, 329.

13. For an able interpretation of progressive currents in the South during the 1920s, see George B. Tindall, "Business Progressivism: Southern Politics in the Twenties," *South Atlantic Quarterly* 62 (Winter 1963): 92–106.

1928. Republicanism in the region dropped during the thirties to the lowest levels since the Civil War.

The Wilson administration had earlier demonstrated how even a liberal Democratic regime in Washington might increase the South's attachment to the Democratic party. While Wilson's administration contributed to the liberalization of southern politics and tended to involve southern politicians in national affairs, it did not seriously challenge the South's political unity. Wilson discovered that it was necessary to cooperate with conservatives from the South in order to enact his legislative program, and the result in many instances was to strengthen the entrenched elements in the region at the expense of those challenging the status quo.[14] White Southerners in general, moreover, found much in the Wilson program to applaud and little that threatened the institutions and ideas that sustained the Solid South.

Franklin D. Roosevelt's leadership and program tended to broaden and nationalize the outlook of southern congressmen, forced New Deal issues into state and local political contests, and threatened the South's traditional social and economic structure far more than had the Wilson administration. Yet the section's response to Roosevelt and the New Deal was ambivalent. Southerners were "so painfully in need of succor," as Frank Freidel has said, "that they desperately sought federal aid; yet the New Deal inevitably threatened to upset the status quo and alter some of the cherished institutions upon which they fervently believed the very existence of Southern civilization depended."[15] At the same time, Roosevelt found it necessary to make concessions to southern leaders in Congress, who once more dominated committee chairmanships and exerted great influence on all parliamentary matters.[16] Although the economic conservatism of these men led them increasingly to

14. On this point see Arthur S. Link, "Woodrow Wilson and the Democratic Party," *Review of Politics* 18 (April 1956): 146–56.

15. Freidel, *F.D.R. and the South* (Baton Rouge, 1965), p. 35.

16. According to James MacGregor Burns, Roosevelt was "the prisoner of the concessions he had made to the regulars—especially Southern Democrats—in gaining the nomination. He had recognized and hence strengthened conservative Democrats in Congress who had gone along with his program." Burns, *The Deadlock of Democracy: Four-Party Politics in America*, Spectrum ed. (Englewood Cliffs, N.J., 1963), p. 173.

In the Seventy-third Congress (1933–35) Southerners held nine of the fourteen major standing committee chairmanships in the Senate and twelve of seventeen such chairmanships in the House. *Official Congressional Directory*, 73 Cong., 1 Sess. (Washington, 1933), pp. 175–80, 191–203.

criticize the president and to vote against his proposals, there was no open break in the ranks of southern Democracy.[17] Roosevelt's growing preoccupation with the gathering war in Europe, the stimulus the war gave to southern patriotism and internationalism, and the mounting prosperity and economic development of the early 1940s combined to moderate southern discontent with parts of the New Deal. Depression, New Deal, and World War II had brought vast changes to all of America, but on the surface at least, the South's political solidarity seemed almost as great when the war ended as it had been at the dawn of the century.[18]

Perhaps it was fortuitous that just at this time a major study of southern politics should be getting under way at the University of Alabama, supported by a grant from the Rockefeller Foundation.[19] This project resulted in the publication of V. O. Key's magisterial volume, *Southern Politics in State and Nation* (1949), the most systematic and searching analysis of "the electoral process in the South" ever undertaken. For the student of southern political history one of the most valuable aspects of this remarkable book is the fact that it examined southern regional unity at its strongest, or at least before the crevices in the walls of the Solid South had become readily visible. For that reason it provides a convenient summary of all the factors which over the years had become institutionalized in the old order.

Key demonstrated that three-quarters of a century after the end of Reconstruction, race and the position of blacks dominated southern politics; the Negro question continued to suppress any meaningful political divisions among white Southerners. Key showed that the areas of greatest Negro population and fertile soil—the black belts— had long served as the backbone of southern conservatism. He showed how the black counties in a state like Alabama allied themselves with the "big mules" of Birmingham and Mobile to dominate the state's politics, and how these elements used the South's strategic position in Congress, and particularly in the Senate, to promote political regionalism and prevent federal meddling that might

17. For evidence of southern disillusionment with Roosevelt and for the origins of the so-called southern Democratic-Republican coalition, see John Robert Moore, "Senator Josiah W. Bailey and the 'Conservative Manifesto' of 1937," *Journal of Southern History* 31 (February 1965): 21–39.

18. For the persistence of southern sectionalism, see Fletcher M. Green, "Resurgent Southern Sectionalism, 1933–1955," *North Carolina Historical Review* 33 (April 1956): 222–40.

19. See Roscoe C. Martin's Foreword to Key, *Southern Politics*, pp. v–viii.

threaten their control. The greatest cohesive factor among southern congressmen was "a common determination to oppose external intervention in matters of race relations."[20]

Despite the persistence of mountain Republicanism in Virginia, North Carolina, and Tennessee and a perceptible increase of Republican voting in presidential elections in such states as Texas, Florida, and Arkansas, Key noted the general continuation of the ancient prejudice against the Republican party. Although Republicans were strong enough in the upper South to force a measure of discipline and continuity on the majority party, they operated everywhere under serious handicaps. They were confronted with Democratic control of voting procedures, discrimination in the apportionment of legislatures, and congressional gerrymandering. In addition, the infrequency with which Republican primaries, candidates, and campaigns were offered limited the appeal of the party. Even had Republican leaders sought to attract a larger numbers of voters, on many issues they would have had to adopt positions out of line with the conservative state governments provided by the Democrats and with their own party's national conventions. Most southern Republicans did not really want to win elections, except in restricted local areas.[21]

As for the Democratic party in most southern states, Key described it as "merely a holding-company for a congeries of transient squabbling factions, most of which fail by far to meet the standards of permanence, cohesiveness, and responsibility that characterize the political party."[22] Whether the dominant party reflected the bifactionalism of Senator Harry Flood Byrd's Virginia or Florida's atomized "every man for himself" structure or some in-between position, one looked in vain for a continuing statewide organization with a recognizable program. Whether the basic conflict of the state's internal politics involved a clash of disparate geographic sections, the existence of a state machine, factions led by colorful personalities, a modified class politics, or a general free-for-all, the characteristic political system operated within a framework of limited suffrage, a low level of voter participation, the repression of meaningful issues, and the isolation of the South from presidential campaigns. Although the white primaries were under mounting legal and political attack, they had been invaded by relatively few Negroes, and the restricted white electorates were guarded by the

---

20. Key, *Southern Politics*, p. 352.
21. "They have been big fish in little ponds and they have liked it." Alexander Heard, *A Two-Party South?* (Chapel Hill, 1952), p. 97.
22. Key, *Southern Politics*, p. 16.

poll tax (in seven states) and a host of other suffrage qualifications. Rural dominance was widely apparent, made all the more incongruous by a substantial farm population too depressed to play any part in the political process, on the one hand, and powerful commercial farmers who dominated the American Farm Bureau Federation and allied themselves with business interests, on the other. And while growing industrialization and urbanization had brought new concerts of political power in the form of organized business, they had not introduced the urban masses to the practices of democracy. In contrast to the multiplicity of factions in state politics, the Democratic party in national politics was the Solid South, the instrument for conducting the region's "foreign relations" with the rest of the nation. "The suffrage problems of the South," concluded Professor Key, "can claim a closer kinship with those of India, of South Africa, or of the Dutch East Indies than with those of, say, Minnesota."[23]

While demonstrating the impressive continuity of southern sectionalism, Key seemed to find, in the region's recurring intraparty factionalism and particularly in the New Deal's impact, the promise of more rapid political change in the coming years. This acceleration would be the consequence of vast economic and social alterations clearly evident at the time Key wrote, and of the increasing intervention by the national government in the region's affairs. The forces of change, whether originating in impersonal economic factors or in the nation's new federalism, would inevitably upset—perhaps were already upsetting—the balance-of-power enclaves that had long prevailed in the southern states. And when that equilibrium was threatened, the champions of the status quo turned almost instinctively to the race question, the touchstone of white solidarity.

The year before the publication of *Southern Politics* the Truman administration's civil rights program and the forthright civil rights platform adopted by the Democratic National Convention precipitated the first sharp reaction. The Dixiecrat movement of 1948, which repudiated the Democratic ticket and carried four Deep South states, provided the southern unifiers with an opportunity for a kind of reconnoitering venture.[24] In 1948 they could scarcely have perceived

---

23. Ibid., p. 661.

24. The Dixiecrat movement gathered most of its strength from racial fears, though some Southerners found in it a means of expressing their hostility toward New Deal and Fair Deal economic policies without having to embrace Republicanism. See William G. Carleton, "The Fate of Our Fourth Party," *Yale Review* 38 (Spring 1949): 449–59; Sarah McCulloh Lemmon, "The Ideology of the 'Dixiecrat' Movement," *Social Forces* 30 (December 1951): 162–71; and Emile B. Ader, "Why the Dixiecrats Failed," *Journal of Politics* 15 (August 1953): 356–69.

the full potentialities of sectional defiance and southern white unity
that eventually would be available to them. That came with the
Brown v. *Board of Education* decision in 1954 and the crisis that slowly
built up during the years that followed. Since 1954, wrote C. Vann
Woodward in 1965, the South "has been more deeply alienated and
thoroughly defiant than it has at any time since 1877." Tormented by
a "minority psychology and rejection anxiety," it has been "reliving
an old trauma." All of the old fears seemed suddenly to be realized in
a kind of Frankenstein created for the South by unknowing and
uncaring fellow Americans: "Negroes at the ballot boxes, federal
bayonets in the streets, a rebirth of scalawags, a new invasion of
carpetbaggers, and battalions of abolitionists and Yankee school-
marms in the form of Freedom Riders and sit-ins and CORE and
SNCC and COFO." In such a situation a besieged minority "could
not afford the luxury of internal division."[25]

The old defense mechanism was quickly set in motion. The black
belts and other traditional centers of southern unity reached out to
solidify white sentiment in surrounding areas. In these subregions
and throughout the Deep South the race question became the over-
riding issue in politics. Southern recalcitrance manifested itself in
talk of nullification and "interposition," in "massive resistance," in a
"Southern Manifesto" and lengthy southern filibusters in Congress,
in tickets of unpledged presidential electors, in popular acclaim of a
new group of Dixie firebrands, and in defeat of political leaders who
offered any opposition to the program of resistance. So obsessed
were southern legislatures with questions of race that by the end of
1956 no fewer than 106 prosegregation measures had been adopted in
the eleven ex-Confederate states, and the legislative defiance continued without letup.[26] Meanwhile, the burgeoning White Citizens'
Councils spread across the South, joined by a score of other voluntary defense organizations. Fiery crosses lit up the skies, schools and
churches were bombed, and resistance in the Deep South reached
the proportions of an insurrection. The moderation of the old-style
paternalists was overwhelmed by the rampant Negrophobia—and

25. C. Vann Woodward, "From the First Reconstruction to the Second," *Harper's
Magazine* 230 (April 1965): 128–29.

26. For a survey of southern resistance, see Benjamin Muse, *Ten Years of Prelude:
The Story of Integration Since the Supreme Court's 1954 Decision* (New York, 1964). By
1964, reported a writer for the Southern Regional Council, the number of laws enacted
by southern legislatures to circumvent desegregation had reached 379. Margaret Long,
"The Dream—Ten Years Later," *The Progressive* 28 (May 1964): 21–22. See also *Southern
School News* 10 (May 1964): 1B.

the Gavin Stevenses surrendered to the Snopeses.[27] A sinister malaise rolled like a heavy fog over the land, bringing widespread racial estrangement, intimidation of Negroes, and in some states an intellectual blockade that rivaled that of the 1850s.[28]

This was more than a matter of race. A good deal of the South's mass political protest was an expression of resentments and fears originating in stagnant and declining areas. In a more general way southern protest in the fifties and sixties was intensified because the region was propelled almost overnight into an urbanized and industrialized age. The resulting tensions produced political uncertainty, reinforced southern conservatism, and stimulated the nostalgia for traditional values and symbols.[29]

Many well-meaning Southerners rallied to the defense of the "southern way of life," and it was apparent that the old sectional shibboleths retained much of their magic. Yet there was an element of unreality, of parody, in the appeal to hallowed traditions of former years. Take the survival of the Confederate legend. "This legend," remarks Denis W. Brogan, "is now less an heroic memory than poison in the blood; it recalls less Chancellorsville, or even Nashville, than Oxford, Mississippi, with Ross Barnett as the poor man's Jefferson Davis."[30] If southern resistance to internal change and national conformity parodied the traditions which in an earlier day contrib-

---

27. The ironic denouement of this tragedy, writes Walker Percy, was that "the Compsons and Sartorises should not only be defeated by the Snopeses but that in the end they should join them." Percy, "Mississippi: The Fallen Paradise," *Harper's Magazine* 230 (April 1965): 167.

28. One feature of this resistance was a vigorous effort in several states of the lower South to restrict black participation in politics by tightening voter registration laws and purging the voter lists. In many instances the local registrars who applied these measures hardly needed additional weapons to discriminate against prospective Negro voters. See, for example, Joseph L. Bernd and Lynwood M. Holland, "Recent Restrictions Upon Negro Suffrage: The Case of Georgia," *Journal of Politics* 21 (August 1959): 487–513. The voting rights legislation of 1965 was designed to counter these disfranchising tactics.

29. The South's emergence as the section most strongly opposed to foreign aid and most other "international" programs in Congress seems to be a political manifestation of the fears and uncertainties produced by these social and economic changes. There is a decided correlation between the areas of strongest southern "unilateralism" and those most concerned with race politics. See Charles O. Lerche, Jr., "Southern Congressmen and the 'New Isolationism,'" *Political Science Quarterly* 75 (September 1960): 321–37, and *The Uncertain South: Its Changing Patterns of Politics in Foreign Policy* (Chicago, 1964).

30. Brogan, "The Impending Crisis of the Deep South," *Harper's Magazine* 230 (April 1965): 148.

uted to regional solidarity, it was also characterized by a foreknowl-
edge of defeat that differed in a profound way from the expectations
of the past. For however frenzied their defiance and however exhila-
rated they might have been during moments of tactical triumph,
Southerners were not really hopeful. They did not expect to win. In a
sense the South was only playing a role, a role to which it had long
been accustomed. The classic pattern of that role, according to Joseph
Margolis, was fixed far back in the section's history. It was a role
"involving open and organized antagonism construed as the devoted
defense of principle, defeat construed as invasion, moral criticism
construed as the imposition of penalties, and finally continuing loyalty to a lost cause construed as the solidarity of a cultured and
homogeneous people in occupation."[31]

Champions of the status quo and of southern political unity
could find little reassurance in the changes in the region's politics
since World War II. In desperation they themselves set the example of
disrupting the Democratic South in 1948 through third-party action,
and many of them eventually shifted to the Republican party. The
1950s brought the two-party system in presidential elections to the
South; in presidential elections since 1948, every southern state except Arkansas and North Carolina voted Republican at least once. In
the meantime, southern influence in the Democratic party continued
to decline, and southern congressmen were repeatedly unable to
prevent the passage of civil rights legislation which the national
party had recommended. Negro voting in most southern states became an important new factor in political life, and in the early 1960s
the reapportionment of state legislatures set in motion by the federal
courts foretold a drastic shift in the locus of political power in state
government. In one way or another all of these developments
threatened the old-time southern sectionalism.

But if the Solid South had disappeared in presidential contests
and if the currents of southern politics were being altered by rapid
social and economic changes, it was still possible in the mid-sixties
to speak of political sectionalism below the Potomac. In the nation's
political arithmetic the South remained a significant factor. Except in
a few scattered localities, the Republican party had not seriously
challenged the entrenched Democrats at the congressional, state, and

---

31. Margolis, "The Role of the Segregationist," *AAUP Bulletin* 43 (December
1957): 610–14.

local levels.[32] Most Southerners continued to think of themselves as Democrats. As late as 1961, 60 percent of the white respondents in a survey carried out by Professors Donald R. Matthews and James W. Prothro characterized themselves as Democrats, as compared with 14 percent who thought of themselves as Republicans.[33]

The tangled skein of traditional loyalties, institutionalized inertia, and vested interests make it difficult for Republicans to extend their challenge below the presidential level. Considerations involving offices and patronage restrain many politicians from leaving the Democratic party; local political elites are naturally determined to maintain their control;[34] and favorable public policies and beneficial concessions often dampen the desire of businessmen for change.[35] The disproportionate power of rural areas and the lack of organization among industrial and urban masses facilitate the domination of state and local government by business interests and other conservative elements. The result is that the most affluent and powerful Southerners, many of whom have long criticized Democratic policies emanating from Washington, find little reason to complain about state and local policies. Nor have they been inclined to support Republican candidates for Congress.

Many Southerners think of the Democratic party in terms of its southern and congressional wing. Southerners constitute the bulwark of what James M. Burns describes as the congressional Democratic party, "the John Garner-Howard Smith-Harry Byrd-John McClellan congressional Democrats" in contrast to "the Roosevelt-

32. In 1965 the thirteen southern states had only 3 Republican senators and 18 Republican representatives (out of 119) in Congress. Oklahoma had the only Republican governor in the region. Although every southern state legislature had at least one Republican member, the total number of Republicans in the region's thirteen legislatures was only 44 senators and 137 representatives. See *Congressional Quarterly Weekly Report* 22 (November 6, 1964): 2644, and ibid. (November 20, 1964): 2709.

33. Matthews and Prothro, "Southern Images of Political Parties: An Analysis of White and Negro Attitudes," in *The American South in the 1960's*, ed. Avery Leiserson (New York, 1964), p. 84.

34. The political power and patronage at the courthouse level in such a state as Texas (with 254 counties) is a weighty factor in resisting change and perpetuating the one-party system.

35. In Arkansas, for example, the utilities, bankers (some of whom have the use of state deposits without paying any interest), wholesale and retail liquor dealers (who benefit from a fair-trade law and guaranteed markups), the American Farm Bureau Federation, and local officials like the county judges (who oppose stringent state regulation of purchases) all act as a drag on positive government at the state level.

Truman-Stevenson-Kennedy presidential Democrats."[36] The typical southern congressman is a conservative, and his powerful position makes him both a source of federal money and an effective instrument in the fight against the national party's liberalism. Southern congressional influence is reflected in the fact that in the current Congress Southerners serve as chairmen of ten of the sixteen standing committees in the Senate and thirteen of twenty such committees in the House.[37] The so-called "conservative coalition" of southern Democrats and Republicans is still an important force in Congress. Southern Democrats and northern Democrats took opposing stands on 24 percent of the 1964 session's roll-call votes on such issues as foreign policy, civil rights, welfare programs, and reapportionment. Although the conservative coalition was evident on only 15 percent of the roll-call votes that year, it had appeared on 28 percent as recently as 1961.[38]

The politics of race, as might be expected, continues to inhibit a more realistic division among Southerners and to perpetuate sectional attitudes and practices. It has been the principal factor in frustrating the liberal inclinations of a sizable group of southern congressmen. In the Deep South the consequences of intense Negrophobia included both the Dixiecrat successes of 1948 and the Goldwater victories of 1964, in addition to a virtual monopoly of state politics. The "New Know Nothingism" went far to gloss over the economic and social cleavages in these states and to impede the halting process of political transformation. Small white farmers and

36. Burns, *The Deadlock of Democracy*, pp. 197, 200. "The congressional Democratic leaders," writes Burns (p. 316), "have an ideal strategy: they can oppose the presidential Democrats in elections and in Washington, all the while benefiting by the victories of liberal congressmen in the North, who will return to Washington to form a coalition in Congress with the congressional Democrats so that the latter may retain their chairmanships and their control of Congress." For Burns's analysis of the southern influence, see ibid., pp. 271–74, 311–16.

37. In addition Southerners serve as chairmen of the Select Committee on Small Business in both houses and as Democratic Whip and secretary of the Democratic Conference in the Senate. *Official Congressional Directory*, 89 Cong., 1 Sess. (Washington, 1965), pp. 243–47, 255–63. In the Eighty-fourth Congress (1955-1957) Southerners held eight of thirteen standing committee chairmanships in the Senate and ten of fifteen in the House. Ibid., 84 Cong., 1 Sess. (Washington, 1955), pp. 207–11, 217–23.

38. In 1961 the coalition won almost 50 percent of these votes in the Senate and 70 percent in the House. See "On Conservative Coalition," *Congressional Quarterly Weekly Report* 19 (November 3, 1961): 1796–1805; "'Conservative Coalition' Appeared on 15% of Roll Calls," ibid. 22 (November 27, 1964): 2741–50; and "Democrats from North and South Split on 24% of Votes," ibid. (December 25, 1964): 2835–40.

members of labor unions frequently succumbed to the blandish-
ments of racist demagogues, and in some areas yesterday's liberalism
became today's reactionary politics.

In Alabama the old regional factionalism rapidly receded as the
northern and southeastern parts of the state joined the black belt in
their racial apprehension.[39] In Louisiana, where the electorate had
long tended to divide along class lines based on economic issues, the
race question disrupted the South's most durable and ideological
bifactionalism; the northern hill parishes, stronghold of the Long
faction, eschewed economic concerns in order to concentrate on
race.[40] In Georgia the old intraparty cleavage disintegrated under the
impact of the race issue, the effects of the county-unit system, and
the emergence of Herman Talmadge as the state's dominant political
leader.[41] Even in Texas, where racial matters are relatively unimpor-
tant, the race issue inhibited the natural tendency of East Texas
politicians to support liberal policies. Meanwhile, Virginia and Arkansas succumbed to the politics of race, showing that the virus of
political racism was not limited to the lower South. In some states
outside the Deep South the civil rights movement brought a reaction
that hurt liberal candidates. While the passage of comprehensive
civil rights legislation has freed southern congressmen in some respects, they remain acutely sensitive in this area, always ready to
rally to the defense of the "southern" position.[42]

39. The penalties of being "hoisted on one's own rhetoric" in a politics of race is
well put by Everett C. Hughes: "To be elected to office a man declares that he will
resist racial change to the death; thus he has made compromise, the essence of politics,
impossible. If he retreats, he will be destroyed, politically and perhaps in other ways
by the extremists whose cause he has espoused." Hughes, "The Sociological Point of
View," in *The Deep South in Transformation: A Symposium*, ed. Robert B. Highsaw
(University, Ala., 1964), p. 72.

40. The religious issue has also been a factor in recent Louisiana politics, separating the Protestant parishes of the north from the Catholic parishes of the south. A
Catholic candidate ran strongly in the Democratic gubernatorial primary in 1960 and
1964, in addition to John F. Kennedy's appearance on the national ticket in 1960. Race
and religion may well have interrupted the shift to rational Republicanism in
Louisiana. See Robert J. Steamer, "Southern Disaffection with the National Democratic Party," in *Change in the Contemporary South*, ed Allan P. Sindler (Durham, N.C.,
1963), pp. 160–70.

41. Joseph L. Bernd, *Grass Roots Politics in Georgia: The County Unit System and the
Importance of the Individual Voting Community in Bifactional Elections, 1942–1954* (Atlanta, 1960).

42. Former Representative Frank E. Smith of Mississippi, himself a victim of the
politics of race, has recently written: "With the rare exception of a few who represent
urban or border districts, all members of Congress from the South for the past fifteen

The course of southern sectionalism since Reconstruction can be roughly divided into three phases. During the first, from the 1870s to the end of the century, regional unity was still being forged. Despite the declining threat of federal intervention, Republicanism remained significant in many areas, and independent movements reflecting longtime social and geographic divisions disrupted the one-party harmony. In turning back the greatest of these insurgent movements, Populism, the champions of Democratic solidarity revived to fever pitch the question of the Negro's role in southern life. They ushered in the second major epoch in the history of modern southern sectionalism, the first three decades of the twentieth century. Although various internal differences were manifest in state and local politics during this period, in national politics southern unity was at its peak. The Wilson administration threatened southern political influence only indirectly, if at all, and the South enjoyed the new experience of contributing substantially to the legislative program of the national government and receiving significant federal appropriations without any real threat of outside intervention.[43] Near the end of this period, in the election of 1928, the gradual growth of the Democratic party outside the South and the economic development of the peripheral states of the section brought a temporary disruption of the Solid South. Ironically, the social and political fears of the Deep South weakened the status of the national Democratic party throughout the region and made it possible for the more diversified rim states to vote Republican.

The New Deal brought the South into still another phase in the evolution of its sectionalism. Momentarily, the Great Depression and the Roosevelt administration reversed the secular trend toward Republicanism on the basis of economic and demographic changes; but in the long run the developments of the 1930s and 1940s encouraged the fragmentation of the Solid South. For one thing, the changing nature of the national Democratic party and the shrinking impor-

---

years have been identified as segregationists and opponents of civil rights legislation. . . . The extremist members are not only accepted as the spokesmen for the South, they are also in a position to keep forcing the Southern position to even further extremes. All other members are their prisoners, because no one can afford a vote which does not coincide with the racist opposition to all civil rights." *Congressman from Mississippi* (New York, 1964), pp. 117–18.

43. There was probably a vague uneasiness in the minds of some southern politicians during the Wilson era concerning the future control of the Democratic party and the possibilities of federal legislation in the interest of truly national purposes.

tance of the South in it began to eat away at the old assumption that Democratic control and defense of the "southern" position were synonymous. Moreover, while the New Deal brought desperately needed federal money to the South, it also brought increasing federal intervention and the slow alteration of internal social and economic relations. The economic expansion of the war years and the postwar prosperity encouraged the region's reaction against the national standards and welfare programs associated with the New Deal. Yet the South remained wedded to the Democratic party until mid-century, when the overt threat of a federally supported movement for Negro rights brought a recrudescence of sectional feeling and resort to all of the old sectional defenses. Paradoxically, this protest was itself the opening wedge in the shattering of southern solidarity and the growing attractiveness of the Republican party.

The potent influence of race, the strategic role of southern congressmen, the predominance of Democrats in state and local politics, and the fact that Lyndon B. Johnson now occupies the White House are all likely to impede the spread of more competitive politics in the South. Nevertheless, it is clear that the region's political solidarity has grown weaker in recent years, and at some point between the forging of the Solid South during the quarter-century after Reconstruction and the middle of the twentieth century the old southern sectionalism reached its zenith and began a slow and uncertain decline. While this was happening, the circumstances that nourished political regionalism underwent a bewildering change. The role of the Democratic party as the guardian of southern solidarity and the role of the Republican party as the perennial threat to southern interests were reversed. The present South no longer has a clearly defined economic interest that sets it apart from the rest of the country. White attitudes toward blacks are widely shared from Virginia to Texas, but individual states and subregions have differed enormously in their political responses to crises in race relations, and Negroes are steadily increasing their leverage in southern politics.

Despite the great transformation of the South since 1945, its political metamorphosis will not be accomplished overnight. This is particularly true of the Deep South, where political affairs are still dominated by racism, demagogic leadership, and economic and cultural backwardness. The most durable political changes seem to be taking place in the upper South and in states such as Texas and Florida, which have experienced rapid economic development while being relatively unconcerned about the race issue. Southern congressmen continue to display a conspicuously regional outlook, though this too is changing in the outer South and the metropolitan areas. For the region as a whole this much can be said: the nationalizing influence of the federal government and the national parties, the emerging role of blacks and other less-advantaged groups in political life, and the state-by-state removal of the race issue as the major determinant in politics will eventually complete the erosion of southern sectionalism.

2

The Southern Bourbons Revisited

Bourbonism is one of those words, like Populism, that resound through the corridors of modern southern politics. Indeed, it became a protean concept in the politics of the New South. While never susceptible to precise definition, the term was widely used by contemporaries to refer to the conservative regimes that dominated politics in the southern states from the end of Reconstruction to the Populist upheaval of the 1890s. Historians have also used the expression, both to describe the post-Reconstruction era and to characterize an enduring element in the region's politics. The Bourbons, it appears, left a heritage of some importance to later generations of Southerners. According to George B. Tindall, they succeeded in reconciling tradition with innovation. "The Bourbons," Tindall wrote in *The Persistent Tradition in New South Politics* (1975), "supplied a thesis, the Populists set up an antithesis, and the Progressives worked out a synthesis which governed southern politics through the first half of the twentieth century." Bourbonism has also been used to identify a political type. Numan V. Bartley, for instance, referred to the politicians and political activists who led the massive resistance campaign as "neobourbons." "Their social, economic, and political outlook was in the tradition of nineteenth century bourbonism," Bartley observed in *The Rise of Massive Resistance: Race and Politics in the South during the 1950's* (1969), "and, as an earlier generation of bourbons sought to end the First Reconstruction, neobourbons strove to crush the Second Reconstruction."

Although scholars continue to differ over the meaning and significance of Bourbonism in southern political history, recent interpretations no longer treat the phenomenon as one-dimensional and stereotypical. Southern Bourbons have scarcely been rehabilitated by this new scholarship, but the character and ramifications of their policies and values in such areas as race relations, economics, and social issues have been explored much more adequately during the last decade and a half. This revisionism was just making its appearance when the following essay was published in 1961. It comments on some of the implications in the early reassessment of the Bourbon era, maintains that Bourbonism should be viewed in juxtaposition with the agrarian revolt of the 1890s, and remarks on the sharp impact and lasting influence of southern Populism.

Readers may be struck by the extent of the fresh scholarly writings on the period dominated by the southern Bourbons. At least three scholarly monographs can now be added to the pioneering state studies of Allen J. Going and Judson C. Ward. These books are William Ivy Hair, *Bourbonism and Agrarian Protest: Louisiana Politics, 1877–1900* (1969); Alwyn Barr, *Reconstruction to Reform: Texas Politics, 1876–1906* (1971); and Roger L. Hart, *Redeemers, Bourbons, & Populists: Tennessee, 1870–1896* (1975). The racial attitudes of the Bourbons are analyzed in these and other works, including Joseph H. Cartwright's solid study, *The Triumph of Jim Crow: Tennessee Race Relations in the 1880s* (1976). Paul M. Gaston's *The New South Creed: A Study in Southern Mythmaking* (1970) also illuminates the age of the Bourbon leaders. While eschewing use of the term *Bourbonism*, Gaston shows that the Bourbons contributed to the formulation of the New South creed and to the program that grew out of what he describes as "a subtle interaction between national ideals and achievements on the one hand and regional aspirations and failures on the other." One scarcely needs to add that if the essay of 1961 were being written in 1978, some additional questions would have to be raised and some new interpretations considered.

FOR a group of leaders referred to by one writer as "figments of medieval imagination," the southern Bourbons exerted a remarkably pervasive and durable influence upon the region south of the Potomac. As Redeemers of the southern states from the

Radical Reconstruction regimes, the Bourbons established a hegemony that prevailed from Richmond to Austin for the better part of two decades. How thoroughly they undid the work of the Reconstruction Radicals is still not altogether clear, but the fact that the dominant features of the New South were developed during the Bourbon era has been incontestably demonstrated in the writings of recent southern historians. As C. Vann Woodward has well said, ". . . it was not the Radicals nor the Confederates but the Redeemers who laid the lasting foundations in matters of race, politics, economics, and law for the modern South."

Biographies of Bourbon leaders, monographic studies of individual states during the period of Bourbon control, and especially the collective portrait of the Redeemers painted by Professor Woodward in his *Origins of the New South, 1877–1913* (1951) have during the last generation sharply drawn the lineaments of the Bourbon countenance. Despite the implications of the term *Bourbon*, these Southerners were not men who had learned nothing and forgotten nothing. Their nostalgia for the past glories of their section was not strong enough to cause them to spend much time looking back. Although they paid homage to the beautiful and the brave in the antebellum South and identified themselves with the romantic cult of the Confederacy, they urged their fellow Southerners to face the future. Convinced that economic progress was the key to the South's problems, they associated themselves with the business interests and became ardent advocates of northern investments in the South, of southern industrialization, and of sectional reconciliation. The state governments under their leadership reduced taxes, starved public service agencies and eleemosynary institutions, and made economy in government a cardinal virtue. They celebrated laissez faire as ardently as any robber baron. They created the Solid South, or at least the illusion of its solidarity, and perfected a working alliance with eastern conservatives in national politics. Although they did not absolutely proscribe Negro participation in politics, they characterized themselves as the defenders of white supremacy, and in their efforts to overcome the independents and dissenters who occasionally challenged their control, their use of the race question took on the character of a fine art. Yet, as modern historians have shown, it was difficult for the Bourbons to secure political unity, and the region paid a high price when it was persuaded to buy their bill of goods.

There is some evidence in a few recent articles and books that historians are beginning to view the southern Bourbons through lenses that are less darkly colored than was true a few years ago. A good example of this new approach is Nash K. Burger's and John K. Bettersworth's *South of Appomattox* (1959), which sketches the lives of ten Confederate leaders during and after Reconstruction. The authors of this work declare that it was "the South that these Confederate leaders shaped and reshaped and to an amazing degree were able to preserve that still lives and asserts itself in the region's concern for its past and the traditional values, its attachment to the land, its opposition to outside interference, and its insistence upon a caste system that manifests itself in racial apartness." Burger and Bettersworth praise the "Brigadiers" and other Redeemers for effecting through their "steadying conservatism" a policy of peace and reconciliation between North and South that silenced the northern radicals and restrained the agrarian insurgents in many southern states. They suggest that it may well have been the rebel "Brigadiers" who saved the country, not the Radicals, who had claimed the honor only to strive for a decade to keep the South out of the Union.

An even more favorable estimate of these leaders is contained in a paper by Francis Butler Simkins on "The Southern Bourbons: An Appraisal," which was presented at the annual meeting of the American Historical Association in 1960. In this provocative paper Professor Simkins calls for a reinterpretation of the role of the Bourbon leaders in southern history. He seems to feel that the present generation of historians (at one point he speaks of "socialist-inclined critics") has unjustly maligned the Bourbons and deprived them of proper recognition as eminently wise and constructive men. He admits that the Bourbons were not angels, but reminds us that their misdeeds were duplicated in other parts of the country during the same era and that they were only reflecting the spirit of the age. In support of his own eulogistic evaluation of these leaders, he asserts that they led Southerners into the mainstream of American capitalism and won the approval of Northerners for their race relations policies—and all without sacrificing "the pageantry and rhetoric of the sentimental South." He has a special word of approbation for the Bourbon Democrats' accomplishment in getting around "the dreaded penalty of obeying the constitutional amendments that supposedly conferred equal civil and political rights upon the Negro." The challenge to Bourbon ascendancy, he says, was brief and ineffective; even the most zealous of the agrarian radicals soon accepted the Bourbon dispensation. The result is that Bourbonism is as strong today as it ever was. Outside capital comes into the region in increasing amounts, and if it brings absentee ownership, it also brings Southerners superior goods, substantial labor opportunities, generous commissions—and all on their own terms, or at least with a minimum of interference with "the Southern way of life." In praising the diplomacy of the Bourbon leaders, Simkins finds a modern parallel in the way Virginia and North Carolina politicians have accepted token integration in public education as a means of encouraging the southward flow of capital investments.

One of the difficulties in attempting an appraisal of the Bourbons is the problem of defining the term. As John K. Bettersworth has said, "One of the most indefinable words ever used to describe Southern persons, places, and things, either solid or liquid, is the word 'Bourbon.' " Some historians have suggested the substitution of the term *New Departure Democrats*, but as so often happens in the case of words susceptible of different interpretations and given sanction through long usage, it has become a symbol to the modern mind altogether too powerful to destroy. Thus, perforce, it remains in the historian's lexicon. But its modern-day currency does not make it any easier to define. Nor was there much agreement among contemporaries as to the meaning of Bourbonism. In Mississippi and some other states, for instance, the old Whig element used it as a term of opprobrium in referring to their dyed-in-the-wool Democratic opponents, who apparently had learned nothing from their venture in secession and war.

Several recent studies, including Woodward's fresh and persuasive treatment, underscore the desirability of going behind the stereotype we have found so convenient in characterizing the post-Reconstruction regimes in the South. Perhaps we have been too quick to categorize southern leaders during the years 1875–90 as either "Bourbons" or "agrarians" and not ready enough to examine carefully the sources of their motivation as individuals and as a group. When we are prepared to generalize more authoritatively in this regard, we will be able to deal more definitively with the old question of just how forward-looking and just how reactionary the Bourbons were. How new were the attitudes of these architects of the New South? In a witty article on "The Urbane Bourbon," published in 1957, Professor Bettersworth argues that the Bourbon was "one and the same person as the South's antebellum ruling class, the planter oligarchy." Bettersworth emphasizes the entrepreneurial elements in the plantation South, points to the planters' capitalistic proclivities and to their respect for cities, and asks if "the New South is not older than the Old South, whether before the Old South ever was, the New South had been."

It would be helpful in appraising the Bourbons if we knew more about their programs and methods and how they changed with the passage of time; if we were better informed with respect to the concessions they were forced to make to their southern opponents; and if we understood more fully the long-range consequences of their leadership. In some states the farmers seem to have obtained a substantial amount of the legislation they sought, and there is reason to believe that at least in some commonwealths the agrarian element in the Bourbon Democracy was more important than is usually recognized. Similarly, there is some evidence that the Bourbons were forced to make concessions to the liberals that we sometimes overlook. Moreover, the new light which recent scholarship has thrown on certain Democratic leaders of this period reveals the inadequacy of the old dualistic classification. Such a man as James Z. George of Mississippi, who is usually assigned a prominent place in the Bourbon leadership of that state, remained at heart a friend of the poor man from whose ranks he rose. He championed legislation for the benefit of the farmer, the laborer, and the consumer, and, according to a study by May Spencer Ringold, "he consistently urged the extension of governmental functions to encompass a control of big business and the regulation of railroads; his tariff policy was hostile to the industrial East; and on the question of bankruptcy and financial legislation, he fostered the interests of the debtor, the consumer, and the small businessman." There is, it would seem, some merit in the plea for a reappraisal, or at least a continuing appraisal, of the southern Bourbons.

Professor Simkins has called attention to the new direction in American historiography and the growing appreciation, after the work of historians like Allan Nevins, of the "constructive" accomplishments of the ill-famed "robber barons." Spiritually, at least, and probably in more tangible ways as well, the Bourbon was the southern counterpart of the northern business leader. Perhaps the Bourbons also had their constructive side. According to Simkins, "They left a lasting record of achievements greater than that of any generation of Southerners since the Founding Fathers of the Republic." This fixes their value at a pretty high level. Not even Holland Thompson was as unrestrained in his praise. "No governments in American history," Thompson wrote in 1919, "have been conducted with more economy and more fidelity than the governments of the

Southern States during the first years after the Reconstruction period." At the same time, he was critical of the Bourbons' obsession with tax reduction and of their niggardly appropriations; and no one has offered a more scathing evaluation of the Bourbon leaders in Congress ("They accomplished little for their section or for the nation. . . . They advocated no great reforms and showed little political vision").

Simkins' own earlier writings contain a more balanced appraisal of the Bourbons than his recent interpretation. In *A History of the South* (1953), he pointed out the limitations of their policies and the oligarchical nature of their political control. He suggested that in some respects the work of Bourbon politicians and their journalist friends had "the earmarks of scalawagism," and that while they achieved some lasting benefits for the South by encouraging "a sort of second generation of carpetbaggers," they paid the price of allowing important resources to fall into the hands of alien capitalists. Professor Simkins now argues that since other Americans during the same period were equally guilty of abuses, the Bourbons have been misinterpreted. This begs the question. Few American governments, as Vann Woodward has written,

have enjoyed such immunity from criticism as those of Redemption. Public curiosity regarding corruption and graft in government had been jaded by the campaign of exposure against the Carpetbaggers. The Redeemers bore the banner of reform and were usually protected by Confederate war records, while the exclusiveness of ring politics spared officeholders the ordeal of defending their records and re-elected them term after term.

Perhaps the most helpful and the best-balanced appraisal of the Bourbons is contained in two comprehensive state studies, Allen Johnston Going's *Bourbon Democracy in Alabama, 1874–1890* (1951) and Judson Clements Ward, Jr.'s unpublished study, "Georgia under the Bourbon Democrats, 1872–1890" (Ph.D. dissertation, University of North Carolina, 1947). We need more monographs like these. Neither was written by what Simkins has called a "scholar-exile" from the South. Both suggest the constructive aspects of southern Bourbonism—the effort to live realistically in the new era, the successful promotion of business, industry, and agriculture, and the way in which the drive toward integration in the national economy hastened sectional reconciliation. They also point out that on occasion the Bourbons were more liberal in their approach to spending than the representatives of small rural counties. But both authors are sharply critical of the Bourbon leaders' policies, their tactics, and some of the consequences flowing from their control. The New Departure Democrats in Georgia, concludes Ward,

became an oligarchy who used their political power selfishly to enrich themselves. They profited personally from the barbarous and benighted convict lease system. They made money from the lease of the state-owned Western and Atlantic Railroad. They refused to shift the burden of taxation from the already overburdened farmer or provide other measures of relief. They increased appropriations somewhat, but even so they failed to provide adequately for schools, roads, charitable institutions, and other public services. They saddled the one-party system on the state. They used white supremacy to crush political differences and prevent the free discussion of public questions. They segregated and discriminated against the Negro. . . . Perhaps the greatest condemnation of the advocates of the New Departure is the heritage they left Georgia of intolerant, bigoted, one-party control; and a weak, parsimonious government unwilling to support in adequate fashion the state's public services. Georgia suffers from this heritage to the present day.

"The Bourbon," according to one of the new interpreters, "is now in the midst of a great awakening." If the writer is referring to the almost unlimited acceptance of the American business system in the region below the Potomac, few will challenge his assertion. But if he means to imply that Bourbonism is triumphant in the sense that the complex of folkways and ideas traditionally associated with the South still retains its old-time power in the region's society, one may question whether he understands either Bourbonism or the profound changes occurring in the present South. Professor Simkins is almost certainly too sanguine in assuming that the forces of business which he thinks are doing so much to perpetuate Bourbon values, whatever they may be, will not ultimately destroy the "southern way of life." For just as the forces of business dominance in the North contributed to the destruction of the southern system in the 1860s, so will similar forces in the twentieth century very likely direct a revolution in the South that goes far beyond economic change. No one can draw a line and by the mere act of doing so determine that innovation will proceed so far and no further!

In one place Francis Simkins speaks of the agrarian revolt as "a strange interlude" in southern history. Does he mean by this to suggest that the agrarian uprising was an aberration? A movement compounded, perhaps, of irrational impulses? Such an interpretation greatly underestimates the significance and influence of the agrarian revolt (which Simkins' own writings do much to document). In arguing that "it was thoroughly abnormal for Southerners to persist in proclaiming the belief that the less privileged class was being oppressed by the more privileged class," he is echoing the thesis advanced by William W. Ball fifty years ago. "In retrospect," Ball wrote in 1911, "the artificiality of the differences of the nineties is plain, and . . . they did not permanently divide the people." The flurry caused by the agrarian radicals soon passed and "the people took up again their accustomed modes of thinking and doing. Though the division of the people was sharp and accompanied with cruel laceration, it was not deep—it was only skin deep." Would the new interpreters go so far as to say that material and ideological differences are nonexistent in the southern social order? Professor Woodward has reminded us that "the classic lines of cleavage in Southern society were not erased magically by Reconstruction." Nor were they erased by the Bourbon Democrats—nor even by the one-party politics of the twentieth-century South. For the basic ingredients of southern politics have been not doctrines of race but socioeconomic groupings like those outside the region—business-minded conservatives, agrarian radicals, middle-class progressives, and the like.

The heritage of agrarian dissent and middle-class progressivism is as important in the South today as is the heritage of Bourbonism. As Professor Simkins himself wrote in 1947:

By overthrowing the Bourbon oligarchies the agrarian movement advanced the cause of political democracy. White masses were taught to exercise more effectively their inherited rights of suffrage and through the white primary were given an adequate means of using this power.

William Garrott Brown, a perceptive Southerner who lived through the agrarian upheaval, had a proper appreciation of the movement's significance. "I call that particular change a revolution," he wrote, "and I would use a stronger term if there were one; for no other political movement—not that of 1776, nor that of 1860–1861—ever altered Southern life so profoundly." In the fundamental elements of the hybrid Democratic party of the South, writes Henry Savage, Jr., one can find "a not inconsequential measure of agrarian radicalism which, from time to time, persists in cropping out to the amazement of those who think the South is ideologically solid."

The agrarian heritage has not always been a constructive or a pretty thing. It may be true, for example, that the southern dema-gogue was the "spiritual descendant" of the embattled farmers of the

1880s and 1890s, as Nash K. Burger and John K. Bettersworth insist, but it is scarcely reasonable to blame them alone for Negro disfranchisement and the stultification of twentieth-century southern politics. To do so is to ignore the roots of the agrarian revolt. For it was the Bourbons who first taught modern Southerners the uses of expediency in politics and whose inadequate program and repressive ideology did so much to call forth the agrarian upheaval of the nineties.

Unless we are careful the effort to find consensus in the southern past—an effort that is probably related to strong trends in American historiography as a whole—is likely to distort the history of the region and to reimpose the old myth of a monolithic South. It has taken southern scholars a generation to destroy this myth and to proceed with the serious business of describing and analyzing past southern societies, which have always been more complex, differentiated, and internally at odds than an earlier school of historians would have us believe. It is well to remember that the issues and cleavages in southern politics have more often than not been those of the larger American politics. But in pointing out the fundamental similarity and the basic identity between southern institutions and ideas and those of other parts of the country, we should not be misled into underestimating the significance of social struggle throughout the history of the South.

It is scarcely necessary to perpetuate the complacent mood of the 1950s or the current fashion for academic togetherness in order to maintain a viable approach to regional history. Southern history will continue for a long time to be a rewarding field of study—at least until the arrival of that day Harry S. Ashmore talks about, when a rich Negro leaves behind a widow with sufficient holdings to justify one of the Snopes boys marrying her for her money! And when that imaginary day arrives, Bourbonism will either be completely triumphant or completely dead.

3

Dinner at the White House: Theodore Roosevelt, Booker T. Washington, and the South

~~~ THE incident discussed in this essay illustrates the regional interplay of opinion in what C. Vann Woodward has called "American Counterpoint," the continuing North-South dialogue involving a variety of interests, issues, and values. The famous Roosevelt-Washington dinner of 1901 provides an example of the interaction of North and South at a significant point in the course of racial policies and attitudes in the United States. In considering the public response to the White House dinner and the subsequent behavior of the two principal actors, this essay points up the persistence of southern sectionalism, the convictions and illusions in white thinking about race relations in and out of the South, and the limits of national concern and presidential leadership in dealing with the "race problem."

Two books published after this paper was written elaborate some of its themes and present a fuller account of certain aspects of the affair. Willard B. Gatewood, Jr., in *Theodore Roosevelt and the Art of Controversy: Episodes of the White House Years* (1970), examines the conflicting versions of the incident and the nature of the southern mythology that grew up in its wake. Gatewood also describes two other racial controversies involving Theodore Roosevelt and white Southerners. Louis R. Harlan includes a chapter entitled "Dinner at the White House" in his biography, *Booker T. Washington: The Making of a Black Leader, 1856–1901* (1972). Harlan places the affair in the context of Roosevelt's southern political strategy and Washington's role as an intimate presidential adviser on southern politics. He also observes that while the White House dinner was of little significance to Roosevelt, it was "a moment of supreme importance" for the Negro leader, "the final crown of success that secured his position as virtual monarch of the black people in the United States."

T HEODORE ROOSEVELT's elevation to the presidency in September 1901 aroused more than usual interest in the South. Ordinarily, Southerners were too firmly committed to the Democratic party and too suspicious of Republicans to pay much heed to Republican presidents, except to denounce them in election years and to condemn their occasional attempts to rejuvenate southern Republicanism. But Roosevelt seemed different. For one thing, the South could attach some claim to him because of his southern family connections, and newspapers from Virginia to Texas suddenly became concerned with the new president's genealogy. His mother was a member of the prominent Bulloch family of Georgia and two of his uncles had been conspicuously identified with the Confederate cause during the Civil War. Roosevelt himself was proud of this southern heritage—he often called himself "half a Southerner"—and people in the South were quick to recall his generous praise of Robert E. Lee and his "noble tribute" to the boys in gray. The president's daring and impetuous nature also appealed to Southerners, and during the early fall of 1901 the region's newspapers devoted much space to his exploits as a soldier and vigorous man of affairs. [1]

The inchoate trust and vague expectations that Southerners had in Roosevelt seemed to be confirmed by his attitude toward the appointment of federal officials in the South. Almost as soon as he assumed the presidency, southern visitors to the White House began to report that Roosevelt had determined to select only the best men for offices in the South, that he would appoint Democrats when he could not find qualified Republicans, and that he hoped to make his party respectable in Dixie. Some commentators declared that he would disregard the notorious "Negro rings of politicians" which

1. See, for example, Atlanta *Constitution,* September 15, 1901; New Orleans *Times-Democrat,* October 6, 1901; Charlotte *Observer,* October 9, 1901; *Literary Digest* 23 (October 12, 1901): 428; Thomas D. Clark, *The Southern Country Editor* (Indianapolis and New York, 1948), pp. 306–7.

had so long dominated the Republican party in the South, and thus put an end to what a New Orleans paper called "one of the scarlet infamies of American politics."[2] The president was quoted as saying, "I am going to be president of the United States, and not of any section. I don't care for sections or sectional lines."[3]

A few weeks after he became president, Roosevelt appointed Thomas G. Jones, a conservative Democrat and ex-governor of Alabama, to a federal judgeship. The South responded enthusiastically to this evidence of "a liberal, broad-minded policy." In one bold stroke, asserted the Montgomery *Advertiser*, Roosevelt had demonstrated that he was president of no one party or section, "but of all parties and of all sections." Many newspapers declared that he was in a better position than any president since the Civil War to encourage the development of the Republican party in the southern states. One journal even predicted that "before his administration is concluded Mason and Dixon's line will be an almost forgotten tradition," while an excited North Carolinian announced the arrival of "the second 'era of good feeling' in American politics."[4]

Just what Theodore Roosevelt hoped to achieve in the way of fundamental reform in the South is not altogether clear. He may not have been certain himself. He undoubtedly hoped to improve the quality of federal appointments and to clean up the party organization in the southern states. But he also wanted to obtain the Republican nomination in 1904, and he knew the importance of the southern Republican delegations in the national convention. To win those delegations he would have to break Mark Hanna's hold on them. How he could realize this objective while simultaneously reforming Republican politics in the South and how he could appeal to white Southerners while at the same time helping to provide American Negroes with a new leadership that would end their long generation of frustration following Reconstruction were questions that Roosevelt must not have studied very carefully.

Yet, in the circumstances, he could scarcely have chosen a man better qualified to serve as a counselor on southern policy than the great Negro educator Booker T. Washington. Roosevelt had known Washington for some time and while vice-president had planned a

2. New Orleans *Times-Democrat,* quoted in *Literary Digest* 23 (October 19, 1901): 456.

3. *Public Opinion* 31 (October 3, 1901): 420–21.

4. Charlotte *Observer,* October 9, 1901, and various newspapers quoted in *Public Opinion* 31 (October 3, 1901): 420, and *Literary Digest* 23 (October 19, 1901): 456–57.

visit to Tuskegee. He cordially endorsed the Tuskegee system, declaring that "the salvation of the Negro lay in the development of the Booker Washington theory." Washington's conservative views on money, labor, and other economic issues appealed to Roosevelt; he referred to the black leader as "a man for whom I have the highest regard and in whose judgment I have much faith."[5] The president knew, moreover, that Washington was widely acquainted with Negroes and whites in the South, that he had to an unusual extent the confidence of southern whites, and that his was the most powerful black voice in America.

On the very day he became president, Roosevelt penned a note to the Alabama Negro. "When are you coming north?" he wrote. "I must see you as soon as possible. I want to talk over the question of possible future appointments in the south exactly on the lines of our last conversation together."[6]

In response to this summons, Booker T. Washington came to the capital during the last week in September for a conference with the new chief executive. The mission caused the Negro educator some misgivings, for he knew that the delicate matter of federal appointments might involve him in politics and endanger his work at Tuskegee. But an invitation from Roosevelt was a command and Washington made the trip to the White House. The president outlined his ideas with respect to appointments, enphasizing his determination to appoint only the best-qualified men even if this meant the designation of some Democrats. Washington strongly urged the appointment of both Negro Republicans and conservative Democrats.[7] It was because of his earnest recommendation, in fact, that Roosevelt announced the appointment a few days later of Thomas G. Jones, and it was the Jones appointment that evoked such widespread enthusiasm in the South.

A few weeks later, while on a tour of Mississippi, Washington received word that the president desired a second conference with him as soon as possible. The Negro leader arrived in Washington on

5. Roosevelt to L. J. Moore, February 5, 1900, and to William Henry Lewis, July 26, 1900, in *The Letters of Theodore Roosevelt*, ed. Elting E. Morison, 8 vols. (Cambridge, 1951–54), 2: 1169, 1364–65; Henry F. Pringle, *Theodore Roosevelt, A Biography* (New York, 1931), p. 230.

6. Roosevelt to Washington, September 14, 1901, in *Letters of Theodore Roosevelt*, 3:149.

7. Booker T. Washington, *My Larger Education, Being Chapters From My Experience* (Garden City, 1911), pp. 170–71; Basil J. Mathews, *Booker T. Washington, Educator and Interracial Interpreter* (Cambridge, 1948), pp. 229–30.

the afternoon of October 16 and immediately went to the home of Whitefield McKinlay, a black friend with whom he often stopped while in the capital. When he reached McKinlay's home, he found an invitation from the president asking him to dine at the White House at eight o'clock that evening. He accepted the invitation but was careful, as he had been in his first conference, to avoid any publicity that might attend his dealings with Roosevelt.[8]

That evening Washington dined at the White House with the president and his family. There was one other guest, a man from Colorado. "After dinner," Booker T. Washington later recalled, he and Roosevelt ". . . talked at considerable length concerning plans about the South which the President had in mind."[9] Later in the evening the educator left the White House and took a train for New York. In the meantime, Washington reporters had noticed the Negro's name on the White House guest list. But their report merely stated that "Booker T. Washington, of Tuskegee, Alabama, dined with the President last evening." In New York the following morning, Washington noticed a similar item in the New York *Tribune*, but he gave it little thought.[10]

Southern correspondents in Washington were more attentive. They furnished their papers reports similar to the following news wire sent to the Memphis *Commercial Appeal*:

Washington, Oct. 16. Booker T. Washington, principal of the Negro school at Tuskegee, Ala., dined with the president this evening. It was largely at Washington's suggestion that ex-Governor Jones of Alabama was appointed a judge on the Federal bench in that State. It is understood that Washington will make a number of recommendations for appointments in the South. . . . He seems to be very influential with the administration.[11]

The South was instantly aroused. The southern white press spoke almost as one voice in condemning the Roosevelt-Washington dinner. Ironically, many of the same newspapers that had recently praised the president for appointing Jones, on Washington's recommendation, now denounced him for having dinner with the man whose advice he had taken. When Roosevelt "invited a nigger to dine with him at the White House," asserted the Memphis *Scimitar*,

8. Washington, *My Larger Education*, p. 175; Emmett J. Scott and Lyman Beecher Stowe, *Booker T. Washington, Builder of a Civilization* (Garden City, 1917), p. 116.

9. Washington, *My Larger Education*, p. 175.

10. Ibid., pp. 175–76; Mark Sullivan, *Our Times, the United States 1900–1925*, 6 vols. (New York, 1926–35), 3:133.

11. Memphis *Commercial Appeal*, October 17, 1901.

he committed the "most damnable outrage which has ever been per-petrated by any citizen of the United States." The New Orleans *States* described the president's act as "a studied insult" to the South, while another newspaper contended that by one foolish decision he had "destroyed the kindly, warm regard and personal affection for him which were growing up fast in the South." A Tennessee journal expressed the opinion that no atonement or future act of the chief executive could remove "the self-imprinted stigma."[12]

The most extreme southern reaction to the White House dinner revolved around the theme of Roosevelt's alleged belief in "social equality." Southern editors suddenly discovered that "Rooseveltism means nigger supremacy." Many of them shared the New Orleans *Picayune's* feeling that the president was "the worst enemy to his race of any white man who has ever occupied so high a place in this republic." It was simply impossible, proclaimed the Columbia (S.C.) *State*, "for a white man of proper ideas to conceive how a white man of culture and refinement could be comfortable under such circum-stances." God erected the barrier between the races, warned the Macon (Ga.) *Telegraph*. "No President of this or any country can break it down."[13]

Some Southerners indulged in an orgy of hysteria. "White men of the South, how do you like it?" vehemently demanded the New Orleans *Times-Democrat*. "White women of the South, how do YOU like it?" The Richmond *Times* said of the incident, "It means the President is willing that negroes shall mingle freely with whites in the social circle—that white women may receive attentions from negro men; it means that there is no racial reason in his opinion why whites and blacks may not marry and intermarry, why the Anglo-Saxon may not mix negro blood with his blood." Another newspaper argued that such a precedent in the South "would lead to the mis-cegenation and amalgamation of the races, and produce a civiliza-

12. Memphis *Scimitar* and Memphis *Commercial Appeal*, quoted in *Literary Digest* 23 (October 26, 1901): 486; Richmond *Times*, quoted in Sullivan, *Our Times*, 3:138; Scott and Stowe, *Booker T. Washington*, p. 117.

13. *Public Opinion* 31 (October 31, 1901): 556; Sullivan, *Our Times*, 3:138; C. Vann Woodward, *Origins of the New South, 1877–1913* (Baton Rouge, 1951), p. 465; Samuel R. Spencer, Jr., *Booker T. Washington and the Negro's Place in American Life* (Boston, 1955), p. 134.

tion, or more exactly a barbarism, in which the virtues of both the white race and the black race would be lost and into which the vices of each would be conserved."[14] Henceforth, declared the Memphis *Scimitar,*

> any Nigger who happens to have a little more than the average amount of intelligence granted by the Creator of his race, and cash enough to pay the tailor and the barber, and the perfumer for scents enough to take away the nigger smell, has a perfect right to be received by the daughter of the white man among the guests in the parlor of his home.[15]

According to "Pitchfork Ben" Tillman, the fiery senator from South Carolina, "The action of President Roosevelt in entertaining that nigger will necessitate our killing a thousand niggers in the South before they will learn their place again." One of the southern cartoons portraying the much-discussed dinner—a savage exhibition that showed Mrs. Roosevelt serving a hideous black monster while the president looked on with a broad smile—was too much even for some white Southerners, who quickly suppressed it.[16]

The violent talk in the South continued for weeks and the furor over the affair ultimately reached international proportions. What a scandal "from one end of America to the other!" exclaimed one French paper. The *Journal des Debats* headed a leading editorial "Une Tempete autour d'un Negre."[17] Not since Lincoln had a president been so bitterly abused in the South. The country editors followed the lead of their city brothers in pouring fire and brimstone over the head of the hapless president. "Let's all take a crack at him!" urged a rural editor from Mississippi. And they did. As Thomas D. Clark has written, "Throughout the South the brief little paragraphs of the country editors cut through the air like the piercing barks of feist dogs snipping at the heels of a bull."[18]

14. *Literary Digest* 23 (November 2, 1901): 523–24; Sullivan, *Our Times,* 3:133–35.
15. Quoted in Clark, *The Southern Country Editor,* p. 310.
16. Sullivan, *Our Times,* 3:135–36; Francis E. Leupp, *The Man Roosevelt, A Portrait Sketch* (New York, 1904), pp. 221–22.
17. Mercer Cook, "Booker T. Washington and the French," *Journal of Negro History* 40 (October, 1955): 319–23, and newspaper clippings in Roosevelt Collection, Widener Library, Harvard University.
18. Clark, *The Southern Country Editor,* p. 310.

Some of the comments in the southern press had their light side. The following from the Raleigh *Post* is an example of the doggerel inspired by the White House dinner:

Booker Washington holds the boards—
    The President dines a nigger.
Precedents are cast aside—
    Put aside with vigor;
Black and white sit side by side,
As Roosevelt dines a nigger.[19]

Young Southerners began to sing a new song:

Coon, coon, coon,
Booker Washington is his name;
Coon, coon, coon,
Ain't that a measly shame?
Coon, coon, coon,
Morning, night, and noon,
I think I'd class Mr. Roosevelt
With a coon, coon, coon.[20]

Although the attitude of the southern white press was one of general disapproval, there were some moderate voices. The Raleigh *News and Observer* called the incident a radical departure from social custom but declared that "a man's home is his castle, whether it be a home in the White House or in an humble cabin. He has the right to choose his guests, and to sit down at his own table with whomsoever he pleases to invite to break bread with him." Several moderate Southerners, such as Governor Charles B. Aycock of North Carolina, noted regretfully that the affair might have a detrimental effect upon Booker T. Washington's work in Negro education by undermining the confidence that white Southerners had in him and laying him open to criticism.[21]

That some white Southerners kept their equilibrium and adopted a fairly temperate attitude toward the notorious dinner is evident in the editorials of several Nashville newspapers. The Nashville *Banner* regretted that the president had defied "the racial social distinction which is so sedulously maintained in the Southern

19. Quoted in Sullivan, *Our Times*, 3:135.
20. Quoted in Spencer, *Booker T. Washington and the Negro's Place in American Life*, p. 135.
21. See the quotations from Raleigh *News and Observer* and other newspapers in *Literary Digest* 23 (October 26, 1901): 486–87; Clark, *The Southern Country Editor*, p. 309.

States" and predicted that his action would tend "to chill the favor with which he is regarded in the South." But, at the same time, the *Banner* seemed to admire Roosevelt's courage and "independence of public opinion."[22] The observations of the Nashville *American*, while characterizing the White House dinner as "an error of judgment and a breach of good taste," were also couched in restrained language.[23] The *Confederate Veteran*, which was published in Nashville, attributed the dinner to Roosevelt's impulsiveness and to Washington's lack of good judgment. The editor's interpretation was an interesting one: "The President's life as a Rough Rider and a hunter, whereby customs are naturally ignored, and his impulsive disposition should induce lenience of popular judgment. The insult to all the best people of America, whether Southern or Northern, was evidently not intended to be as severe as it is in fact, and it should be forgotten as soon as possible. The South has waited in patience so long that this reflection will be borne in the hope that the President may do great good in restoring real sectional peace."[24]

In a long discussion of the affair on October 23, the Nashville *American* elaborated its position and presented an admirable statement of the more moderate opinion in the South. Admonishing those Southerners who had resorted to passionate outbursts of criticism, it declared: "This intemperance of speech and fierce denunciation may win a certain kind of applause which may be very flattering to a certain type of mind, but it puts those who employ it at a decided disadvantage before the world, even though they have the better side of the argument. . . . This is a great weakness with too many Southern writers and speakers." Continuing, the editor observed that "honesty of opinion and sincerity of desire to do no race or section injustice must be accorded those who differ with the Southern view of the negro question. If these do not concede the South the same honesty and desire, then that is their weakness and misfortune. As we see it, our Northern critics have a very erroneous view of the negro question, especially as to the social equality or social feature of it." The Nashville paper then set forth the rationale that underlay its faith in white supremacy:

The South refuses social recognition or equality to Booker Washington not because of any hatred of him, not because of his respectability, but in spite

22. Nashville *Banner*, October 18, 1901.
23. Nashville *American*, October 19, 1901.
24. *Confederate Veteran* 9 (1901): 496.

of it. It denies him social equality because he is a negro. That is the South's reason. It is prepared to defend that reason, which it will not abandon, no matter what all the rest of the world may say or think. . . . A leak in a dam is dangerous to the dam's safety. There is danger that the leak may grow larger until the dam is destroyed and hopeless havoc and ruin are wrought. To accord social equality to negroes of Booker Washington's stamp would be a leak in the dam. It would cause other negroes to seek and demand the same recognition. It would be an example which would encourage the lower classes of negroes and whites to mingle together socially; miscegenation would follow and a mongrel race would be the result. Save the South from that! [25]

Southern white editors and politicians were not too hysterical to recognize that Roosevelt had provided them with the ammunition to repel any Republican invasions of the South which he might have planned with Washington's help. The White House dinner "is not a precedent that will encourage Southern men to join hands with Mr. Roosevelt," observed Josephus Daniels in the Raleigh *News and Observer*. The Memphis *Scimitar* declared that the president had rudely shattered "any expectations that may have arisen from his announced intention to make the Republican party in the South respectable. He has closed the door to any accessions of Southern white men to the Republican ranks." [26] In Alabama, where a new disfranchising constitution was being debated, the Roosevelt-Washington affair was made the theme of discussion by the ratificationists and the incident appeared to be "cementing the white forces in opposition to the negro." A few weeks later, during the Virginia constitutional convention, which was also preoccupied with the question of Negro disfranchisement, antidisfranchisement men found themselves embarrassed by all the talk about the White House dinner. In other parts of the South there were rumors that the old guard Republicans in the region, upset over the implications of the Jones appointment, were quietly rejoicing over the whole thing. [27]

The southern outburst brought a strong reply from the North, and the sectional caldron was soon boiling. The New York *Press*

25. Nashville *American*, October 23, 1901.
26. *Literary Digest* 23 (October 26, 1901): 486–87.
27. Clippings from Boston *Herald* (about October 22, 1901) and other papers in Roosevelt Collection, Widener Library, Harvard University.
In 1903 Roosevelt noted that Arthur Pue Gorman, the Democratic stalwart from Maryland, was reported to be making effective use of a campaign button showing the president and Washington at dinner. Roosevelt to Lyman Abbott, October 29, 1903, in *Letters of Theodore Roosevelt*, 3:638–39.

described the outraged Southerners as the "arrogant old plantation strain," while the Boston *Transcript* asserted that "the hysterical and horror-stricken Southern Shriekers" were the victims of "old ingrained prejudice."[28] The Washington *Bee,* a Negro journal, declared:

The Southern Democrats hoped and expected to blarney the President so as to continue unrestrained in their wicked reign of terror and proscription against the coloured race. They are shocked, boiled, smitten, and exasperated. In one fell swoop Mr. Roosevelt has smashed to smithereens their fondest idol. They are fuming with dire imprecations against him, and all because he took a meal of victuals with a coloured gentleman who had been entertained by the nobility of England, and the best people of America.[29]

In general the northern press provided an unqualified defense of the president, though some papers questioned the wisdom of the White House dinner. Northern newspapers pointed out that Booker T. Washington had been entertained by Queen Victoria and other notable people while visiting Europe, and that he was one of the most learned and eloquent men of the day. Many individuals and a number of organizations also rallied to the support of Roosevelt and Washington. Pondering the nature of southern racial prejudice, the New York *World* thought it a curious thing that a people could be allowed to die for their fellowman and yet not eat with him. A Boston paper expressed the hope that the shock would not prove fatal to white Southerners "but that after a little further reflection they will settle down to the conclusion that life is still worth living, and that if the country does go to pieces it will be owing to some mightier cause than the fact that a gifted, interesting, and attractive olive-skinned Christian gentleman has broken bread and eaten salt at the President's table."[30]

Many northern newspapers were suspicious of the motives involved in the southern outburst. But the *Literary Digest* was inclined to believe, after carefully reading many southern expressions on the subject, that there was real apprehension in the South about the incident's effect on race relations.[31] A race riot in Louisiana, late in

28. *Literary Digest* 23 (October 26, 1901): 487, and ibid. (November 2, 1901): 523.

29. Quoted in John Hope Franklin, *From Slavery to Freedom: A History of American Negroes* (New York, 1947), p. 427.

30. Boston *Transcript* and other newspapers, quoted in *Literary Digest* 23 (October 26, 1901): 487; New York *World,* October 20, 1901.

31. *Literary Digest* 23 (November 2, 1901): 523.

October 1901, that resulted in the death of nine Negroes and two white men was attributed by some Southerners to the White House dinner. "There is no doubt that the negroes have been lately aroused to aggressiveness by the intemperate expressions in both the Northern and Southern press over the recent Booker Washington dinner with the President," declared the New Orleans *Picayune*, "and doubtless not a few have been told that the affair means an active revival of Federal inter[f]erence and intervention in their behalf."[32]

Meanwhile, Mr. Dooley had been discoursing to his friend Hennessy about the president's "havin' a coon to dinner at the White House." The dinner incident was "goin' to be th' roonation iv Prisident Tiddy's chances in th' South," meditated Mr. Dooley. "Thousan's iv men who wudden't have voted fr'm undher anny circumstances has declared that undher no circumstances wud they now vot f'r him. He's lost near ivry State in th' South." Mr. Dooley himself hardly gave the affair a thought. "But it hit th' Sunny Southland," he told Hennessy. "No part iv th' counthry can be more gloomy whin it thries thin th' Sunny Southland, an' this here ivint sint a thrill iv horror through ivry newspaper fr'm th' Pattymack to th' Sugar Belt."[33]

The gales of criticism from the South that lashed the president and his Negro guest in the wake of their dinner meeting were all a little bewildering to the two principals involved. Neither of them would say anything publicly during the clamorous period that followed the incident. Several years later Washington recalled that "for days and weeks I was pursued by reporters in quest of interviews. I was deluged with telegrams and letters asking for some expression of opinion or an explanation; but during the whole of this period of agitation and excitement I did not give out a single interview and did not discuss the matter in any way."[34] Meanwhile, a drawer full of threatening letters arrived at Tuskegee, and Washington's secretary, Emmett J. Scott, later reported an abortive attempt by a group of white men in Louisiana to have Washington assassinated.[35]

No black leader had ever achieved such widespread respect among white Southerners as had Washington. By consistently opposing any agitation for social equality, by renouncing northern inter-

---

32. Quoted in ibid. (November 9, 1901): 559.
33. *Literary Digest* 23 (November 23, 1901): 636.
34. Washington, *My Larger Education*, p. 176.
35. Scott and Stowe, *Booker T. Washington*, pp. 117–18; Mathews, *Booker T. Washington*, pp. 233–34.

vention and acknowledging the validity of dominant white ideas, and by emphasizing his primary interest in industrial education and economic opportunities for his people, he had stamped the impression of his leadership on the mind of the South. He seemed to accept the South as it was, and he appealed to southern sentiment with great success. "I love the South," he often said. "I was born in the South and I understand thoroughly the prejudices, the customs, the traditions of the South—" [36]

Booker T. Washington's belief in moderation and conciliation had led him to avoid offending the white South. In the South he had always conformed to the native social customs, and even in the North he had avoided "purely social" functions. "You have no idea," he once told a friend, "how many invitations of various kinds I am constantly refusing or trying to get away from because I want to avoid embarrassing situations. . . ." Nevertheless, when outside the South the Tuskegee educator was unwilling to be governed entirely by southern social views. He had been entertained by some of the most distinguished people in the country, and even in his own section he had for years ridden Pullman cars and on occasion had visited in the compartments of northern friends without any objection from white Southerners.[37] Perhaps these experiences led him to misjudge, for a moment, the force of the southern prejudices he knew so well.

Although Washington was roundly abused in the South for his "presumption" in dining with the president, Theodore Roosevelt received far greater condemnation. M. Jules Huret, a French journalist who wrote a book in 1904 entitled *De New-York á la Nouvelle-Orléans*, found that New Orleans white men praised the black educator and the Tuskegee program but criticized Roosevelt for having invited a Negro to dine with him.[38] Several years later Washington gave a good illustration of the curious nature of a southern white man's racial prejudice. He told of a trip he made through Florida some weeks after the White House dinner. Since it was generally known along the railroad line that Washington was on the train, he was met at nearly every station by groups of people who boarded the train to greet him. At one little station near Gainesville, a white man whose dress and manner revealed him to be a small farmer entered the train, shook hands cordially with the Negro

36. Washington, *My Larger Education*, pp. 179–80.
37. Spencer, *Booker T. Washington and the Negro's Place in American Life*, pp. 130–32.
38. Cook, "Booker T. Washington and the French," pp. 326–27.

leader, and said: "I am mighty glad to see you. I have heard about you and I have been wanting to meet you for a long while." Pleased at this hearty reception, Washington was rather surprised to have the farmer look him over and exclaim: "Say, you are a great man. You are the greatest man in this country!" The educator protested mildly but the farmer insisted: "Yes, sir, the greatest man in this country." Finally Washington asked him what he had against President Roosevelt, saying that in his opinion Roosevelt was the greatest man in the country. "Huh! Roosevelt?" his new friend demanded. "I used to think that Roosevelt was a great man until he ate dinner with you. That settled him for me."[39]

Other situations inevitably developed which allowed newspaper editors and politicians in the South to portray Booker T. Washington as a violator of southern social customs. None of these incidents quite rivaled the White House dinner but several were momentous enough to rearm the sentinels on the southern ramparts. One such episode occurred in 1903 when Washington and a group of Negro teachers en route to an educational conference in North Carolina were invited into the main dining room of a railroad cafe in Hamlet, North Carolina, while a handful of white passengers were served in private dining rooms. Another incident happened in the same year when the black educator stopped at the English Hotel in Indianapolis, a lodging house which did not customarily accept Negro guests. The white chambermaid assigned to care for Washington's room refused to perform her duties, declaring that she "would not clean up after a nigger." The management then fired her. A hotel in Houston, Texas, immediately offered her a position, and several southern towns and cities began a subscription fund for the "self-respecting girl."[40]

Two years later Washington accepted an invitation to dine with the wealthy merchant John Wanamaker and his daughter at a hotel in Saratoga Springs, New York, and the southern press again berated the Negro from Tuskegee.

Leaving out of the question the lack of delicacy and self-respect manifested by Wanamaker and his family [asserted one southern paper], blame must rest upon Washington, because he knows how deep and impassable is the gulf between whites and blacks in the South when the social situation is in-

39. Washington, *My Larger Education,* pp. 177–78.
40. Clark, *The Southern Country Editor,* p. 312; Scott and Stowe, *Booker T. Washington,* pp. 125–26.

volved. He deliberately flaunts all this in the face of the Southern people among whom he is living and among whom his work has to be carried on. He could have given no harder knock to his institution than he gave when he marched into that Saratoga dinner room with a white woman and her father.[41]

Such accidental occurrences as these and especially the ill-fated White House dinner led many white Southerners to question Booker T. Washington's motives. Washington's popularity with these Southerners declined. He became a marked man in the southern white press—not because of his pioneering work in Negro education but because he was "the saddle-colored coon" who had the insolence to eat a meal in the White House. One reason white Southerners continued to attack Washington, no doubt, was his ascendancy as the chief patronage referee for federal appointments in the South during the Roosevelt and Taft administrations.[42] But fortunately Washington's work at Tuskegee suffered no real harm, and in the long run most Southerners retained their confidence in the great Negro leader and his work.

Theodore Roosevelt was less stoical than his Negro friend in his attitude toward the southern outcry over the White House dinner. He found it hard to believe that the southern hysteria and the letters of censure were not some kind of nightmare. "The outburst of feeling in the South about it is to me literally inexplicable," he declared. On another occasion he wrote, "I really felt melancholy for the South at the way the Southerners behaved in the matter." At the same time, he was angered by the attacks against him and let it be known privately that he would have Booker T. Washington "to dine just as often as I please"—he would not be intimidated by "the idiot or vicious Bourbon element of the South." "If these creatures had any sense they would understand that they can't bluff me," the president wrote his friend Henry Cabot Lodge.[43]

Roosevelt's braggadocio did not quite hide the chagrin he felt

---

41. Unidentified paper, quoted in Scott and Stowe, *Booker T. Washington,* p. 122.
42. Spencer, *Booker T. Washington and the Negro's Place in American Life,* pp. 135–37; Woodward, *Origins of the New South,* p. 359; Clark, *The Southern Country Editor,* p. 312; Franklin, *From Slavery to Freedom,* p. 427.
43. Roosevelt to Lucius Nathan Littauer, October 24, 1901, to Curtis Guild, October 28, 1901, and to Henry Cabot Lodge, October 28, 1901, in *Letters of Theodore Roosevelt,* 3:181, 184–85; Joseph Bucklin Bishop, *Theodore Roosevelt and His Time Shown in His Own Letters,* 2 vols. (New York, 1920), 1: 165; Pringle, *Theodore Roosevelt,* p. 249.

over the affair. He told Lodge and others that he had invited Washington to dinner as "a matter of course." As he explained to one correspondent, "I had no thought whatever of anything save of having a chance of showing some little respect to a man whom I cordially esteem as a good citizen and good American." But in a letter to Albion W. Tourgée three weeks after the incident the president admitted that he had felt "a moment's qualm on inviting him because of his color," but this "made me ashamed of myself and made me hasten to send the invitation."[44] Roosevelt assured his friends that he regarded the scurrilous attacks with the "most contemptuous indifference," but he told James Ford Rhodes that he would not make such a mistake again. When he wrote to invite Finley Peter Dunne to dinner in November 1901, he added ruefully: ". . . you need *not* black your face." In a letter to Booker T. Washington he declared, "By the way, don't worry about *me*; it will all come right in time, and if I have helped by ever so little 'the ascent of man' I am more than satisfied."[45]

Despite Roosevelt's defiance of the Southerners in the friendly company of his friends, he invited no more Negroes to dine at the White House. Furthermore, he went to considerable lengths to point out that he had appointed fewer Negroes and more white Democrats to federal positions than any previous Republican president. Yet this solicitude for the feelings of southern whites, if such it was, appeared to have little effect in softening Dixie rancor toward Roosevelt, and two subsequent episodes provoked white Southerners to new assaults on the president.

One of these agitations grew out of Roosevelt's appointment in 1903 of a Negro named William D. Crum to be collector of the port of Charleston. Although Crum was a respected black leader, the white South reacted strongly against his selection and Senator Tillman violently attacked the president for it. Year after year he prevented senatorial confirmation of the nomination, only to have the president keep Crum in office with a series of recess appointments. Roosevelt maintained that unless some valid reason could be advanced against Crum, he would not withdraw the nomination. In the end, just be-

44. Roosevelt to Lucius Nathan Littauer, October 24, 1901, and to Tourgée, November 8, 1901, in *Letters of Theodore Roosevelt*, 3:181, 190; Pringle, *Theodore Roosevelt*, p. 250.

45. Scott and Stowe, *Booker T. Washington*, pp. 118–19; Pringle, *Theodore Roosevelt*, p. 249.

fore Roosevelt left office, Crum resigned without ever having had his appointment confirmed.[46]

The other incident began with the closing of the post office at Indianola, Mississippi, after the Negro postmistress, Effie Cox, submitted her resignation in the face of opposition from local rowdies in the fall of 1901. The Post Office Department refused to accept Mrs. Cox's resignation. When she would not serve, the post office was closed, and the Indianola mail was sent to Greenville, which was twenty-five miles away. To many Southerners this appeared to be a clear case of spite and white southern editors condemned the president's act as "a high-handed outrage." The northern press answered by denouncing the people of Indianola for having "intimidated and bullied" the postmistress into resigning. Eventually the Indianola post office was allowed to reopen, under a white postmaster, and Southerners could claim the final decision.[47] In 1906 Roosevelt admitted to a friend, "I am not satisfied that I acted wisely in either the Booker Washington dinner or the Crum appointment, though each was absolutely justified from every proper standpoint save that of expediency."[48]

But Theodore Roosevelt found some satisfaction in noting that white Southerners were far from logical in their behavior and attitudes. He liked to tell, for instance, how the very Charlestonians who had objected most forcefully to the Crum appointment later assured him that Crum was one of the city's best citizens and that they would have had no objection to his appointment as collector of some other city, say Savannah. The president gleefully described an occasion in 1903 when a mixed group of Episcopal bishops from the

46. Woodward, *Origins of the New South*, p. 464; Alfred Holt Stone, *Studies in the American Race Problem* (New York, 1908), pp. 246–47.

47. Franklin, *From Slavery to Freedom*, p. 428; Stone, *Studies in the American Race Problem*, pp. 247–48.

48. Roosevelt to Owen Wister, April 27, 1906, in *Letters of Theodore Roosevelt*, 5:227.

In the spring of 1905 Roosevelt wrote Jacob McGavock Dickinson of Tennessee to thank him for some recent suggestions on the "negro question." The president agreed with the Tennessean in his feeling that there was no "perfect solution of the question." As Roosevelt wrote, ". . . so far as I have any theory in the matter at all, my theory is to get hold of southerners with your ideas and then back them as heartily but as unobtrusively as possible. . . . I am very keenly aware of the blunders I have at times committed, but I do hope that the net result has been good rather than evil." Roosevelt to Dickinson, May 2, 1905, in Dickinson Papers, Manuscripts Division, Tennessee State Library and Archives.

South called on him and Mrs. Roosevelt in the White House. Yet "nobody shrank from them; nobody seemed to think it unnatural that I should receive them in the White House."[49] Writing of the Indianola controversy some years later, Roosevelt declared with heavy sarcasm:

Bands of valorous "southrons" from Arkansas and other seats of culture volunteered to rush to the defense of the imperiled white race in Indianola, and join in mobbing or killing the colored postmistress who had already served there for six years and who was backed by all their decent citizens. . . . Now the fantastic fools and moral cowards who encouraged or permitted the mob to turn her out are depositing their funds in the husband's bank and have him as a director in a white bank, and she and her husband own one of the best houses in Indianola and one of the best plantations in the neighborhood.[50]

Looking back on this period, one can see somewhat better than could the baffled Roosevelt the reasons for the white South's emotional reaction. The early years of the century happened to be the years in which southern racism reached its peak, exacerbated no doubt by northern efforts to pass the Force bill of 1890, and by the bitter conflicts between regular Democrats and Populists in the nineties. This was the period in which the disfranchisement movement swept to its climax, in which the annual lynching toll sometimes exceeded one hundred, and in which an epidemic of race riots occurred in the southern states. And this was a time when demagogues began to plow the fertile fields below the Potomac and to raise up a new intensity of racial feeling. Gustavus Myers, who made a tour of the South in 1901, declared that a person could not travel "through the cities or backwoods districts of the South without being confronted on every hand with the most conspicuous evidences of the intensity of race feeling. All other matters seem subsidiary."[51]

Roosevelt's challenges to southern folkways were not numerous but they were spectacular and exceedingly well publicized, and however unwittingly, the president succeeded in offending the white South as had no other public man in a generation. It must be remembered, of course, that southern spokesmen and agitators seized on

49. Roosevelt to Lyman Abbott, October 29, 1903, in *Letters of Theodore Roosevelt,* 3:638–39; Owen Wister, *Roosevelt, the Story of a Friendship, 1880–1919* (New York, 1930), pp. 254–55.

50. Roosevelt to Owen Wister, June 21, 1906, in *Letters of Theodore Roosevelt,* 5:310.

51. *Literary Digest* 23 (November 9, 1901): 559.

such incidents as the White House dinner for purposes that had nothing to do with white supremacy.

Roosevelt was anything but consistent in his approach to the southern situation. As C. Vann Woodward says, "Quixotic reformism mingled strangely with an old brand of practical politics from the start."[52] The president courted at various times and sometimes simultaneously Black-and-Tan Republicans, lily-white Republicans, and conservative Democrats. While he talked about improving the quality of federal officeholders in the South and publicly acknowledged Booker T. Washington as his adviser, he sought to win control of the Republican "rotten boroughs" in the South in order to ensure his nomination in 1904. The immediate significance of the Roosevelt-Washington dinner, as John M. Blum has suggested, was the political nature of Booker T. Washington's mission. Relying on the black educator's advice, Roosevelt tried to give Negroes a fairer share of federal offices and to improve the federal service, but he also used Washington with marked success in helping Postmaster General Henry C. Payne and James S. Clarkson as they maneuvered to loosen Hanna's grip on southern Republican delegates. The twistings and turnings of Roosevelt's southern policy did have one element of consistency: they helped guarantee the president's firmer control of the Republican party.[53]

During the early years of Theodore Roosevelt's administration, American Negroes responded to his leadership with great enthusiasm, referring to him as "our President—the first since Lincoln set us free." But ultimately the shifting nature of Roosevelt's policies in the South and especially his quondam endorsement of lily-white Republicans disturbed many Negroes and caused Booker T. Washington hurriedly to use his influence to reassure his people of the president's fairness. Roosevelt's action in ordering the discharge without honor of three companies of black soldiers, in the notorious Brownsville affair of 1906, caused many Negroes to become disillusioned with him.[54] Although Washington disagreed with the Brownsville order, he remained on close terms with Roosevelt throughout his administration. He continued his role as presidential adviser during the Taft administration.

52. Woodward, *Origins of the New South*, p. 463.
53. John Morton Blum, *The Republican Roosevelt* (Cambridge, 1954), pp. 44–47.
54. Franklin, *From Slavery to Freedom*, pp. 428, 434; Woodward, *Origins of the New South*, pp. 463–65.

The optimistic forecasts, indulged in so freely at the beginning of Roosevelt's term, that envisaged a new nationalism in the South and a rapid flocking of white Southerners to Roosevelt's banner were never realized. Instead, the president was violently abused in and out of political years, and made the butt of an endless number of stories. He gained few political adherents in Dixie, although many Southerners admired his bold policies on such questions as the Panama Canal and railroad regulation. Personally, T. R. was as irresistible in the South as elsewhere. On an extended tour of the region in 1905, he was warmly greeted by Southerners; he reciprocated by discussing southern problems and praising southern traditions. "I am as proud of the South as I am of the North," he told a friend sometime later. "The South has retained some barbaric virtues which we have tended to lose in the North. . . ."[55] The president said nothing about the race question on his southern tour. As the historian William Garrott Brown said, "If there has been any conversion on that subject, it is rather the President than the South that has seen a new light."[56]

Southerners could be an exhilarating audience when Theodore Roosevelt addressed them in person; they could even demonstrate a growing capacity to think in other than racial terms by their response to his discussion of important national problems. But apparently they could never really forget the first episode that had turned them against the youthful president. As Alfred Holt Stone wrote in 1908, "That episode tinged for the South every subsequent act of his in which the Negro was concerned."[57]

55. Roosevelt to Owen Wister, April 27, 1906, in *Letters of Theodore Roosevelt*, 5:224.

56. Brown, "President Roosevelt and the South," *Independent* 59 (November 9, 1905): 1089.

57. Stone, *Studies in the American Race Problem*, p. 315.

4

Three Violent Scenes in Southern Politics

Historically, violence has been an American and not merely a southern phenomenon. But in some respects the tradition of violence and its vitality as a cultural pattern have contributed to southern distinctiveness. After reviewing homicide rates in the southern states during the late nineteenth century, C. Vann Woodward concluded, in *Origins of the New South, 1877–1913* (1951), that "the South seems to have been one of the most violent communities of comparable size in all Christendom." The Southerner's insistence upon autonomy in personal relations and his habit of self-redress no doubt fostered the fearful toll that resulted from individual encounters, not to mention the actions of lynching mobs, night riders, whitecappers, and other vigilante groups. The long frontier experience and the presence of a large black population probably abetted the inclination toward violence in the region, but Sheldon Hackney has offered a more fundamental explanation: "the development of a southern world view that defined the social, political, and physical environment as hostile and casts the white southerner in the role of the passive victim of malevolent forces." For whatever reason, the attitudes of white Southerners toward the private use of force and violence continue to differ appreciably from those of other white Americans. John Shelton Reed notes in *The Enduring South: Subcultural Persistence in Mass Society* (1972) that the South still manifests "a subculture of violence" and remains the most violent part of an increasingly violent nation.

One strain of southern violence has taken the form of physical assault and even murder in politics. Political assassination and other kinds of extremism are not peculiar to the southern states, of course, but the three examples discussed in this essay reveal some distinguishing characteristics of the prevailing political culture in the South early in the twentieth century. The very nature of politics in the various southern states—atomistic, disorganized, based on loose and shifting factional groupings—enhanced the importance of personality, the emergence of demagogues, and the "hell-of-a-fellow" complex in political campaigns. These tendencies were related to a second, somewhat paradoxical, feature of southern politics: the democratization of the political process for white men. Despite the conformity engendered by the one-party system and the effective disfranchisement of many poor whites as well as most blacks, the role of primary elections and the tenor of campaign rhetoric directed toward the "common man" had their effect upon the thinking of ordinary white Southerners. This effect was heightened by a third development of the late nineteenth and early twentieth centuries—the official proscription and widespread degradation of southern blacks. All of these factors played a part in the political excesses and occasional eruption of violence illustrated in this paper.

Two comprehensive works are useful for the study of violence in the United States: Hugh Davis Graham and Ted Robert Gurr, eds., *Violence in America: Historical and Comparative Perspectives* (1969), and Richard Maxwell Brown, *Strain of Violence: Historical Studies of American Violence and Vigilantism* (1975). The first of these studies includes a thoughtful analysis of "Southern Violence" by Sheldon Hackney. The milieu, circumstances, and aftermath of N. G. Gonzales' death—one of the episodes described in the following pages—are dealt with more fully in Lewis Pinckney Jones, *Stormy Petrel: N. G. Gonzales and His State* (1973).

Scene I

I N January 1900 Frankfort, Kentucky, wavered on the edge of violence. The city had recently become the center of a stormy political contest over the governorship of the state. It was tense with excitement and expectation; the air was filled with reports of political moves and countermoves, blown everywhere by the shifting winds of rumor. The governor was flanked by the state militia, the members of the general assembly were armed, and the bars and beer parlors were crowded with angry men. Then, on January 30, it happened.

As William Goebel, leader of the liberal Democrats in Kentucky, and two of his political supporters approached the capitol that cold morning, the sharp report of a rifle rang out from a nearby building. Goebel uttered a quick, involuntary cry of pain and made a futile attempt to draw his own revolver as he sank to the pavement, with a bullet through his chest. Rapidly several other shots were fired by the concealed assailant but they struck the brick sidewalk without taking effect. The wounded man was taken to a hotel in the vicinity and given medical aid. Four days later he died and the news sped throughout Kentucky: "They killed Goebel." For a long moment the state moved perilously close to civil war.

The train of events that led to William Goebel's assassination on the capitol grounds at Frankfort was long and complicated, but three developments were particularly important in the formation of the political milieu in which the crime took place. For one thing, Kentucky's political affairs had been dominated for many years by powerful corporations, most notably the Louisville and Nashville Railroad Company. Inevitably this condition provoked political rebellion and demands for reform. A second key to an understanding of Kentucky politics in 1900 is to be found in the agrarian unrest and radicalism of the 1890s. The Populist program and the emergence of William Jennings Bryan precipitated a sharp cleavage in the Democratic party in the state. Although Bryan lost the election of 1896, his reform proposals and his leadership enlisted the support of many Kentuckians during the following years.

A third significant factor in the Kentucky situation was the rise of a powerful reform leader within the state. This man was William Goebel, probably the most controversial figure in modern Kentucky history. The son of German-born parents of modest means, Goebel was a taciturn and determined lawyer from north Kentucky who had served in the state senate for a dozen years. He emerged rapidly after

1896 as the strongest Bryan Democrat in Kentucky and the leader of the reform forces in the legislature. He demonstrated his power in 1898 by securing the passage of a new election law which his opponents claimed would give him and his friends a determining voice in the outcome of state elections. Although he was strongly opposed by conservative Democrats and business interests, Goebel conducted such a skillful campaign at the state convention in 1899 that he won the Democratic nomination for governor.

The campaign that followed was one of the bitterest in the annals of Kentucky politics. Goebel made a vigorous appeal to the voters; he advocated numerous reforms and scathingly criticized the domination of state politics by corporations like the L & N Railroad. So hostile were some anti-Goebel Democrats to their party's nominee that they put forward a candidate of their own—a "solid-gold, freedom-loving, honest election" man. The Republican candidate, William S. Taylor, was the beneficiary of the division in the Democratic party and of powerful business support. He was narrowly elected, receiving some 2,400 more votes than Goebel, out of a total of about 400,000 votes cast.

Goebel leaders immediately charged fraud. But the state election commission, created by the Goebel Election Law, authenticated the Republican victory, and Taylor was inaugurated on December 12, 1899. Goebel and his friends refused to give up, however, and early in 1900 took their case to the Democratic-controlled legislature, arguing that the election had been corrupted by the railroads and other corporations. It soon became apparent that the Democratic majority in the general assembly was going to unseat the Republican administration. By this time the atmosphere in Frankfort was indescribably tense. The town was full of the partisans of both sides. More than a thousand mountaineers, apparently given free transportation by the L & N, and well armed with "moonshine" and "squirrel guns," poured into Frankfort determined to prevent the Goebelites from "stealing" the governorship. Rumors had long been circulated to the effect that the Democratic leader would never live to be inaugurated, even if he won the disputed election. On the eve of the legislature's decision Goebel was shot.

While Goebel lay fighting for his life in a stuffy room in the Capitol Hotel, the Democratic members of the legislature, barred from the capitol by Governor Taylor's orders, met in the same hotel and declared Goebel the legally elected governor of Kentucky. On the day after he was shot, the stricken leader was propped up in his bed and sworn in as governor. Meanwhile Taylor, having adjourned the legislature and directed it to meet in a Republican stronghold in eastern Kentucky, had entrenched himself in the governor's offices behind the bayonets of the state militia. On February 3 Goebel died. An hour later the Democratic lieutenant governor, J. C. W. Beckham, was sworn in as his successor. Kentucky still had two governors, and men all over the state were urging a resort to pistols and rifles.

Somehow the threat of civil war passed. The political deadlock was ultimately broken by the courts in favor of the Democrats. With the martyred Goebel as their symbol, the vengeful Democrats soon passed a stringent railroad control law, but it proved to be far more difficult to enforce than it had been to enact. The Goebelites also pressed the search for their leader's assassin. He was never identified, although three men, including the Republican secretary of state, Caleb Powers, were tried and convicted for the crime.

William Goebel's assassination became a *cause célèbre* in Kentucky politics. It sharpened the bifactionalism in the state's Democratic party, but at the same time, by promoting an extravagant personal politics, tended to gloss over the more fundamental economic and social cleavages which had helped make possible Goebel's rise.

Scene II

A few minutes before two o'clock on January 15, 1903, the lieutenant governor of South Carolina, James H. Tillman, met his bitter enemy, Narciso G. Gonzales, at the corner of Main Street and Gervais in Columbia. Tillman, the nephew of the famous "Pitchfork Ben" Tillman, had just left the state capitol after presiding over a session of the senate. Gonzales, brilliant editor of the Columbia *State* and critic of Tillmanism, was walking home for lunch, following his usual route through the city.

When Tillman saw Gonzales, he drew a pistol and shot the editor in the chest. As Gonzales staggered back against a transfer station, Tillman coolly wiped his gun on his coat sleeve and raised the weapon a second time. At this the wounded man, who was unarmed, cried out, "Shoot again, you coward." Tillman then lowered his revolver, and several passersby rushed up to assist Gonzales. Within a few minutes great excitement prevailed in the city, as the word was passed along the streets that Jim Tillman had shot N. G. Gonzales. Four days later Gonzales died.

James H. Tillman was the son of Benjamin R. Tillman's brother,

George D. Tillman. Jim Tillman, as he was called, was a man of striking appearance, a reckless but affable braggart, clever and ambitious, eager to follow in his uncle's footsteps. Ben Tillman said that he had "as many brains as any Tillman I ever knew." But Ben's biographer notes that he was "a free spender of his own and other people's money, a gambler, a drinker, a rascal who sometimes tried to wear the cloak of righteousness." Despite his erratic conduct, Jim moved steadily up the ladder of South Carolina politics, in part because of his uncle's power and prestige, in part because his demagoguery appealed to upstate textile workers and other dispossessed South Carolinians. By 1902 he was ready to try for the governorship.

Meanwhile, Jim Tillman's politics came under strong attack from Narciso G. Gonzales in the Columbia *State*. Gonzales, the son of a Cuban patriot who married into a prominent South Carolina family and served bravely in the Confederate Army, had launched the *State* as an anti-Tillman journal in the wake of the Tillman revolution of 1890. A man of firm integrity and high ideals, N. G. Gonzales had early recognized the dangers inherent in Tillmanism and the possibilities it held for demagoguery and reaction. In Jim Tillman's career he saw his worst fears being realized. Always bold and outspoken, he determined to expose the younger Tillman for what he was and to save his state from this species of Tillmanism.

Gonzales' harshest criticism of Jim Tillman came in the Democratic campaign of 1902, in which Tillman was a candidate for governor, but the enmity between the two men went back many years. As early as 1890, young Tillman had accused the "wily Spaniard" of falsely reporting some of his uncle's speeches; soon afterward Gonzales had remarked that Jim Tillman was "unfit for association with gentlemen." He ignored the hotheaded Tillman's challenge to a duel. During the campaign of 1902, Gonzales attacked Tillman in editorial after editorial, calling him a "proven liar, defaulter, gambler and drunkard," a "blackguard," a "criminal candidate," a "disgrace to his uncle, a double disgrace to his father." As Francis Butler Simkins says, "Jim Tillman was disgraced before the people and defeated in his candidacy for governor." Jim never forgot this humiliation. "But for the brutal, false and malicious newspaper attacks headed by N. G. Gonzales," he declared, "I believe I would have been elected."

Four months after the election Gonzales was assassinated. Despite the indignation expressed in the state and throughout the country, Tillman was acquitted after a trial in which he made a farcical plea of self-defense. "This is as gross a miscarriage of justice as has ever been witnessed in any part of the Union," declared the New York *Evening Post*. Yet many South Carolinians felt that the shooting was justified. As John Temple Graves put it in the Atlanta *News*, "the better man had hounded the worser to a point that justified the worser in this act."

The Baltimore *American* described Gonzales' murder as "the natural corollary of the rise of the Tillmans to power and influence in South Carolina." There was an implication in this evaluation that did an injustice to the constructive side of Benjamin R. Tillman's work in South Carolina, but the *American*'s statement was not without a certain validity. For in arousing the common white man to a realization of his potential importance in the state's politics, Ben Tillman opened the door to irresponsible men like his nephew who would cater to the worst passions and prejudices of the people in order to further their own political ambitions.

The political impact of the murder in South Carolina was similar to that of the Goebel assassination in Kentucky. It exacerbated the friction between the major political factions in the state, while diverting attention from more fundamental economic and social questions. There was plenty of passion and considerable vigor in South Carolina politics, but the passion and vigor were too often absorbed in political feuds and personal politics.

Scene III

On the afternoon of November 9, 1908, Edward Ward Carmack, the crusading editor of the Nashville *Tennessean*, was walking north on Seventh Avenue in Nashville, Tennessee. Ahead of him and to his right, up the hill a few hundred yards, loomed the state capitol. It was shortly after four o'clock, and Carmack was on the way to his boardinghouse, having just left the offices of his newspaper. In front of the Polk Flats he paused to exchange greetings with a friend, Mrs. Charles H. Eastman. According to Mrs. Eastman's later testimony, the voice of Col. Duncan Brown Cooper suddenly interrupted them: "Now we've got you all right, sir; we've got the drop on you."

At the sound of Cooper's voice, Carmack sprang clear of Mrs. Eastman and drew his pistol, wounding Colonel Cooper's son, Robin, in the shoulder. Robin Cooper, meanwhile, fired three bullets into Carmack's body, and the editor sank into the gutter, fatally wounded. The elder Cooper, whose right hand was crippled, had not participated in the exchange of shots. A curious crowd quickly gathered at the scene, and the word flashed over Nashville that the Coopers had killed Ned Carmack.

Carmack's death was the sequel to a bitter political contest in 1908. A fiery orator, prohibitionist, and opponent of corporations, Carmack had sought unsuccessfully to win the Democratic nomination for governor in that campaign. He had lost to Governor Malcolm R. Patterson, a confident and courageous politician who opposed statewide prohibition and advocated a conservative approach to the question of corporation controls.

After serving as editor of several Tennessee newspapers, Edward W. Carmack had won a contested election to Congress in 1897. He was reelected in 1898 and sent to the Senate two years later; in the upper house he made a name for himself as a staunch anti-imperialist and as a critic of President Theodore Roosevelt. A growing schism in the Democratic party of Tennessee was a factor in Carmack's defeat for reelection in 1906. Aside from personalities, the most important issue in the division among Tennessee Democrats was prohibition, which dominated state politics by 1908.

As the champion of prohibition, Carmack aggressively attacked Governor Patterson in the campaign of 1908, asserting that the Patterson "machine" was the tool of the liquor interests and the corporations, and that it opposed the direct primary as a means of nominating state officials. Carmack and Patterson engaged in a series of joint debates in various parts of Tennessee. So violent were some of these discussions that the two men almost came to blows, and on several occasions a general melee broke out in their audiences. Patterson, who controlled the party machinery, defeated Carmack in a close race, but prohibitionists took heart a few weeks later when they won a majority of the legislative seats.

After his defeat, Carmack became editor of the Nashville *Tennessean;* he pledged himself to bring statewide prohibition and other reforms to Tennessee. He continued to denounce the Patterson "machine" and many of the governor's friends, including Col. Duncan B. Cooper. A Confederate veteran and erstwhile friend of Carmack, the colonel was at this time a lobbyist for the Louisville and Nashville Railroad and an influential behind-the-scene figure in state politics. During the campaign Carmack had referred to Cooper as "a little bald-headed angel of hell," and in the fall of 1908 he criticized him sharply for his connection with the Patterson faction. On the day of his death the editor penned a particularly caustic editorial "To Major Duncan Brown Cooper, the great diplomat of the political zweibund." Cooper had already warned Carmack to keep his name out of the *Tennessean*; he now determined to have a full measure of revenge.

Following Carmack's death, the Coopers were tried and convicted of second degree murder; each man received a sentence of twenty years' imprisonment. Upon appeal to the state supreme court, the case of Robin Cooper was remanded to the lower court, but a retrial was never held. Colonel Cooper's conviction was upheld but Governor Patterson immediately pardoned him, observing that "it took the Supreme Court 72 days to decide this case and it decided it wrong; it took me but 72 minutes and I decided it right." By this time Tennessee was in a state of bitter political turmoil.

Meanwhile, Edward W. Carmack had become a martyr to "the holy cause of prohibition." Many Tennessee prohibitionists agreed with the man who declared that Carmack's blood would be "the seed from which thousands of Carmacks will arise and snatch the flag of Democracy from the beer keg and bear it in triumph to our capital festooned in the white ribbon of their mothers." This was a prophetic statement, for early in 1909 the Tennessee legislature enacted a statewide prohibition bill over Governor Patterson's veto.

From this time until the election of 1910, the cleavage in the ranks of Tennessee Democrats widened rapidly. In the spring of 1910, the anti-Patterson Democrats launched an independent movement and refused to participate in the state convention that renominated Patterson. Ultimately, many of the Independents fused with the Republicans on a reform platform stressing prohibition and elected the Republican gubernatorial candidate, Ben W. Hooper. The Solid South had been cracked for the first time in many years, and Tennessee had its first Republican governor since the early 1880s. Carmack's murder was a dramatic factor in a long chain of events leading up to the political revolution of 1910 and important developments that came in later years.

Epilogue

In death the three victims in these violent scenes achieved martyrdom and a certain triumph. Monuments were erected to their memory, and they were immortalized as shining knights who fought the good fight against the evils of politics. Their enemies fell on evil days. In Kentucky Governor William S. Taylor was forced to flee the state, Secretary of State Caleb Powers was tried four times for Goebel's murder, and Republicans were long associated in the public mind with the crime. In South Carolina many people always blamed Tillmanism for Narciso G. Gonzales' death, and as Francis B. Simkins says, "The ghost of the dead man pursued Jim Tillman the rest of his unhappy days." In Tennessee prohibition was adopted and the Patterson faction was driven from power. Governor Patterson had to retire from politics, in part, according to a story that still circulates in Tennessee today, because Carmack men cleverly took advantage of his personal weaknesses and maneuvered him into a compromising position by way of alcohol and women of ill repute. Colonel Cooper died and his son was mysteriously beaten and killed about a decade after he shot Carmack.

Carmack, Gonzales, and Goebel were in a sense their own assassins. They were all aggressive, unrelenting, crusading men and, particularly in the case of Goebel, had a violent background. The Kentuckian was a master of vituperative and biting speech, a man of remorseless determination who had killed an enemy in a gun fight in 1895. Gonzales had no such record, but he was sometimes overbearing and self-righteous, almost fanatical, in controversies with his opponents. Carmack was a practitioner of impetuous journalism, a man of caustic wit, unexcelled in sarcastic rejoinder. His bitter and personal journalism led him into many controversies, one of which resulted in an abortive duel.

Contemporary observers, especially those outside the South, placed these political crimes in the broader pattern of violence that had long characterized the region below the Potomac. An individual in the South, wrote Walter Hines Page in 1903, "assumes that he and not the organized community is dominant." This assumption of personal sovereignty was especially evident when a matter of "personal honor" was involved. "Except in rare cases," asserted the Charleston *News and Courier*, "the killing of one white man by another is the safest crime that can be committed in South Carolina." This was a harsh judgment but it had a solid core of reality.

The rise of the common white man to a place of influence in southern politics and the important role that personalities played in southern political affairs probably contributed to the frequent resort to violence in the region. Under the spell of the emotional oratory of numerous demagogues who appealed to their worst passions, many Southerners found it all too easy to match violent words with violent deeds. Certainly there were many instances of assault and murder growing out of political controversies. The South was not the only section of the country in which human life was often held cheap, but as one newspaper noted, "in the South the feuds of politicians easily pass into a homicidal mood not so commonly encountered elsewhere."

5

Black Patch War:
The Kentucky and Tennessee
Night Riders, 1905–1909

Violence in the early twentieth-century South was sometimes the product of agricultural distress. Tobacco farmers in the Black Patch of Kentucky and Tennessee, long plagued with low prices and economic hardships, were finally driven to seek relief through organization. Their desperation was exacerbated by a powerful monopoly movement directed by the American Tobacco Company. Their plight was made even more dismal by the seeming incongruity between the ruinous prices tobacco growers were receiving for their product and the improving prices other types of farmers were getting for their crops. The tobacco farmers set out to apply legitimate force in the market through cooperative methods; they intended to use economic and political pressure to attain their objectives. But the aroused farmers eventually resorted to a campaign of terror and lawlessness which proved counterproductive. Thus there were elements of conservatism as well as economic radicalism in the behavior of the Black Patch farmers.

Two other aspects of the Black Patch War are particularly noteworthy. One was the fact that the Planters' Protective Association reflected the larger organizational efforts undertaken by American farmers during this period. In the South the most important of the new agricultural groups was the Farmers' Union, but there were numerous other rural organizations, including bands of whitecappers who employed terrorist tactics to drive black farmers off the land they owned or rented. Most of the farm organizations in the South, like their counterparts in other regions, avoided third-party movements, relied on pressure-group politics, and tried to exert economic force to improve their position. Another notable feature of the tobacco belt revolt was its anticorporation campaign. While the antimonopoly sentiment expressed in the Black Patch was more virulent and sharply focused than was the case in most parts of the South, it was part of an intense and pervasive southern attitude during these years.

Readers of this essay may find it helpful to consult Theodore Saloutos' *Farmer Movements in the South, 1865–1933* (1960), the basic work on the subject. Another example of southern night riding in this period is described in Paul J. Vanderwood's *Night Riders of Reelfoot Lake* (1969). This is an account of the struggle waged by small farmers and fishermen in northwest Tennessee to prevent a private monopoly from controlling Reelfoot Lake and its environs and to preserve their way of life against a changing society.

DURING the first decade of the twentieth century one of the most bizarre episodes in modern American history came to a climax in the tobacco region of western Kentucky and Tennessee. For more than two years this dark-leaf tobacco country had been the scene of violence and destruction by night riders. Armed and masked, these grim horsemen destroyed their neighbors' tobacco beds and tobacco barns, brutally whipped those who opposed them, and even resorted to murder. They dynamited and burned warehouses and factories of the big tobacco corporations, captured and terrorized half a dozen towns, and created fear and suspicion in a large area of the tobacco belt. "By night," wrote a contemporary, "bands of masked men are roving the State [Kentucky] with flaming torches and ready revolvers, leaving behind them a trail of devastation and bloodshed."

The night riders performed on a stage built by the despair of economic hardships and the frustration of unrealized hopes. In the post-Civil War years tobacco farming was stimulated by the discovery of new types of leaf, the use of improved methods of production, and the revolution in transportation. Yet the tobacco farmers became increasingly less self-sufficient and more dependent upon the cash sale of their tobacco. Many of the Kentucky and Tennessee tobacco producers were poor and illiterate tenant farmers who relied on the staple as the principal source of their scanty income. The tobacco area, like other farm regions, had suffered from overproduction and recurrent hard times during the latter part of the nineteenth century, but while most farm prices improved during the early years of the new century, dark-leaf tobacco prices dropped to an average of four cents per pound, less than it cost the toilworn farmer to produce it. The explanation most farmers gave for this situation was the "Tobacco Trust"—the monopoly of the tobacco business established by the American Tobacco Company and the European companies associated with it. Having gained control of almost all phases of the industry, the "trust" was moving toward full integration by destroying competition on the farmer's market. As independent dealers disappeared and prices dropped, tobacco growers raised the bitter cry, "The trust is robbing us of our tobacco."

By 1904, many planters were threatened with ruin and the tobacco country of Kentucky and Tennessee faced a crisis. For several years, farm leaders in the tobacco belt had advocated united action by tobacco farmers; they urged the repeal of discriminatory federal taxes, the adoption of an acreage restriction plan, and an investigation of the "trust" by the government. Several local associations of tobacco farmers were organized, and an abortive effort was made to hold the tobacco crop off the market until prices rose. At this point, on September 24, 1904, a great rally of dark-leaf tobacco growers was held at the fairgrounds in Guthrie, Kentucky, to consider what might be done. Five thousand farmers, representing all classes of tobacco producers in the Black Patch—the dark-tobacco district of western Kentucky and Tennessee—agreed to join the Dark Tobacco District Planters' Protective Association. The organization was the brainchild of a wealthy Tennessee planter named Felix G. Ewing, who became general manager of the association. The leaders of the Planters' Protective Association hoped to persuade most of the tobacco raisers in the Black Patch to pool their tobacco, that is, pledge it to the association and store it in association warehouses until the entire crop could be sold by the organization. The farmers were going to organize "a trust against a trust."

Association leaders launched a vigorous campaign to win the support of the dark-leaf growers. Speakers and organizers toured the Black Patch lambasting the "trust" and painting a glowing picture of the new era the association would usher in. The response was encouraging. In some counties more than 90 percent of the producers pledged their crops. The county branches of the association perfected arrangements for storing pledged tobacco and attempted to give their members a cash advance to hold off the mortgage collectors and the village creditors. Slowly and painfully, in the face of many obstacles, the association demonstrated that it could benefit the tobacco farmers. By September 1906, when 25,000 people attended an association rally at Guthrie, there were twenty-five counties in Kentucky and Tennessee affiliated with the organization. Ultimately, the membership in the two states reached 30,000, with an additional 5,000 members in the dark-leaf region of Virginia. Meanwhile, a similar association had been organized at Henderson, Owensboro, and Bowling Green, with approximately 20,000 members, and the American Society of Equity had established the Burley Tobacco Society with the same objectives in the burley belt of central Kentucky. It had a membership of about 35,000 farmers.

All of this was heartening to association champions, but a number of formidable problems stood in the way of complete victory. The organization's precarious financial condition, the opposition of the tobacco "trust," and the stubborn unwillingness of some producers to join the association combined to present a serious threat to the organized farmers. Since the association was forced to hold the tobacco of its members for long periods of time, it was hard put to obtain adequate financial backing. As for the American Tobacco Company and its European associates, they fought the farm movement with every weapon at their disposal. During the first few months they refused to buy tobacco from the association; instead, they sent their agents through the tobacco belt offering attractive prices and special inducements to farmers who would sell to them. It was the nonassociation farmer who posed the greatest danger to the program of the Planters' Protective Association. Some of these men were financially burdened tenants, while others were simply lethargic and indifferent; some were dubious of the association's value, while others were too independent to participate in the pool. Ironically, when prices began to rise as a result of the pooling agreements, these "hillbillies," as the association men derisively called the non-signing tobacco growers, became the chief beneficiaries of the movement against the tobacco monopoly. Some of the association members, seeing how independent farmers were receiving remunerative prices while they themselves were suffering, quietly disposed of their tobacco to the "trust" dealers in order to share in the higher prices.

At first membership in the Planters' Protective Association was purely voluntary; there were no plans for coercion or intimidation, though boycotts of unfriendly merchants were occasionally attempted. Organizers and friends of the association sought to convince nonmembers of the benefits of cooperation. They begged, cajoled, and sometimes even prayed with farmers to join the association. But eventually it became obvious that some producers simply would not pledge their tobacco, particularly after the tobacco companies began to offer higher prices. And the association would never achieve its goals unless most of the tobacco farmers agreed to join in the undertaking.

It was frustrating indeed for the association members to stand by helplessly while the hillbillies brazenly refused to take part in the cooperative movement and sold their tobacco to the "trust" at high prices. In the Henderson, Owensboro, and Bowling Green districts of the Black Patch, and in the burley region, large groups of "day riders," calling themselves "armies of peace," rode from farm to farm urging men to support the American Society of Equity's program. But long before the "armies of peace" rode abroad, a more effective means of enforcement was being used in the dark-tobacco belt. The new force was the organization known as the night riders, which picked up where the association left off and relied on "the mask, match, lash, and hoe."

During the latter part of 1905, there were reports of secret meetings in the dark-leaf area and rumors of a secret society being organized to force farmers to pool their tobacco. In October 1905, thirty-two association men in the Stainback School District of Robertson County, Tennessee, formed the "Possum Hunters Organization" to bring pressure on the agents of the "trust" and the hillbillies. The night visits of the Possum Hunters in Robertson County soon spread to neighboring counties in Kentucky and Tennessee, and acts of violence began to occur in various parts of the Black Patch. The term *night riders* quickly came into general use, and in 1906 these anonymous bands began to operate on a larger scale. They enjoyed their greatest influence in 1907 and early 1908, when their number probably approached 10,000 men.

The night riders were elaborately organized as a secret, fraternal order known to initiates as the Silent Brigade. Although the Planters'

Protective Association disclaimed responsibility for the night riders' activities and publicly condemned their depredations, most of the riders were members of the association and their announced purpose was to compel all tobacco growers to join the association and to force tobacco dealers to cooperate with it. The order had a distinct military cast, with a general and a lieutenant commander in central command and a colonel in charge of each county. Members of each local "lodge" elected a captain to serve as their leader. Every night rider was required to take a "blood oath," swearing to obey all orders and never to reveal the secrets of the Silent Brigade. The initiation of new members was marked by a mysterious ritual, and the organization made use of a comprehensive set of passwords, signs, and signals. As a rule the riders disguised themselves by wearing black masks, slouch hats, or false beards. They were heavily armed, equipped with good saddle horses or mules, and usually operated in bands of fifteen to fifty men.

The center of the night-riding activity was in the Kentucky counties of Trigg, Caldwell, and Lyon. It was in this region that Dr. David A. Amoss, a physician and prominent association leader later identified by renegade riders as the general of the organization, lived and practiced his profession. The night riders and their friends justified their deeds by invoking the Boston Tea Party and the Ku Klux Klan as precedents. "To burn the warehouses and factories of the trust, and its agents," Dr. Amoss was supposed to have told his men, ". . . is taking no more from them than they have taken from you."

The night riders used a variety of methods to enforce their demands. In some cases a warning was sufficient to bring cooperation. Nonassenting farmers would awake some morning to find that a warning had been left during the night at the door or gate. It might be some cartridges with a crude sketch of a railroad track, a picture of a coffin with the words "At Rest," or some matches and a brief statement "Think it over." Often there would be a bundle of switches with such a message as this:

You *all will please* put your tobacco in the association and stop so much talk against it. And stopp now. . . . If you D[on't] we will WHIP y[ou] sure.
Dam You
and oblige
THE KIRKSEY NIGHT-RIDERS.

When a farmer ignored such threats, or opposed the night

riders, he was inviting trouble. His valuable tobacco plantbeds might be sown with salt or grass seed, or more likely "scraped"; his livestock might be destroyed, his farm machinery blown up, or his crops laid waste. Barn burnings and floggings became almost nightly occurrences in some Black Patch counties. A favorite night-rider tactic was to surround the home of a hillbilly late at night, call him out, and give him a severe beating. A typical case was that of a Trigg County farmer named Stephen Moseley, who had been laggard in joining the Planters' Protective Association. On a July night in 1907, he and his family were awakened by hundreds of bullets crashing into their farmhouse. Moseley was forced to come outside, where he was whipped and warned not to seek legal redress. One of the most brutal floggings in night-rider annals was that administered to Henry Bennett, a prominent farmer and trader from Crittenden County. His tobacco factory and distillery in Dycusburg were burned, and he was tied to a tree and unmercifully lashed with thorn bushes. When he died in 1910, his marker in the Dycusburg cemetery was inscribed with the legend: "KILLED BY THE NIGHT-RIDERS."

The night riders proved to be surprisingly effective. Their ruthless acts forced many independent tobacco raisers into the association and brought the capitulation of some tobacco dealers. The larger tobacco purchasers did not surrender, but they found it necessary to be eternally vigilant if their lives and property were to remain safe. Furthermore, it was no longer possible to insure tobacco warehouses and factories in some Black Patch counties.

Inevitably the night riders' assaults led to uncontrolled violence and terror in the Black Patch. The campaign of intimidation fostered distrust and suspicion; much of the neighborliness disappeared from village and countryside, and a pervasive tension settled over the tobacco region. It was no longer safe for a stranger to be abroad after sunset. One Kentuckian remembered that "a man feared to lie down at night without a loaded shotgun in reach under the edge of his bed." No man, not even an association member, knew when he might be the object of some secret attack, prompted by a real or fancied slight. Once things got out of hand, as was bound to happen, there was no way to draw the line between "justifiable" and "unjustifiable" violence. Thus innocent Negro families were threatened, whipped, and even murdered in some Kentucky counties because of the general dislike of blacks in the area. Many landlords with Negro tenants were secretly warned not to renew their contracts.

The Black Patch became a perfect stage for those rowdy and lawless men who had long wandered along the edge of violence. As an opponent of the riders recalled:

The secret and mysterious rituals, the regalia and military formations, the swift and silent rides with arms at night into strange neighborhoods to attack an alleged foe in the enemy's country, the opportunities for leadership, with the high-sounding titles and authority of office, in many cases the opportunity to gratify a spirit of revenge and spite, called not only the young and thoughtless, but the evil-minded and vicious into an oath-bound organization which . . . controlled the courts, distributed political favors and dominated the social and material interests of the community.

And, as Dr. MacDonald, the commander of the night riders in Robert Penn Warren's novel of that name, said: " . . . the good Lord never got any thousand or so men together for any purpose without a liberal assortment of sons-of-bitches thrown in. . . . Not even for the purpose of burning tobacco warehouses. . . ."

The night riders did not stop with assaults on individual hillbillies. They also attacked hostile tobacco dealers and "trust" agents. At first, those who refused to cooperate with the association were visited by bands of night riders and warned; later, some of them were whipped and many of their warehouses were destroyed. For example, the factory of James Chestnut, Italian Regie agent in Trenton, Kentucky, was burned in December 1905. On at least one occasion a group of masked men stopped a passenger train to search it for tobacco buyers. Local officials who dared to oppose the riders were likely to receive a midnight visit. An unruly judge and city marshal in Eddyville, Kentucky, for instance, were captured by a large band of riders early in 1908 and savagely lashed with buggy whips.

The Klan-like riders went so far as to raid and terrorize entire towns and villages. Their first show of armed strength came without warning early on the morning of December 1, 1906, when 250 men seized the town of Princeton, in Caldwell County, Kentucky, and burned two large tobacco factories. A year later the riders staged their most spectacular raid when they invaded Hopkinsville, Kentucky, a large town in Christian County and a stronghold of the big tobacco companies. It had long expected the night riders. At least 250 horsemen converged on the town from four directions to be met by spies who had earlier slipped into the place. Moving with military precision, the raiders quickly took possession of all communication facilities, seized the armory, and captured the police force and the fire department. One squad of men burned two large tobacco factory warehouses. Another wrecked the offices of the local newspaper, which had criticized the "Silent Brigade." Some of the invaders shot and fatally wounded a brakeman of the Louisville and Nashville Railroad, while others dragged a tobacco buyer from his home and beat him almost to death. Meanwhile, the streets were filled with masked men who kept up a continuous rattle of gunfire, smashing windows and shooting out lights. Few residents ventured out of their houses to investigate, for they knew without being told that the night riders were there. When a person was observed looking out of a window he was commanded, "Take your damn head in and put out the light." After finishing their work, the night riders held an assembly in the middle of Hopkinsville and then marched out of town singing "My Old Kentucky Home."

Bands of masked horsemen invaded several other small communities, usually to dynamite and burn the warehouses of unfriendly agents or to visit personal punishment upon hillbilly leaders. Early in January 1908, fifty-five night riders raided Russellville, in Logan County, Kentucky, burning two tobacco factories and indiscriminately shooting up the town. Other leading tobacco towns in the Black Patch, such as Clarksville, Tennessee, lived in momentary fear of night-rider raids, and a contagion of dread spread north and east from Hopkinsville. Even the towns in the burley belt, where night riding never became common, guarded their warehouses and factories against the time when secret men would rise up out of the night, armed with revolvers and torches.

Although the night riders dominated much of the Black Patch during the years 1906 to 1908, forcing many people to cooperate with the association or leave the area, there were some men who refused to be intimidated and who openly opposed the masked riders. The hillbillies never formed an effective counterorganization, but in some places they retaliated by scraping the tobacco beds and burning the barns of association members. Here and there in the dark-leaf territory, patrols were initiated to guard against the night marauders. The hillbillies delivered tobacco to the "trust" buyers in Hopkinsville by forming armed caravans from surrounding counties. One of the outstanding hillbilly leaders was Ben H. Sory, who operated a tobacco factory in Robertson County, Tennessee. He became known as the "King of the Hill Billies." After moving to Clarksville in 1906, Sory became the moving spirit of the opposition to the night riders in that city. He planted spies in the association, took charge of the city guards, and built up such a stout defense that the riders never risked an invasion of Clarksville. On one occasion Sory and his men ambushed a group of night riders returning from a raid on another town and shot two of them.

The night-riding practice soon spread beyond the tobacco belt. A national periodical reported in the fall of 1908 that "night riders are becoming a menace throughout many parts of the South." One of the most notorious areas outside the tobacco belt where night riders were active was the Reelfoot Lake country in the extreme northwestern section of Tennessee. The poor fishermen and hunters who inhabited this wild region, made reckless by their bitter controversies with the West Tennessee Land Company and the Reelfoot Lake Fish Company over fishing and grazing rights, became night riders. These men and others in nearby counties committed more than a hundred crimes before their movement came to a climax on an October night in 1908, when a band of riders seized two prominent lawyers at a lodge near the lake, ruthlessly killed one of them, and would have killed the other had he not miraculously escaped by diving into the lake. This incident aroused public opinion and brought the governor and state troops of Tennessee to Reelfoot Lake. The night riders were rounded up, more than one hundred indictments were obtained, and eight men were tried and found guilty of murder. That ended the night riding around Reelfoot Lake.

Meanwhile, the original night riders were encountering difficult times. A new Kentucky governor, Augustus E. Willson, proved more determined than his predecessor in his efforts to deal with night riding. Willson and Governor Malcolm R. Patterson of Tennessee hurried state troops to various parts of the Black Patch, and they slowly began to curb the "Silent Brigade." The militia garrisoned several tobacco towns, commenced regular patrols, raided nightrider lodges, and began to arrest some members of the secret order. Several night riders turned traitor, and Dr. Amoss, the commander in chief, had to flee from his home in Cobb. Public opinion had also begun to turn against the masked men. The press grew increasingly hostile, and a Law and Order League was organized, with branches in all the tobacco counties. Finally, the secret society began to experience serious legal challenges.

The night riders had often boasted that they feared "no judge or jury," a boast that reflected their almost complete control of local officials and courts in the dark-tobacco belt. But, in the spring of 1908, they were suddenly confronted with civil suits in the federal courts, brought by some of their victims who had left Kentucky to establish residences in other states. The riders lost the first of these suits, the famous Hollowell case. One of the features of this trial was the testimony of an ex-rider named Sanford Hall, who served as a witness against the defendants and revealed a great deal of inside information about the "Silent Brigade." The night riders, now attacked in distant courts which they could not control or intimidate, were soon faced with other damage suits in the federal courts. Many of these they lost. Eventually, in 1910, Dr. Amoss and five others were indicted and tried for participating in the Hopkinsville raid, but they were not convicted.

Sporadic night riding continued for a time, but by early 1909 law and order had returned to the Black Patch. The famous plea of the *Black Patch Journal* had finally been heard: "Rider, turn the reins of your horse's head homeward and there dwell in peace. The human heart can not condemn your zeal, but common sense and decency does your foolishness."

Although the night riders disbanded and the Planters' Protective Association ultimately deteriorated, as did the Burley Tobacco Society, the "tobacco strike" was partially successful. The farm organizations did help raise prices, the American Tobacco Company was dissolved, as a monopoly, by the federal courts, and some marketing reforms were made. More important in the long run, perhaps, was the fact that the dark-leaf and burley-tobacco producers demonstrated for the first time that they could achieve a measure of cooperation. Part of the association's success in the Black Patch was the result of night-rider activities but, as C. Vann Woodward has said, it "was bought at an appalling cost in property, suffering, life, and moral deterioration."

The organization of the tobacco farmers and the subsequent night-riding activities were part of a broader protest during the early 1900s against the corporations and monopolies. That protest took many forms, but none was more extreme or dramatic than the Black Patch War.

6

Southern Progressives and the Racial Imperative

Historians generally agree that the major reforms of the progressive era were not much concerned with the burdens and inequities of the Negro's place in American life. There is no reason to doubt the essential validity of this interpretation, particularly in the case of the South, where most blacks still lived in the pre-World War I period. But if the amelioration of the black condition was not an important objective of southern progressives, the Negro's presence and the prevailing consciousness of race became an inescapable factor in the reformers' approach to every other organized campaign of social improvement. Indeed, this racial imperative strongly influenced the rationale, objectives, and tactics of southern progressivism, whether the reform cause involved the treatment of prison inmates, child labor in industry, support for public education, the adoption of statewide prohibition, or the liberal measures of the Wilson administration in Washington. In these and other reform endeavors, white progressives in the South were impelled in varying degrees by their preoccupation with the need for social controls, especially of black people.

This essay adumbrates the connection between race and reform in the early twentieth-century South. Although virtually all white progressives in the region subscribed to the ideology of white supremacy, they differed among themselves in their racial assumptions and prescriptions. This essay suggests a tentative classification of the southern reformers. Three other themes should perhaps be mentioned. The first is the way in

which race and racist thinking assumed an instrumental role in
southern progressivism: as an impetus to greater social control,
as an aspect of a *Herrenvolk* democracy for whites, and as part
of the widespread white view of the "race settlement" as a
reform that would free the South to pursue other needed
changes. A second theme concerns the contribution southern
liberals made to the development of a national consensus on
the race question around the turn of the century. A third theme
has to do with the response of southern blacks to the
progressive impulse. It is increasingly clear, as a result of such
books as Lester C. Lamon's *Black Tennesseans, 1900–1930* (1977),
that Negro men and women in the South were not simply acted
upon by white society; they responded in their own right to the
challenges and opportunities of their time, creating
institutions, organizations, and instruments of their own. They
supported numerous reform causes and fashioned their own
version of progressivism.

This paper was presented as the Rembert W. Patrick
Memorial Lecture at Guilford College in March 1975.

T HE "racial problem" and the status of the Negro were crucial
elements in the thinking and activities of southern reformers
during the progressive era. Indeed, the relationship between
whites and blacks was at the heart of the social philosophy of the
region's progressives. As Guion Griffis Johnson once observed, the
place of blacks in southern life was "the *raison d'être* of any controversy which arose involving the general welfare of the South or
the relation of the South to the federal government."[1] Mississippians
boasted that they were the first Southerners to solve the "problem"
of white supremacy by constitutional means, yet they continued to
torture the issue in their political campaigns and public discourse.
The same was true in varying degrees in the other southern states. It
made no difference, remarked one national journal of the Mississippi

---

1. Johnson, "The Ideology of White Supremacy, 1876–1910," in *Essays in Southern
History*, ed. Fletcher Melvin Green (Chapel Hill, N.C., 1949), p. 125.

situation, whether a politician won power "by the votes of ignorant blacks or by the denunciation of them." In either case, the Negro still dominated the state's politics.[2] Despite nuances and shadings of opinion, a remarkable white consensus on racial matters had developed in the South by the early twentieth century.

This consensus reflected the widespread conviction among white Southerners that disfranchisement and the rising walls of formal segregation represented a workable settlement of the region's perplexing racial dilemma. Negro disfranchisement was finally undoing the "mischief" of Reconstruction, and with the proliferating Jim Crow laws, it promised to inaugurate a more dependable system of social control over black people. Meanwhile, as the historian William A. Dunning noted in 1901, the North had acknowledged that "its views as to the political capacity of the blacks had been irrational," and thus Northerners "manifested no disposition for a new crusade in favor of Negro equality."[3] A non-Southerner such as Bourke Cockran could appeal in 1900 for justice to the black man in one breath and advocate the repeal of the Fifteenth Amendment in the next, while the journalist Ray Stannard Baker could say some years later that the North, "wrongly or rightly, is today more than half convinced that the South is right in imposing some measure of limitation upon the franchise." Writing in 1909, Hilary A. Herbert of Alabama confidently asserted that "intelligent public opinion at the north is at this writing so thoroughly with us that there is now no longer any danger of interference with us from Washington, either legislative or executive, so long as we do not, by harsh or unjust treatment of the negro, now at our mercy, alienate the sympathies of the majority section of our union."[4]

But if white proscription of blacks in the South was steadily increasing, the two races were also becoming more estranged from each other than at any time since Reconstruction. White Southerners frequently complained during the early years of the century that Negroes of the younger generation were deteriorating morally. "The South is to-day overrun with a shiftless, vagabond, ignorant, vicious to the last degree, type of savage," declared the president of Wofford

2. "How the Negro Rules in Mississippi," *World's Work* 6 (October 1903): 3941.

3. Dunning, "The Undoing of Reconstruction," *Atlantic Monthly* 88 (October 1901): 447.

4. Quoted in Dewey W. Grantham, "The Progressive Movement and the Negro," *South Atlantic Quarterly* 54 (October 1955): 475.

College in 1904.[5] Edgar Gardner Murphy explained that these younger blacks had been reared "away from the shadow of 'the great house,' and we are confronted by the first generation which has come to maturity out of all contact, direct or indirect, with the domestic constraint and example of the stronger race."[6] "Everywhere I went in Atlanta," Ray Stannard Baker wrote of his study of southern race relations in this period, "I heard of the fear of the white people, but not much was said of the terror which the Negroes also felt. And yet every Negro I met voiced in some way that fear."[7]

Black Southerners had reason to be afraid. More than 1,100 Negroes, most of them in the South, were lynched between 1900 and the beginning of the First World War. An outbreak of race riots and near riots took place around the turn of the century, the most sensational occurring in Atlanta in the wake of a bitter and race-laden gubernatorial campaign in 1906. Deprived of the ballot, confined by law to a separate place in society, and discriminated against in virtually every aspect of life, including economic employment and the administration of justice, southern blacks were also victimized by peonage, a new form of bondage spreading through the Deep South during these years.

The volatile nature of southern white opinion on matters involving the race question was also manifested in numerous controversial incidents early in the century. Several of these grew out of President Theodore Roosevelt's actions, including his notorious White House dinner with Booker T. Washington in 1901 and certain of Roosevelt's appointment policies in the South. Another of these racially tinged episodes resulted from the publication of an article in the July 1902 issue of the *Atlantic Monthly* by the Reverend Andrew Sledd, a professor of Latin at Emory College in Georgia. In "The Negro: Another View," Sledd stated his belief in the natural inferiority of blacks, but he was sharply critical of the conditions under which southern Negroes had to live, and especially the "dehumanizing" of the black man for political gain; he condemned the practice of lynching and boldly asserted that Negroes were, "in everything save color, superior to many white men." For this heretical opinion the professor was pub-

5. Henry N. Synder, quoted in H. Shelton Smith, *In His Image, But . . . Racism in Southern Religion, 1780–1910* (Durham, 1972), p. 272.

6. Murphy, "The Task of the Leader: A Discussion of Some of the Conditions of Public Leadership in Our Southern States," *Sewanee Review* 15 (January 1907): 17.

7. Baker, *Following the Color Line: Negro Citizenship in the Progressive American Era* (New York, 1964), p. 7. Originally published in 1908.

licly excoriated, accused of "treason" to the South, and quickly forced to resign his position.[8]

A similar but more widely publicized controversy was precipitated in the fall of 1903, following the appearance of John Spencer Bassett's article, "Stirring Up the Fires of Race Antipathy," in the *South Atlantic Quarterly*. Bassett, a professor of history at Trinity College and editor of the *Quarterly*, spoke out strongly against southern racism and delivered an encomium to Booker T. Washington—"a great and good man, a Christian statesman, and take him all in all the greatest man, save General Lee, born in the South in a hundred years. . . ." Bassett and the *South Atlantic Quarterly* were part of an embryonic intellectual community in the South, one that was critical of the region's prejudices and parochialism and that urged a more rational approach to social problems, including the status of Negroes. Yet this manifestation of a more liberal spirit in North Carolina occurred in an atmosphere still inflamed by the Republican-Populist control of the nineties, the white supremacy campaigns of 1898 and 1900, and the success of the disfranchisement movement. Thus the Bassett article brought Trinity College under sharp attack from such critics as Josephus Daniels in the Raleigh *News and Observer*, and for a time Bassett's fate seemed to hang in the balance. The college stood behind him, however, and the principles of free speech and academic freedom won the day.[9] Nevertheless, blunt criticism of southern racial patterns like that of Bassett was rarely voiced in the years that followed, and Bassett himself soon left the region to accept the comfortable cloister of a northern professorship.

Worsening race relations, the prevalence of mob violence against black people, and the occurrence of incidents like the Bassett affair were all borne along by the strong current of anti-Negro thought that welled up in the aftermath of the turbulent nineties. Numerous books and articles proclaimed the Negro's degenerate state and contended that the race was retrogressing instead of advancing. Darwinist concepts of racial degeneracy and extinction gave this line of thought a patina of scientific support. The most virulent anti-Negro writings at the turn of the century pictured the black man as "a wild beast," "a fiend," "a monstrous beast" of uncontrollable sexual pas-

8. Henry Y. Warnock, "Andrew Sledd, Southern Methodists, and the Negro: A Case History," *Journal of Southern History* 31 (August 1965): 251–71.

9. Earl W. Porter, *Trinity and Duke, 1892–1924: Foundations of Duke University* (Durham, 1964), pp. 96–139. Quotation on p. 118.

sion. Thomas Dixon, a North Carolinian who wrote a series of novels on race conflict, depicted the Negro as a creature

with a racial record of four thousand years of incapacity, half-child, half-animal, the sport of impulse, whim and concert, pleased with a rattle, tickled with a straw, a being who, left to his will, roams at night and sleeps in the day, whose native tongue has framed no work of love, whose passions once aroused are as the tiger's. . . .[10]

Dixon's first novel, *The Leopard's Spots* (1902), was a story of Reconstruction, Redemption, and disfranchisement in North Carolina. It became an immediate best seller and the center of much controversy. *The Clansman* (1905), which later became the basis for the moving picture *The Birth of a Nation* (1915), provoked an even greater storm. Several other novels followed, portraying the black man as a threat to honest democratic government and to racial purity. The Negro was pictured by the novelist as an amoral creature, unable to discriminate between right and wrong, at best only a good child. He was dominated by a powerful sex impulse, an irrational and elemental force. Any effort to reverse the laws of nature by artificially equalizing the relations between the two races, Dixon cautioned, would only lead to the disintegration of the white man's world.[11] A strong imperialist, Dixon was convinced that a great national racial crisis was developing in the United States, precipitated by such alien forces as racial degradation and urban-industrial materialism. Writing from within the tradition of white democracy, Dixon attempted to justify his racial views on scientific and humanitarian grounds. In his novels the North Carolina writer brought together most of the themes that were embodied in a powerful mythological view of the southern past. These concepts included reconciliation (the idea that the South's suffering and humiliation had given it great strength of character), southern burden (the notion that the terrible burden of the past and of the Negro offered a compensatory guidance and inspiration for the future), and southern mission (to eliminate the black

10. Dixon, "Booker T. Washington and the Negro," *Saturday Evening Post* 178 (August 19, 1905): 1–2.

11. Maxwell Bloomfield, "Dixon's *The Leopard's Spots*: A Study in Popular Racism," *American Quarterly* 16 (Fall 1964): 387–401; Raymond A. Cook, "The Man Behind 'The Birth of a Nation,' " *North Carolina Historical Review* 39 (October 1962): 519–40.

man from politics and society and to preserve the nation's racial purity).[12]

In the spring of 1900 a group of professional leaders, businessmen, and politicans convened a well-publicized conference on the race question in Montgomery, Alabama. The conference was the product of the Southern Society for the Promotion of the Study of Race Conditions and Problems in the South. The society, which was organized in January 1900, intended "to furnish, by means of correspondence, publication, and particularly through public conferences, an organ for the expression of the varied and even antagonistic convictions of representative Southern men" on the race problem.[13] The timing of the Montgomery conference was significant, for it conincided with the wave of disfranchisement campaigns, the growing awareness of the racial implications of the nation's new imperialism, southern eagerness to facilitate regional economic development, and heightened concern among some white Southerners over mob violence and harsh abuse of blacks in the administration of justice. The promoters of the conference took pains to make the meeting representative and nonpartisan. But they failed to include a spokesman for the mass of white laborers and farmers, and they decided against any Negro participation. Booker T. Washington was consulted, however, and he praised the conference as an expression of the "Silent South." Writing shortly after the Montgomery meeting, the Tuskegee principal noted that "for years we have heard the voice of the North, the voice of the negro, the voice of the politician, and the voice of the mob; but the voice of the educated, cultivated white South has been too long silent."[14] Thus a forum was provided for the region's "best" white elements to speak out.

Several of the speakers during the three-day conference in Montgomery were pessimistic about prospects for improved race relations in the South. Dr. Paul B. Barringer of the University of Vir-

---

12. F. Garvin Davenport, Jr., "Thomas Dixon's Mythology of Southern History," *Journal of Southern History* 36 (August 1970): 350–67, and *The Myth of Southern History: Historical Consciousness in Twentieth-Century Southern Literature* (Nashville, 1970), pp. 23–43.

13. For accounts of the conference, see Hines H. Hall III, "The Montgomery Race Conference of 1900: Focal Point of Racial Attitudes at the Turn of the Century" (M.A. thesis, Auburn University, 1965), and Hugh C. Bailey, *Edgar Gardner Murphy: Gentle Progressive* (Coral Gables, Fla., 1968), pp. 29–50.

14. Washington, "The Montgomery Race Conference," *Century Magazine* 60 (August 1900): 631.

ginia, for example, characterized the history of blacks since Emancipation as one of complete retrogression. He suggested that they would eventually disappear as a separate racial entity. Other speakers were more optimistic, holding that material prosperity and the advance of knowledge would ultimately solve the race problem. The participants attributed the corruption in recent southern politics to unrestrained Negro suffrage; disfranchisement was approved as a reform that would purify the political process, encourage political debate, and ease racial tensions. Some speakers did advocate the uniform application of suffrage tests to both races. The main point was that black men ought to forsake the lure of political privilege and get on with the important business of economic development. A great deal of attention was given in the various sessions to questions of Negro criminality, and the alarming crime rate was interpreted by several participants as evidence of black retrogression. Lynching was discussed at length, and in a notable address by Alexander C. King, an Atlanta lawyer, the practice was condemned on several grounds. Lynching, King asserted, discredited the law and the courts, diverted notice from the crime itself and generated attention for the victim of the lynch mob, blunted the moral sense of the community, created additional race antagonism, and destroyed the safeguards against injustice to the accused.

The Montgomery society did not survive very long, and despite efforts to arrange another conference in 1901, no further meetings were held. The conference of 1900 is significant because it was the first organization established by white Southerners to deal specifically with the race issue. It also opens a revealing window into the mind of the southern moderate at the turn of the century. One scholar has aptly concluded that the Montgomery meeting was "essentially an effort by the conservative, propertied interests of the South to reach an understanding through which the outstanding racial difficulties could be removed as impediments to the economic progress and political stability of the region."[15]

The moving spirit in the organization of the Montgomery Conference on Race Relations—the major source of its inspiration, plans, and publicity—was the young Episcopalian minister Edgar Gardner Murphy. The Negro's place in southern life absorbed much of Murphy's thought and energy, and race relations occupied a central place in his reform rationale. He provides a surpassing example of a

15. Hall, "The Montgomery Race Conference of 1900," p. 2

moderate approach to racial orthodoxy in the early twentieth-century South. As early as 1893, during his ministry at Christ Church in Laredo, Texas, Murphy had organized a public protest against the lynching of a black man by a local white mob. The leading role he assumed in the Montgomery conference, at about the time he was becoming involved in the movement to restrict child labor and in the campaign for public schools, broadened and reinforced his interest in the South's perennial problem. During the following decade Murphy wrote extensively on the "race question," and black-white relations constitute a pervasive theme of his two books, *Problems of the Present South* (1904) and *The Basis of Ascendancy* (1909). The first of these works, a volume of eight essays dealing with the race question, child labor, and education, reflected the author's faith in the possibilities of regional progress and enlightened white leadership in effecting social improvements in the South. The second, addressed mainly to Southerners, was a plea for restraint and self-awareness on the part of white inhabitants. The determination of ascendancy, or downfall, Murphy declared, must rest with the "stronger race." "In my new book," the minister wrote Booker T. Washington, "I have exhausted every power at my command to 'knock out' once and for all the whole philosophy of *repression*." [16]

An accommodationist, a friend of Booker T. Washington, and a moralist with a keen appreciation of the role of the past in human thought and behavior, Edgar Gardner Murphy worked for interracial harmony and cooperation. By "cooperation" he meant paternalism, toleration, benevolence, and charity toward the "weaker race." "The real South," the Alabama minister declared in 1901, "—the South of the businessman, the educator, the churches, the schools, the homes—is helping the negro today as never before since the moment of emancipation." [17] Murphy's racial humanitarianism was mirrored in these words from an article published in 1907: "Here is this colored man whom you and I know to be 'a good negro'—industrious, sensible, self-respecting. He is making his way. He counts for something. We know him and we know we can trust him. He is right here with us on the soil of the same State. Do we want him? We do. Do we want him to stay? We do. How shall we deal with him? Treat him

16. Murphy to Washington, June 4, 1909, Booker T. Washington Papers, Manuscript Division, Library of Congress.
17. Murphy, "The Freedman's Progress in the South," *Outlook* 68 (July 27, 1901): 724.

justly. Give protection to his life and property. Give his children a chance. Let *him* vote."[18] Murphy began with the conviction that the two races were decidedly unequal in their current condition and state of development. But he believed in Negro progress, or at least in the possibility of such progress. If blacks were given economic and educational opportunities, if they were encouraged to develop their own self-sufficient social and cultural life, he argued, they would demonstrate their latent genius, evolve a sound separate culture, and lose any desire they might have to amalgamate with whites. The surest safeguard for the integrity of each race, he wrote in *The Basis of Ascendancy*, was the development of racial self-confidence. Accepting the idea that racial consciousness was universal, Murphy considered blacks to be a "backward and essentially unassimilable people." While opposing racial hatred, he thought that a mutual antipathy between the races was both inevitable and potentially good. But he did not regard racial conflict as unavoidable.

Education was basic to the minister's reform efforts. As he said, "Education is the process by which the irresponsible are bound into the life of the responsible . . . by which a people is changed from a mob into a society."[19] The school, he believed, was indispensable for economic progress, individual development, and a more democratic society. Murphy's support of the campaign for public education was strengthened by his fear of the South's illiterate white masses. That was one reason for his willingness to give priority to white education. The clergyman and other southern humanitarian progressives believed that the removal of white ignorance represented the best hope for improved race relations. Southern education reformers contended that to educate the white masses would make them more tolerant of blacks; on the other hand, a substantial increase in the education of blacks would only increase the anti-Negro hostility of ordinary white Southerners. Murphy, however, advocated schools for blacks, particularly of the Tuskegee type. Education, in his opinion, would also prepare Negroes for the right discharge of their duties as citizens. The question was simple: "Shall we keep him in the condition which best fits him to follow vile leaders, with low appeals and evil passions, to bad government; or shall we guard him against that day by educating him enough to make him amenable to

18. Murphy, "The Task of the Leader," p. 11.
19. Quoted in Daniel Levine, "Edgar Gardner Murphy: Conservative Reformer," *Alabama Review* 15 (April 1962): 111.

the influence of reason and right?"[20] Murphy wanted to develop the "higher life and feeling of our colored people," he declared in 1909, for ". . . my sympathy with the higher element among our colored people is intense and my faith in them profound."[21]

Despite his moderation and goodwill, Murphy's racial policy rested on his firm belief that Negroes were inferior to whites. This conviction accounted for his fear of "racial fusion" and his emphasis on the maintenance of "racial integrity." As he asserted in 1903, "The doctrine of race integrity, the rejection of the policy of racial fusion is, perhaps[,] the fundamental dogma of southern life."[22] The Negro must remain a separate caste. Murphy therefore found no fault with segregation laws, the dual system of public education, or the legal disfranchisement of virtually all blacks. Reconstruction had shown the failure of unlimited suffrage, the Alabama minister declared, and thus it was hardly surprising that white Southerners should regard the black man "not merely as the symbol of their social humiliation, but as the representative of administrative incompetency."[23] "The illiterate among the white population and, more especially, the great masses of illiterate blacks," he observed, "make suffrage restriction the starting point of all our responsible statesmanship."[24] Murphy also advocated the modification of the Fifteenth Amendment.

In theory Murphy opposed unequal enforcement of the suffrage restrictions, which he regarded as establishing for blacks and whites alike an incentive to education and the ownership of property. Yet he eventually decided that some illiterate white men deserved the ballot, since, he asserted, the white man "excels the negro voter by the genius of his race, by inherited capacity and by a political training which has formed part of the tradition of his class."[25] Murphy also conceded that the "experiment" of black enfranchisement should be tried again, but only under "wise restrictions and conservative safeguards." In 1901 he expressed the opinion that "the Negro as a 'menace to good government' is passing out of the imagination of the South."[26]

20. Quoted in Claude H. Nolen, *The Negro's Image in the South: The Anatomy of White Supremacy* (Lexington, Ky., 1967), p. 130.

21. Murphy to Booker T. Washington, July 16, 1909, Washington Papers.

22. Quoted in Nolen, *The Negro's Image in the South*, p. 119.

23. Murphy, "The Freedman's Progress in the South," p. 723.

24. Murphy, "Shall the Fourteenth Amendment Be Enforced?" *North American Review* 180 (January 1905): 122.

25. Quoted in Smith, *In His Image*, pp. 288–89.

26. Murphy, "The Freedman's Progress in the South," p. 723.

Early in the century Edgar Gardner Murphy seemed to be optimistic about the chances of greater racial tolerance, interracial cooperation, northern assistance, developing black leadership, and Negro progress in the areas of economic enterprise and education. But through the years Murphy was less optimistic about the future than many other southern progressives. He distrusted the philosophy of material progress, did not consider education a social panacea, and had only modest expectations as far as the various reform movements were concerned. Indeed, his hopes were tinged with anxiety resulting from his feeling that a great crisis threatened the South, especially in race relations. These forebodings reflected his concern over the upsurge of the region's white masses, the exploitative character of the burgeoning industrial system, and the disappearance of the old restraints which he associated with the social order, self-discipline, and *noblesse oblige* of the Old South. Injustice against Negroes, Murphy warned, would harm whites by spawning hate and lowering the standards of southern social, economic, and political life. Aggression against the black man would destroy "not the negro, nor the white man only, but society itself,—society as a sufficient instrument of equitable and profitable relations."[27] The young minister, who died in 1913 before his forty-fourth birthday, followed the path of reconciliation. He sought to reconcile blacks and whites, the middle class and the white masses, the North and the South. He hoped until the end that the democratization of the white South and a policy of white unity would bring southern poor whites into "the conscious movement of civilization."

Among political leaders James K. Vardaman of Mississippi represented a strain of agrarian radicalism that strongly conditioned southern progressivism. He was also a zealous champion of Negro proscription. Vardaman shrewdly capitalized on the political awakening of the white masses and the smoldering racial antagonisms that lurked just below the surface of the social order in Mississippi. Long sympathetic with Populist principles and an exponent of William Jennings Bryan's Democracy, the Mississippian combined an attack on the trusts and special "interests" with an assault upon the hapless black man. The Negro, Vardaman warned, belonged to "a race inherently unmoral, ignorant and superstitious, with a congenital tendency to crime, incapable unalterably of understanding the

27. Quoted in George M. Fredrickson, *The Black Image in the White Mind: The Debate on Afro-American Character and Destiny, 1817–1914* (New York, 1971), p. 297.

meaning of free government, devoid of those qualities of mind and soul necessary to self-control."[28] In his incendiary speeches on the race question Vardaman drew a graphic picture of the Negro as a "predatory animal," of a black aggressor race that was being misled by the policies of leaders such as Theodore Roosevelt, whom the Mississippian denounced as a "coon-flavored miscegenationist." Vardaman invoked the danger of black criminality and described the "impending crisis" resulting from the desire of Negroes for social and political equality. He spoke of the "monstrous folly of filling the head of the nigger" with a lot of useless learning, demanded the repeal of the Fifteenth Amendment and the modification of the Fourteenth, and was not averse to defending the practice of lynching. As a candidate for governor, Vardaman advocated the distribution of the school fund between the races according to the taxes paid by each.[29] Southern demagogues such as Vardaman, Theodore Roosevelt lamented in 1908, had taught the young men who came under their influence to believe that "yelling, foul-mouthed vulgarity," "coarse abuse in the most violent terms of all opponents," and "crass and brutal class selfishness" were necessary to achieve success.[30]

Somewhat surprisingly, Vardaman proved to be an able governor during his tenure between 1904 and 1908. Although he remained an outspoken Negrophobe, his proposals for retrenchment in educational expenditures for blacks were not adopted. On several occasions the governor intervened to prevent the lynching of Negroes, and he helped eradicate a form of racial terrorism against blacks in south Mississippi known as "whitecapping." Early in 1913, at the height of his influence in Mississippi politics, Vardaman entered the United States Senate. Although his record as a senator was in many respects distinctly progressive, it also reflected his intense racism. He was a vocal opponent of black appointments by the Wilson administration and a strong advocate of racial segregation in the executive departments in Washington, as were most southern con-

28. Quoted in William F. Holmes, *The White Chief: James Kimble Vardaman* (Baton Rouge, 1970), p. 193.
29. Holmes, *The White Chief*, pp. 34–39, 88–90, 102–103, 132–33, 187–88, 193–94, 197–99; Eugene E. White, "Anti-Racial Agitation in Politics: James Kimble Vardaman in the Mississippi Gubernatorial Campaign of 1903," *Journal of Mississippi History* 7 (April 1945): 91–110.
30. Roosevelt to Ray Stannard Baker, June 3, 1908, in *The Letters of Theodore Roosevelt*, ed. Elting E. Morison and others (Cambridge, Mass., 1952), 6: 1047.

gressmen for that matter. While supporting a national program of agricultural extension, he joined with several other southern congressmen in an effort to ensure white control of such expenditures in the South. His concern over the prospect of Negro women exercising the ballot caused him to delay endorsing a national woman suffrage amendment until 1918. On the other hand, his fear of the evil consequences of alcohol among blacks was one reason for his support of national prohibition. His racial attitudes reinforced his longtime anti-imperialism, and in the aftermath of the Great War they strengthened his abhorrence of Woodrow Wilson's League of Nations. Vardaman was a genuine spokesman for and champion of the white masses, and that fact lies at the heart of his paradoxical career. He was, as his biographer William F. Holmes writes, both "the master demagogue who fanned the flames of hatred" and "the dedicated reformer who worked for programs he believed benefited small white farmers, laborers, and businessmen."[31]

The juxtaposition of reform and racism was also conspicuous in the progressivism of Josephus Daniels, the foremost political editor of North Carolina early in the twentieth century. As editor of the Raleigh *News and Observer*—the "Nuisance and Disturber," according to some North Carolinians—the amiable and enthusiastic Daniels was tireless in his advocacy of reform causes. Probably no Southerner surpassed him as an exponent of Bryanism in the late nineties and early years of the twentieth century. An "apostle of righteous discontent" and an ardent and resourceful critic of big business, he carried on a vigorous campaign against the Southern Railway Company and the American Tobacco Company. He condemned the practice of granting free passes and the powerful railroad lobbies, while urging the establishment of a stronger railroad commission, lower railroad rates, a more equitable tax system, and various other reforms, including statewide prohibition, expanded public education, and child labor legislation. While unrivaled in his partisanship, his reform attitudes made him a frequent critic of Bourbon Democracy. As Joseph L. Morrison has written, the Tarheel editor "spoke and fought for virtually everything sought by the predominantly middle class reformers of that era."[32]

Daniels became a zealous supporter of Woodrow Wilson's

31. Holmes, *The White Chief*, p. xii.

32. Morrison, *Josephus Daniels Says . . . An Editor's Political Odyssey from Bryan to Wilson and F.D.R., 1894–1913* (Chapel Hill, 1962), p. 149.

nomination in 1912, and perhaps no one symbolizes better than the North Carolinian the reciprocal nature of the relationship between Wilsonian politics and southern progessivism. Daniels served ably in Wilson's cabinet as secretary of the navy. He attempted to purify and democratize the navy as well as to make it more effective, and as secretary he revealed his old fears of monopolies in his determined battles against the armor-plate manufacturers and the oil interests. Daniels' liberalism was no passing phenomenon. It remained with him, and it became more comprehensive as time passed. The North Carolina editor was not unwilling to use sectional themes, and he was quick to criticize outsiders who sought to patronize or reform the South. Yet, as E. David Cronon has suggested, Daniels provided "a direct link between the simple Bryan agrarianism of the 1890's, the broader Wilsonian idealism of the Progressive Era, and the still more complex New Deal of Franklin D. Roosevelt."[33]

Josephus Daniels' progressivism was manifested in his "faith as a democrat" as well as his anticorporation attitudes and economic radicalism. His son Jonathan remembered that his father was "scornful of any supposed elite. He kept an almost mystic faith in the people themselves."[34] But Daniels' democracy stopped short of the color line, and in fact his political ideology contained a pronounced Negrophobia. So lurid and sensational were the editor's journalistic assaults on the fusionist government of North Carolina in the 1890s that his enemies derisively labeled him "the State Saviour."[35] His efforts on behalf of Negro disfranchisement were cut from the same cloth. Unless blacks were removed from politics, Daniels contended, they would be a continuing temptation to corrupt white politicans. From time to time in the years that followed the Raleigh editor revealed the narrowness of his views in such outbreaks as the Bassett affair at Trinity College. Like many white Southerners, Daniels showed affection for blacks in a paternalistic way, and he was an admirer of Booker T. Washington. After the Negro "settlement" in North Carolina at the turn of the century, Daniels frequently praised black progress in education and business, emphases that fitted into the Tuskegee philosophy. In later years Daniels seemed to be less preoccupied with the race question, but there is no evidence that he

33. Cronon, "A Southern Progressive Looks at the New Deal," *Journal of Southern History* 24 (May 1958): 176.
34. Jonathan Daniels, *The End of Innocence* (Philadelphia, 1954), p. 17.
35. Josephus Daniels, *Editor in Politics* (Chapel Hill, 1941), pp. 253–58.

experienced any real change during the progressive era in his belief that the well-being of southern society demanded the segregation and subordination of blacks.

Another variety of social reformer in the early twentieth-century South is illustrated in the careers of two remarkable New Orleans women, the sisters Kate and Jean Gordon. Members of a prominent local family, the sisters worked for virtually every reform movement in Louisiana during the progressive period.[36] In 1896 they were instrumental in founding the Equal Rights Association (the Era Club). Kate Gordon, as the dominant figure in the Era Club, led the organization to concentrate its energies in a continuing effort to advance woman suffrage, for Kate believed that woman's emancipation would bring with it the uplifting of all society. She headed the Louisiana state suffrage association from 1904 to 1913. Meanwhile, she had begun to work for the National American Woman Suffrage Association, serving as its corresponding secretary for several years. She was influential in the decision to hold the NAWSA convention of 1903 in New Orleans and was active in promoting the suffrage cause in other states. A strong champion of "states rights suffrage," Miss Gordon eventually became a vigorous opponent of the federal amendment plan, contending that it would allow the national government and probably the Republican party to control southern elections.

Four years younger than Kate, Jean Gordon was less absorbed in the woman suffrage movement than her sister. In working as a volunteer for the Charity Organization Society of New Orleans, she became aware of the child labor problem in the Crescent City. With the help of other Era Club members, she began an investigation of the problem and took a leading part in an energetic campaign for an effective child labor statute. The result was the child labor act of 1906 and an amendment to the state constitution permitting women to become factory inspectors. She herself became the first such inspector for Orleans Parish. In 1908 she drafted and helped secure the enactment of a more comprehensive child labor statute, and during the following year she was involved in arranging a successful conference of southern governors to consider the problem of child labor in industrial work. Miss Gordon's concern over working conditions

36. For the activities of the Gordon sisters, see the biographical sketches by L. E. Zimmerman, in *Notable American Women, 1607–1950: A Biographical Dictionary*, ed. Edward James and others (Cambridge, Mass., 1971), 2: 64–68.

brought her into the National Consumers' League, and she organized a Louisiana branch of the League in 1913.[37] She opened a day nursery in 1909 to aid working women, took the lead in establishing a home for retarded girls, helped launch the School of Applied Sociology in New Orleans, served as president of the Louisiana Woman Suffrage Association during the years 1913 to 1920, and assisted in organizing the New Orleans Central Council of Social Agencies in 1921. Like her friend John M. Parker, this warm and dynamic woman joined Theodore Roosevelt's Progressive party in 1912.

The Gordon sisters, while dedicated social reformers, were typical of most southern whites in their racial attitudes. Indeed, they sometimes employed racial prejudice to advance their reform causes. In supporting the enactment of a compulsory education law in 1908, Jean Gordon declared: "As far as my experience goes, I have yet to find a Jew or a negro child in a mill, factory or department store. They are at school, well nourished, playing out in our glorious Southern sunlight, waxing strong and fat; it is only your white-faced, sunken-chested, curved backed little Christians who are in the mills and department stores."[38] Kate Gordon and other suffragists complained that Negro men could still exercise the ballot in some areas while white women could not. Suffragist leaders, North and South, repeatedly argued that white women ought not to be the political inferiors of black men and that woman suffrage would ensure or at least in no way threaten white supremacy in the South. This was emphatically the position taken by Kate Gordon.[39] The "race question" was clearly a major factor in her strenuous campaign to win the ballot for women through state rather than federal action. By 1907 she had also become fearful of black women's influence in the NAWSA and expressed her adamant opposition to the national association's operating upon anything but a white basis. "Lord knows," she explained on one occasion, "we had enough trouble to exclude the negro man from voting in the States where it really amounts to an issue, and the only hope I see in the near future for gaining [woman]

37. "The New Child Labor Law For Louisiana," *Outlook* 90 (November 7, 1908): 507–8; "Personals," *Survey* 28 (June 22, 1912): 465.

38. Jean M. Gordon, "Why the Children Are in the Factory," Supplement to *Annals of the American Academy of Political and Social Science* 32 (July 1908): 68.

39. Aileen S. Kraditor, *The Ideas of the Woman Suffrage Movement, 1890–1920* (New York, 1965), pp. 173–85, 212.

suffrage in the South will be that through the white woman's vote we can establish an honest white supremacy, and get rid of the fraudulent conditions which lend a permanency to so many of the corrupt conditions still surrounding our Southern political right to vote."[40]

On the other side of the color line most white progressives in the South admired the leadership of Booker T. Washington, whose moderation and conciliatory social philosophy strongly appealed to them. Hero of *Up From Slavery*, builder of Tuskegee Institute, deliverer of the Atlanta Compromise address, Washington offered a felicitous formula for interracial cooperation. No Negro of his generation had greater faith in the beneficence of material progress; he pictured himself as "the black version of the American success-hero."[41] The Tuskegean's emphasis on the importance of industrial education and manual training for his race brought him southern goodwill and northern philanthropy. Advocating patience and gradualism, he consistently adopted a cheerful and optimistic outlook in his many public appearances. "As I have traveled through the southern states from time to time," Washington wrote in 1910, "nothing has been more encouraging and at times surprising than the change of feeling on the part of certain individuals of the better class of white men toward the Negro."[42]

The black response to mounting white prejudice and discrimination during this period involved, as August Meier has shown, both accommodation and protest, a dichotomous theme that runs throughout American history.[43] Booker T. Washington was the most striking symbol of the accommodationist ideology during the progressive era. He appealed not only to most black Americans but also to the white middle class. He emphasized bourgeois virtues like individual initiative, education, and uplift. The Tuskegee principal, Louis R. Harlan has remarked, "endorsed not only the beatitudes but all the platitudes—the Sunday school lesson, Polonius, Poor Richard, and the Gospel of Wealth."[44] He also accepted segregation, urged

40. Kate M. Gordon to Laura Clay, October 11, 1907, Laura Clay Papers, University of Kentucky Library.

41. Louis R. Harlan, "The Secret Life of Booker T. Washington," *Journal of Southern History* 37 (August 1971): 394.

42. Washington, "Negro Life in the South," *Outlook* 96 (December 10, 1910): 831.

43. Meier, *Negro Thought in America, 1880–1915: Racial Ideologies in the Age of Booker T. Washington* (Ann Arbor, 1963). See also Louis R. Harlan, *Booker T. Washington: The Making of a Black Leader, 1856–1901* (New York, 1972).

44. Harlan, "The Secret Life of Booker T. Washington," p. 394.

stability within the caste system, and agreed to the black man's subordination in politics, although he wanted the various suffrage tests
to be applied fairly to both races. He called for "justice" for his
people and the easing of racial and sectional animosities. He spoke of
a bargain between the Negro, the southern white man "of the better
class," and the northern capitalist.

Washington was much more complex and far subtler in his racial
leadership than this characterization suggests. Behind the scenes he
was sometimes more militant than conciliatory. Thus he privately
opposed the disfranchisement laws and secretly directed court cases
against segregated railroad facilities, peonage, and the exclusion of
Negroes from jury panels. He fought a hard but losing battle to stem
the tide of the lily-white movement in the southern GOP. In his
correspondence he occasionally revealed his dissatisfaction with the
alleged reforms of southern progressives. "Much of the advance in
the direction of white education," Washington complained in 1909,
"is being made at the expense of Negro education, that is, the money
is being actually taken from the colored people and given to white
schools. The conditions in some sections of the rural South so far as
Negro education is concerned are pitiable."[45]

Nevertheless, accommodation was Washington's game, and
when militant leaders such as William E. B. Du Bois began to challenge his leadership, he marshaled his great influence and the powerful resources of his Tuskegee "machine" to nullify their moves. But
Washington's critics persisted. Oswald Garrison Villard, one of the
founders of the National Association for the Advancement of Colored
People, complained after the Tuskegean spoke at a Lincoln Day dinner in 1909: "It is always the same thing, platitudes, stories, high
praise for the Southern white man who is helping the negro up,
insistence that the way to favor lies through owning lands and farms,
etc., etc.; all note of the higher aspiration is wanting."[46] Still, as
Professor Meier concludes, Washington's philosophy unquestionably "represents in large measure the basic tendencies of Negro
thought in the period under consideration."[47]

Booker T. Washington was also a social reformer, and his ideas
both shaped and illustrated black progressivism in the South. He

45. Washington to George Foster Peabody, July 30, 1909, Washington Papers.
46. Villard to William Lloyd Garrison, February 24, 1909, Oswald Garrison Villard
Papers, Harvard University Library.
47. Meier, *Negro Thought in America*, p. 102.

supported such reform causes as prohibition, antivice campaigns, and the southern education movement. Through farmers' conferences, the National Negro Business League, land-purchasing revolving funds, all-black towns, and countless public addresses and magazine articles, he sought to encourage economic and moral development and to foster racial pride, self-help, and personal autonomy among blacks. His concern for family organization, education, and improved community life was reflected in his many schemes for black strength and mutual aid. He represented an emerging Negro middle class, and with similar black reformers in the South he "strove for an expanded concept of social justice, a more efficient pattern of living, and a greater emphasis upon local organizations."[48]

The black approach to racial progress and better social conditions was critically dependent upon the examples of the most widely known Negro leaders. Washington was preeminent among these leaders, but in every state there were locally influential advocates of self-help like the Reverend Richard Carroll of Columbia, South Carolina. These men served as the focal point for the expression of Negro attitudes and aspirations. The role of such institutions as Tuskegee, Hampton, and Fisk was also responsible for the emergence of racial self-consciousness among Negroes. In the late nineteenth and early twentieth centuries many southern black leaders, frustrated with the failure of Reconstruction and the intensification of Jim Crow, turned to the school and church as institutions in which their hopes for self-help, race pride, and separation might be realized. By 1915 the drive for black autonomy had resulted in 60 percent of the teachers being Negro in all the secondary schools and colleges in the South founded by or receiving support from northern missionary sources, though the white influence was still paramount in the major colleges.[49]

Negro newspapers like the Nashville *Globe* and the Richmond *Planet* and such pioneering research ventures as the *Publications* directed by Du Bois at Atlanta University were vitally important as agents of black progressivism. The Nashville *Globe* was the voice of black men who, being resigned to the white demands for a system

---

48. Lester C. Lamon, "Was Progressivism 'For Whites Only'? A Close Look at Black Nashvillians" (unpublished paper in possession of its author).

49. See James M. McPherson, "White Liberals and Black Power in Negro Education, 1865–1915," *American Historical Review* 75 (June 1970): 1357–86.

based on caste, became advocates of a parallel black "system" with its own board of trade, self-sufficient business community, "equal" schools, segregated parks, and pride in its own race. The editors of the *Globe* recognized the depressed status of southern Negroes but rejected the ideas of racial inferiority and dependence upon white paternalism. They were optimistic, aggressive in tone, and determined to stress the potential strength of the black population rather than its moral and economic weaknesses.[50]

One manifestation of such black power was a series of boycotts organized against Jim Crow streetcars early in the century. Although these protests were usually unavailing, they were organized in at least twenty-five southern cities between 1900 and 1906. The black reform spirit was also apparent in such civic betterment bodies as Negro boards of trade, equal rights associations, ward improvement associations, and law and order leagues. Welfare activities in the black community included orphanages, old folks' homes, hospitals, day nurseries, and settlement houses. Self-help cultural societies also existed. The Phyllis Wheatley clubs were affiliated with the National Federation of Colored Women's Clubs. The National Urban League, which was organized in 1911 with the support of white philanthropists, became the principal welfare agency among blacks. George Edmund Haynes, a young Negro professor at Fisk University, became the League's director of southern field activities. Haynes quickly decided to found a training school for black social workers and to use the League as a means of coordinating the welfare efforts of Negro women's clubs, the business efficiency programs of the boards of trade and business leagues, the morality crusades of the "colored" ministerial alliances, and the housing and school improvement appeals of other black community organizations. He tried unsuccessfully to form a "State Wide City Community Betterment Organization."[51]

Most Negro leaders in the progressive period were moderates who recognized the reality of racial segregation but hoped to curb racial violence and intimidation, promote justice to black people in the courts, build educational facilities for Negroes, enlarge economic opportunities for the race, and strengthen black institutions and race

50. Lester C. Lamon, *Black Tennesseans, 1900–1930* (Knoxville, 1977), ch. 1.

51. Lamon, *Black Tennesseans*, ch. 10; August Meier and Elliott Rudwick, "The Boycott Movement Against Jim Crow Streetcars in the South, 1900–1906," *Journal of American History* 55 (March 1969): 756–75.

pride. These spokesmen tended to be optimistic about Negro prospects and to think progress would result from hard work and a
cooperative attitude on the part of blacks. A certain ambivalence in
outlook was a natural consequence of their race pride and their resentment over the discrimination they suffered at the hands of white
Southerners. They were forever confronted with pressures both overt
and subtle to see themselves through the eyes of the dominant
whites—as an inferior race and as a problem to the white society and
even to themselves. The degree to which they resisted these pressures was a measure of their autonomy and self-respect.

By the beginning of the second decade of the twentieth century,
the "race problem" began to assume a somewhat less somber prospect in the minds of many white Southerners. There were various
reasons for this heightened mood of optimism, but one of the significant factors in creating the changed outlook was the nomination and
election of Woodrow Wilson, the first native son to be elected president since the Civil War. Southern enthusiasm for Wilson embodied
more than the expectations associated with his party leadership and
platform; they also rested on a widespread perception of him as a
man of "southern" culture and ideas. Wilson cultivated this impression among Southerners. "My earliest recollection," he remarked in
1909, "is of standing at my father's gateway in Augusta, Georgia,
when I was four years old, and hearing some one pass and say that
Mr. Lincoln was elected and there was to be war."[52] Reared and
partially educated in the South, Wilson was indelibly marked by the
southern culture. Even though he early became an ardent nationalist,
he identified himself with southern people, southern history, and
even the romantic mythology about the Old South. The South, he
once confided, was the only place in the world where nothing had to
be explained to him. Arthur S. Link has noted that Wilson "imbibed
the Southern love of locality and adherence to State rights. He inherited attachment to the Democratic party and a low tariff, and shared
his society's feeling of *noblesse oblige* toward women and Negroes,
along with its belief in segregation of the races."[53] As president of
Princeton Wilson barred blacks from admission as students, and he
sometimes told dialect stories in a Negro accent. Still, while he re-

52. Quoted in Arthur S. Link, *Woodrow Wilson: A Brief Biography* (Cleveland and
New York, 1963), p. 15.
53. Ibid., p. 18. See also Arthur S. Link, "Woodrow Wilson: The American as
Southerner," *Journal of Southern History* 36 (February 1970): 3–17.

garded Negroes as a backward race, he considered them capable of advancement through education, vocational guidance, and better economic opportunities.

Wilson, as the Democratic nominee during the campaign of 1912, appealed with some success for Negro votes, promising to deal justly with black Americans if he were elected. But this proved to be more difficult than he had anticipated. The new southern ascendancy in the federal government brought with it an intensified race consciousness in Washington. A flood of segregation proposals moved into Congress, and southern race concepts and practices gained greater currency. Wilson's leadership in dealing with this racial crisis was intermittent and wavering. Although the president resisted the most extreme proposals of white supremacists, he capitulated to many of their demands. He appointed only a few Negroes to federal offices, despite his campaign promises of just treatment of blacks, and his administration dismissed or downgraded many black civil servants. Wilson sanctioned and made more official a policy of racial segregation in federal employment. He refused to appoint a National Race Commission to study race relations in the United States, after initially appearing "wholly sympathetic" toward the idea. The political situation would not permit him to act, the president informed Oswald Garrison Villard, who had presented the plan to Wilson.[54]

The racial policies of the Wilson administration angered and disillusioned black leaders. Booker T. Washington, who had stated early in 1913 that Wilson favored "the things which tend toward the uplift, improvement, and advancement of my people," admitted a few months later that he had "never seen the colored people so discouraged and bitter as they are at the present time."[55] Strong protests from the Negro community and from white liberals forced the administration to retreat somewhat in its segregation policies. The policies were not reversed, however, and President Wilson even defended them as being in the "interest" of blacks. He contended that "by putting certain bureaus and sections of the service in the charge

54. Arthur S. Link, *Woodrow Wilson and the Progressive Era, 1910–1917* (New York, 1954), pp. 63–66; Link, *Wilson: The New Freedom* (Princeton, 1956), pp. 243–54; Kathleen Long Wolgemuth, "Woodrow Wilson's Appointment Policy and the Negro," *Journal of Southern History* 24 (November 1958): 457–71; and Nancy J. Weiss, "The Negro and the New Freedom: Fighting Wilsonian Segregation," *Political Science Quarterly* 84 (March 1969): 61–79.

55. Washington to Oswald Garrison Villard, August 10, 1913, Woodrow Wilson Papers, Manuscript Division, Library of Congress.

of negroes we are rendering them more safe in their possession of office and less likely to be discriminated against."[56] It was probably a specious argument, for only a few months later the president confessed: "I say it with shame and humiliation, but I have thought about this thing for twenty years and I see no way out."[57] Yet basically Wilson's position was one best described by George B. Tindall: "In the best tradition of Southern paternalism, he clearly wished Negroes no harm, but the whole question was peripheral to his concerns and he drifted willingly in the current of the times."[58]

The "race problem" was a crucial element in the thinking and reform efforts of southern progressives. Even so, the region's progressives differed among themselves on the race question. Political reformers, including racial extremists like James K. Vardaman, were usually, though not always, advocates of repressive measures aimed at Negroes. Progressives of the humanitarian type such as Edgar Gardner Murphy, although no less obsessed with the search for social controls, tended to be more moderate than the politicians and sought to apply "understanding" and "reason" to race relations. A third group of southern reformers, which became more evident in the second decade of the twentieth century, was more aware of the need for new approaches to the South's racial dilemma and more hopeful about the future. While assuming that blacks were racially inferior to whites, they interpreted the Negro's position as the result of environmental conditions as well as heredity.[59]

But whatever their differences over solutions to the "race problem," southern progressives were not social radicals; they were reformers within the framework of the established society. Thus, as Carl N. Degler contends, they were not dissenters in the same sense that Republicans or scalawags or Populists were.[60] Social justice progressives in the South were much like Gunnar Myrdal's later description of southern liberals: they were "inclined to stress the need

56. Wilson to Oswald Garrison Villard, July 23, 1913, in Ray Stannard Baker, *Woodrow Wilson: Life and Letters* (Garden City, N.Y., 1931), 4: 221.

57. Quoted in Lawrence J. Friedman, *The White Savage: Racial Fantasies in the Postbellum South* (Englewood Cliffs, N.J., 1970), p. 165.

58. Tindall, *The Emergence of the New South, 1913–1945* (Baton Rouge, 1967), p. 143.

59. See the categories suggested by I. A. Newby, *Jim Crow's Defense: Anti-Negro Thought in America, 1900–1930* (Baton Rouge, 1965), pp. ix–x.

60. Degler, *The Other South: Southern Dissenters in the Nineteenth Century* (New York, 1974), pp. 368–69.

for patience and to exalt the cautious approach, the slow change, the organic nature of social growth."[61] Furthermore, they were seldom reluctant in appealing to southern values and traditions as a means of winning support. Like the opponents of social reform in the region, they frequently employed racist arguments and rhetoric.

Anti-Negro attacks as a tactic were used by southern progressives in almost all of their reform campaigns. Insurgent politicians such as James K. Vardaman and Hoke Smith made effective use of racial fears and prejudices in their rise to power, though they appealed to other emotional issues as well. Josephus Daniels' vituperative treatment of John Spencer Bassett in 1903, to take another example, was probably in considerable part the Democratic editor's desire to get at the Duke family and the American Tobacco Company for reasons of partisanship, antitrust feeling, and distrust of privately supported colleges.[62] In the campaign for a child labor law in North Carolina the reformer Alexander J. McKelway strengthened the reform cause with a collection of photographs showing black children on their way to school while white children were working in the textile mills of Charlotte. Kate Gordon and other suffragists invoked racial prejudice as a means of broadening the support for their movement. Southern prohibitionists did likewise. During the Wilson administration racial considerations did a great deal to determine southern congressional votes on such matters as immigration restriction, agricultural extension, and woman suffrage. Even when white reformers avoided overt use of anti-Negro sentiment, they often sacrificed the black man's well-being in favor of white interests. This was true of the public education movement, for instance. "As a matter of absolute justice," Wallace Buttrick, the executive secretary of the General Education Board, wrote in 1904, Negroes ". . . ought to participate proportionately with the whites. But we are confronted 'with a condition and not a theory.' . . . We shall err and invite defeat, if, in the present state of public sentiment, we demand too much from the white people of the South."[63]

The impulse to reform in the early twentieth-century South was to some extent charged by fear—a fear whose scapegoat was the

61. Myrdal, *An American Dilemma: The Negro Problem and Modern Democracy* (New York, 1944), 1:470.

62. Morrison, *Josephus Daniels Says*, pp. 123–48.

63. Quoted in Louis R. Harlan, "The Southern Education Board and the Race Issue in Public Education," *Journal of Southern History* 23 (May 1957):195.

Negro, the corporation, or some other menace.[64] In a narrow sense, race provided an impetus to reform. The race settlement of the 1890s and early 1900s was, as Jack T. Kirby contends, a fundamental part of southern progressivism. Disfranchisement, segregation, and Negro proscription not only constituted a workable system of racial control but also brought a measure of social stability and public calm. Middle-class Southerners profited most from this racial "reform," according to Kirby, and became the "most articulate reformers."[65]

Many white Southerners did regard racialism as the very foundation of progressivism. Since black participation in the late nineteenth century was divisive and unsettling, architects of the new southern politics confidently asserted that the political restriction of Negroes would lead to interracial peace. It would purify politics by removing the illiterate black man as a political pawn. Nor was that all. Disfranchisement would promote a healthy division among white voters on the basis of real issues and interests, and it would make possible the enactment of badly needed local reforms. "Already there is a breath of freedom in the air," Alexander J. McKelway wrote of the North Carolina situation in 1900, "and with the shadow of negro domination no longer impending, men will divide on national questions as in the old days when the State sometimes voted for the Democrats and sometimes for the Whigs."[66] Experience soon demonstrated the illusory nature of these claims. Rather than encouraging rational debate on issues and meaningful division among white voters, disfranchisement fastened the one-party system on the South more securely than ever. The great race settlement did not eliminate demagoguery or foster better race relations. Instead it worsened the status of black people. One of the North Carolina disfranchisement leaders noted in 1902 that he was "very much surprised at the small number of Negroes who have registered [under the new suffrage provisions]. I fear that the shrinkage in the number will make the Negro absolutely indifferent to his political interests and welfare and the whites will be emboldened to oppress him in his material and

64. On this point see Robert L. Brandfon, *Cotton Kingdom of the New South: A History of the Yazoo Mississippi Delta from Reconstruction to the Twentieth Century* (Cambridge, Mass., 1967), p. 168.

65. Kirby, *Darkness at the Dawning: Race and Reform in the Progressive South* (Philadelphia, 1972), pp. 4–8.

66. McKelway, "The North Carolina Suffrage Amendment," *Independent* 52 (August 16, 1900): 1957.

educational interests." [67] That is exactly what happened. The passage of the suffrage regulations, Edgar Gardner Murphy wrote in 1907, "so far from resulting in a more general willingness to afford the Negro an educational opportunity, has been followed by an attack on practically every privilege he possesses." For example, "No sooner had the new laws been enacted than the cry arose, 'Down with the negro school!' " [68] And, as John Spencer Bassett had said during the campaign for disfranchisement in North Carolina, "It is one more step in the educating of our people that it is right to lie, to steal, & to defy all honesty in order to keep a certain party in power." [69]

Southern reformers during the progressive era reflected class interests as well as racial predispositions, and sometimes the two were inextricably connected. White Southerners differed, however, far more in their attitudes toward questions involving class than in their racial beliefs. Murphy's views on Negro voting, for instance, were not entirely concerned with race. He was an elitist, "an unabashed aristocrat who feared the mob." [70] J. Morgan Kousser has recently contended that southern progressivism, with its infusion of racism, was in reality a "revolt against democracy" for whites as well as blacks, since racial proscription and most other "reform" movements tended to enhance the position of the middle class and the economic elites. [71] The woman suffrage movement in the South and elsewhere, as Aileen S. Kraditor has written, "was essentially from beginning to end a struggle of white, native-born, middle-class women for the right to participate more fully in the public affairs of a society the basic structure of which they accepted." [72]

Talk of a democratic upheaval among white men and the revolt of the red-neck in the South undoubtedly exaggerated the extent of such changes. Yet there was an increase in popular democratic consciousness among ordinary white Southerners in the 1890s and early 1900s—a growing awareness of at least the possibility and desirabil-

67. Henry G. Connor to George Howard, November 3, 1902, quoted in William Alexander Mabry, " 'White Supremacy' and the North Carolina Suffrage Amendment," *North Carolina Historical Review* 13 (January 1936): 23.

68. Murphy, "The Task of the Leader," pp. 21–22.

69. Bassett to Herbert Baxter Adams, February 13, 1899, John Spencer Bassett Papers, Duke University Library.

70. Levine, "Edgar Gardner Murphy," p. 108.

71. Kousser, *The Shaping of Southern Politics: Suffrage Restriction and the Establishment of the One-Party South, 1880–1910* (New Haven, 1974), pp. 251–64.

72. Kraditor, *The Ideas of the Woman Suffrage Movement*, p. x.

ity of counting for more in politics and community decisions. Some contemporary observers such as the muckraking journalist Ray Stannard Baker held that the militant anti-Negro leaders represented "a genuine movement for a more democratic government in the South."[73] Alexander J. McKelway put the matter succinctly when he asserted in 1900, "it is well known that the illiterate whites of the mountains are far better citizens and far more intelligent voters than the illiterate Negroes."[74] Several years later a southern educator observed that "the more white men recognize sharply their kinship with their fellow whites, and the more democracy in every sense of the term spreads among them, the more the negro is compelled to 'keep his place'—a place that is being gradually narrowed in the North as well as in the South."[75] Such views were based upon the doctrine of hierarchical biracialism, a theory of society William Lowndes Yancey had aptly characterized on the eve of the Civil War as resting on two fundamental ideas: first, that "the white race is the citizen, and the master race, and the white man is the equal of every other white man," and second, that "the Negro is the inferior race."[76] The idea of *"Herrenvolk* democracy"—a democratic society for whites only—was pervasive in the South during this period. Thus southern suffragists saw nothing incongruous in linking the "consent of the governed" argument with appeals to white supremacy. Some southern reformers resisted the notion of *Herrenvolk* democracy, but they made little headway in overturning it in the white community.

Southern progressivism, C. Vann Woodward wrote in *Origins of the New South* (1951), was "for whites only." In a strict sense, Woodward was right, for blacks had little discernible influence on the various reform campaigns or the enactment of progressive legislation. Yet black men and women were not simply acted *upon* by white society; there was a black version of southern progressivism. Not surprisingly, black progressivism in the South, like its white counterpart, was strongly marked by middle-class ideas and leaders. Newspaper editors, ministers, teachers, and businessmen were the most articulate and influential spokesmen for the black community.

73. Baker, *Following the Color Line*, p. 238.
74. McKelway, "The North Carolina Suffrage Amendment," p. 1957.
75. Thomas Pearce Bailey, *Race Orthodoxy in the South, and Other Aspects of the Negro Question* (New York, 1914), p. 40.
76. Quoted in Fredrickson, *The Black Image in the White Mind*, p. 61.

Although black reformism stressed self-help, economic efficiency, accommodationist ideas, and racial solidarity, it included a strain of protest. Furthermore, the roots of the "New Negro" movement following World War I can be found in the social and intellectual currents of the Age of Booker T. Washington.[77] Most Negro progressives in the South resented compulsory segregation but at the same time were eager to establish racial distinctiveness and racial pride among blacks.

White racism clearly weakened or perverted many southern reform movements during the progressive era. Moreover, the "race problem" was employed by southern leaders of various political and social outlooks as the basis for white agreement and interclass reconciliation. For some white progressives the formulation of new and more effective social controls for the handling of blacks became the most vital "reform" on their agenda. Racial moderates among the southern progressives probably had some influence in preventing even greater discrimination against Negroes in such areas as education. They began an organized campaign against lynching. Although they made other modest gains during the second decade of the twentieth century, the interracial movement that took shape in the aftermath of World War I was their major contribution to the expansion of social justice for Negroes in the South. But not even the churches, themselves the captives of the dominant regional culture, were able to move beyond that limited program. In fact, organized religion in the prewar period was dominated by spokesmen who held firmly to a belief in Negro inferiority, and who thus maintained that "the system of black-white separation represented the normal development of a divinely implanted instinct."[78]

Ironically, most southern progressives seemed unaware of their own racism. They did not appreciate the fact that like the white masses they too were under "the sway of a set of controlling assumptions and mythologies."[79] The failure of southern liberals to see themselves in a realistic light was partly the result of their own self-confidence and class bias. They found it easy to attribute racial prejudice and mob violence to demagogic politicians and the easily aroused mass of poor whites. In addition they were bolstered by the

77. Meier, *Negro Thought in America*, pp. 258–60.
78. Smith, *In His Image*, pp. 304–5.
79. Bruce Clayton, *The Savage Ideal: Intolerance and Intellectual Leadership in the South, 1890–1914* (Baltimore, 1972), p. 215.

growth of scientific racism, the cult of Anglo-Saxon supremacy, and the support of southern white Protestantism. They were also encouraged by the widespread approval given their racial ideas in other parts of the country. George M. Fredrickson has suggested that the southern accommodationists helped establish a new national consensus of "enlightened" and "liberal" opinion on the race question. Thus it could be said that they lost the South to the extremists but won the North to their way of thinking.[80] The struggle to advance that position below the Potomac and the Ohio would absorb much of the energy of southern liberals in the 1920s and 1930s.

80. Fredrickson, *The Black Image in the White Mind*, pp. 298–99, 304.

7

Ray Stannard Baker's
Report on American Negro Citizenship
in the Progressive Era

Many of the ideas and convictions that entered into the "racial imperative" of the South were explored in Ray Stannard Baker's *Following the Color Line* (1908). Baker was a well-known muckraker, and his informative book, the product of close observation, extensive interviewing, and a period of total immersion in the study of current attitudes and practices, was probably the outstanding work of its kind devoted to race relations during the progressive era. The journalist's account is a valuable historical document, noteworthy for its broad scope, open-minded search for answers, and understanding of the American color line. The rising interest in Afro-American history in the 1960s led to a rediscovery of Baker's volume, which had long been out of print, and to its publication in a new, paperbound edition in 1964. The essay that follows was written as the Introduction to the new edition.

R A Y STANNARD BAKER had already gained an enviable reputation as a magazine reporter before he retired from journalism following the First World War and turned his attention to the writing of his many volumes on Woodrow Wilson. One of the writers discovered by Samuel S. McClure, he became a practitioner of the new journalism and a member of the famous muckraking team that wrote for *McClure's Magazine*. Baker investigated a variety of social problems in early twentieth-century America, and his articles on labor organizations and on the railroad question brought him praise from experts in those fields and something of the status of a public-servant-at-large. On occasion the effervescent Theodore Roosevelt invited him to the White House to sound him out before forming public policy. In the fall of 1906, the serious and energetic young Midwesterner turned to a new subject: the Negro in American life. The result was *Following the Color Line,* his most notable achievement as a journalist.

Shortly before Baker began his investigation of the Negro question he had joined with several other leading staff members of *McClure's* in the purchase of the *American Magazine.* The new venture desperately needed the kind of articles that Baker and Lincoln Steffens and Ida M. Tarbell had formerly written for *McClure's.* Baker's search for material that would help make the new magazine an "assured success" brought him to the race problem, a topic of growing national interest in an era marked by the completion of the Negro's political proscription in the South, the erection of an elaborate structure of Jim Crow legislation in the region below the Potomac, and the perpetuation and even worsening of a pattern of violence and brutality in the treatment of southern blacks. Baker had long been interested in the problem of lawlessness and mob violence, and in earlier years he had made a few excursions into Negro folklore. He had traveled to Georgia to interview Joel Chandler Harris and with the help of "Uncle Remus" had talked with some of the "ancient Negroes" who remembered the old stories. In the fall of 1904 he visited the scene of four widely publicized lynchings—in Georgia, Alabama, Ohio, and Illinois—while preparing two articles on lynching for the January and February 1905 numbers of *McClure's.* During the next two years the reporter's earlier interest in the Negro and lawlessness was reinforced.

By the early years of the twentieth century the capitulation of the South to extreme racism was virtually complete, in part because of the steady erosion of indigenous restraints during the period since Reconstruction and in part because of the acquiescence of northern liberalism as expressed in the press, the courts, and national politics. The terrible toll of mob violence against blacks in the South was producing a growing harvest of bitterness and fear; Negro migration and racial conflict also led to race riots in several northern cities; and the country as a whole seemed to be awakening to the realization that it faced "a new Negro problem." What *should* be the status of the

Negro in American life? In announcing the forthcoming appearance of Baker's articles, the editors of the *American* answered one rhetorical question with another: "Could there be anything more necessary— North or South—than light and information and publicity?"

At the outset Baker considered the possibility of confining his investigation to one southern state, perhaps South Carolina, but he quickly abandoned that idea for one treating the question in a national setting. Once the journalist settled on a subject, he could absorb himself in it completely. Reading, traveling, interviewing, collecting statistics, and filling his notebooks with information and impressions, he accumulated a mass of material from which he fashioned more than a dozen substantial magazine articles. After he had spent several weeks in the field gathering material, he would retire to his home in East Lansing, Michigan, to think and write. From the time he began his research in late October 1906 until the appearance of his last article in the September 1908 issue of the *American,* the Negro in America was Baker's major preoccupation as a journalist.

Baker began his intensive work in Atlanta on November 1, 1906, only a few weeks after a terrible race riot occurred in that city. That event became the subject of his first article and set the stage for the rest of the series. From Atlanta Baker moved on to the black belt of Alabama and Georgia, visiting such places as Tuskegee and the plantation of J. Pope Brown. Eventually he visited most of the southern states. He also followed the color line in half a dozen or more of the great northern cities, as well as in some smaller towns and communities north of the Ohio River. The subject grew more complicated and more difficult as he got into it. Wherever he went, he talked with public officials, leading spokesmen of the two races, and students of the race question. Among those he interviewed or corresponded with were Booker T. Washington, William E. B. Du Bois, Edwin A. Alderman, William E. Dodd, Edwin Mims, Alfred Holt Stone, Oswald Garrison Villard, Albert Bushnell Hart, and Mary White Ovington. His project attracted so much attention, particularly in the South, that people sent him unsolicited information and sought him out in person to offer help or advice. Baker drove himself, sometimes working sixteen hours a day, but he became increasingly excited over the prospects of his series. "I believe," he wrote his father on November 22, 1906, "I am going to be able to do a real public service with these articles. . . ."

The first article, profusely illustrated with photographs, appeared in the April 1907 number of the *American*. It was followed during successive months by four more pieces on the Negro in the South, after which, to the delight of the southern press, Baker shifted his attention to race relations in the North. The first article in this group appeared in the February 1908 issue, and the series continued until September of that year with monthly installments devoted to the Negro in the North and race relations in the United States generally. The articles were an immediate success and interest in them increased as they were published. The February and March 1908 numbers of the *American* were completely sold out. Newspaper comment was generally favorable, especially in the North, and the author observed to one correspondent that while some southern journals had given him "the anticipated fits," others had been "unexpectedly appreciative." Southern liberals and moderates applauded the series. Alexander J. McKelway, a North Carolina progressive, described the articles as "eminently fair." A northern liberal, Oswald Garrison Villard, who was later to be one of the founders of the National Association for the Advancement of Colored People, termed the first article "very successful indeed." Booker T. Washington and W.E.B. Du Bois were both complimentary in their evaluation of the series, although Du Bois had reservations about a few of Baker's points. There were a few astringent notes: some of the more militant black spokesmen were critical of an interpretation that seemed to stress the duty of Negroes to the neglect of their rights.

While the magazine articles were still appearing, Baker reached an agreement with Walter Hines Page to have them brought out as a book by Doubleday, Page & Company. The articles were arranged in *Following the Color Line* in the order of their appearance in the *American Magazine*, except for the inclusion of the two articles on lynching from *McClure's*, which were combined as chapter 9 of the book. Few revisions were made in the articles for book publication. As a book the work is somewhat episodic and lacks clear unity. Yet it is a comprehensive account, possessing a balance and objectivity unusual for its time. The style is characteristically readable and lively, and the narrative reveals Baker's insatiable curiosity about the human condition. The book's publication evoked the enthusiasm of scholarly as well as popular critics. The reviewer for the *American Journal of Sociology*, for example, described it as "remarkable for its objectivity and psychological insight." It was, students of Ray

Stannard Baker agree, the most significant of his publications prior to his biography of Woodrow Wilson.[1]

Baker, as he said, was trying "to get at the *facts*," trying to picture conditions as they actually existed during the first decade of the twentieth century. He was an indefatigable and a talented newspaperman—keen, observant, and imaginative. He took pains to express all views on the question and his frequent use of the phrase "South or North" provides a clue to his determined search for balance. Although he eschewed the role of sociologist or historian, his constant effort to understand the data he had collected and the observations of his own eyes gave his essays a dimension lacking in most journalism. These qualities were most important, perhaps, in making his account authentic and comprehensible to the average reader. The work does not always probe deeply, but it has much to commend it: the analysis of race relations in a national context, the description of concrete social situations from which racial strife arose, the graphic portrayal of the lynching mob in action, the appraisal of Negro migration, the realistic account of Negro town life, the interpretation of the opposing parties among black leaders, the recognition of the "wide and deep" chasm developing between the best elements of the two races, and the insight into the nature of racial prejudice and discrimination in South and North.

Following the Color Line was a moderate and in many respects even a conservative appraisal of the problem it surveyed. To some extent this was a tactical decision of the *American Magazine*. As John S. Phillips, one of the magazine's editors, reminded Baker in April 1907: "For the sake of effect we must keep the interest and friendliness of Southern readers. After all, they are the people whom we wish to reach and enlighten." One observer suggested that Baker was "rubbing it in" just enough to make Southerners "face the situation." Yet, fundamentally, the journalist expressed his honest convictions. They were not essentially radical in character. Baker's associations in the South tended to be with well-meaning moderates,

---

1. See John Erwin Semonche, "Progressive Journalist: Ray Stannard Baker, 1870–1914" (Ph.D. dissertation, Northwestern University, 1962), p. 173. I am indebted to this careful study of Baker's career as a journalist not only for the author's discussion of the writing of *Following the Color Line* but also for his perceptive treatment of Baker's broader role during the years 1892–1914.

men who joined with northern philanthropists in the annual Conferences for Southern Education during this period, and his interpretation reflects the paternalism and optimism associated with the current vogue of the Booker T. Washington school.

Southern white readers of whatever disposition on the race
question could find much to please them in Baker's book. His interpretation of Reconstruction as a time of chaos and corruption was
favorable to the southern white leaders. He agreed that for the time
being some segregation was necessary, and he frankly said that Negroes "as a class are to-day far inferior in education, intelligence, and
efficiency to the white people as a class." While he asserted that both
the approach of Booker T. Washington and that of W.E.B. Du Bois
were valuable, he obviously preferred the Tuskegee idea of education for service over Du Bois' more aggressive program. As a backward race Negroes would have to go forward primarily under the
tutelage of white men. Genuine progress would come only with
"time, growth, education, religion, thought." Baker also held other
assumptions that were common during the period of his investigation. At times he fell into the familiar southern habit of characterizing blacks as a race in various particulars. When he used the word
"Southerner," he meant *white* Southerner; he did not include the
Negro. It was this assumption, accepted naturally and perhaps even
unconsciously by Baker, that led Du Bois to remark to him in April
1907:

Of course, as I have said to you personally, the great trouble with anyone coming from the outside to study the Negro problem is that they do not
know the Negro as a human being, as a feeling, thinking man; that they do
know the Southerners, have met them in their homes and have been intimate with them and the result is that while they speak of the Southerner in
the second person, they continually regard the Negro as in the third person,
a sort of outside and unknown personality.[2]

Although Ray Stannard Baker thought of himself as an objective
reporter, he was intensely interested in educating his readers, in
being a "maker of understandings." "The best thing," he wrote a
few months before beginning his exploration of the color line,
"seems to be more publicity, more information, more preaching in
the wilderness." Like many other progressives, Baker had a pro-

2. Du Bois to Baker, April 3, 1907, Ray Stannard Baker Papers, Manuscript Division, Library of Congress. It might be noted that even Du Bois used the word
"Southerners" to mean southern whites.

found faith in the possibility of awakening and regenerating the individual citizen, "his intelligence, his unselfishness, his social responsibility." Yet during the years he was working on *Following the Color Line* Baker was becoming increasingly convinced of the necessity of a collectivist approach to social action, and his book presented a class analysis of historical movements.[3] Clearly there was some contradiction in the journalist's acceptance of a Washingtonian philosophy of improvement by individual effort and his class interpretation of history. The contradiction is never reconciled in *Following the Color Line*. But in answering Theodore Roosevelt's vigorous criticism of his division of society into the "Few" and the "Many" and of his thesis that the Negro problem was really part of a larger struggle for democracy, Baker insisted that the political revolution in the South offered proof that *"class action is a condition now existent."*

Although Baker contended that the Vardamans and Jeff Davises represented "a genuine movement for a more democratic government in the South," his interpretation was scarcely an endorsement of southern conditions. He criticized the old aristrocratic leadership in the region as being selfish and undemocratic, but he also realized that the new "men of the people" like Vardaman would exploit the passions and prejudices of the white masses. Yet he was hopeful. He found democracy at work in the overthrow of the old leadership and believed that it would not stop at the color line: "once its ferment begins to work in a nation it does not stop until it reaches and animates the uttermost man." In this sense Baker's work was anything but prosouthern. In fact, a note of impending political change runs strongly through the book. And despite his darker fears, he thought the South was ready for change and that the ferment of democracy would soon bring the Negro into more active participation in American society.

If Baker subscribed to many of the conservative ideas about race so commonplace in his day, he was nevertheless able to transcend much of the racism of his contemporaries. His genuine concern over the distressing conditions of American blacks, his sympathy for the downtrodden, his ardor for justice, and his basic optimism were inseparable from the argument of *Following the Color Line*. His broad

3. For a suggestive essay on Baker's search for a philosophy, see David Chalmers, "Ray Stannard Baker's Search for Reform," *Journal of the History of Ideas* 19 (June 1958): 422–34.

humanity embraced the Negro, and he considered racial conflict a spiritual as well as a social and economic problem. His very inconsistencies revealed as much. Thus it was impossible for him to reconcile his emphasis on the growing separation of the two races, into which he tried to read hopeful signs, with his belief in democracy and brotherhood. It was this confusion, this dilemma, that gave his chapter on the mulatto in America—the man caught in between—rare sensitiveness and pathos. The prophetic quality of *Following the Color Line* cannot compare with such a volume as Du Bois' *The Souls of Black Folk* (1903), but its very ambivalence makes it one of the most revealing documents of the progressive era. Baker had no ready solution for the American Dilemma; he could only suggest "a gradual substitution of understanding and sympathy for blind repulsion and hatred." But he was convinced that "the white man as well as the black is being tried by fire." And throughout his book he demonstrated a conviction that "the man farthest down" could be helped only if all Americans expressed a democratic spirit.

In the decade following the publication of *Following the Color Line* Baker retained his interest in the problem of the Negro in the United States, writing and speaking on the subject and stressing his conviction that the problem was basically one of democracy. For a time his optimism about an ultimate solution mounted. Thus in 1913 he predicted the early breakup of the Solid South, the entrance of many blacks and poor whites into politics, and a rejuvenated southern political life in which basic issues could be attacked and solved. But events soon pricked the bubble of his optimism. In the fall of 1914 he conceded that in its patronage and segregation policies the Wilson administration had "surrendered a stronghold of democracy in the treatment of the Negro & given new territory to the occupation of the idea of caste in America." In 1916 he expressed alarm over the growing economic competition between the races in the South, the increasing migration of blacks to northern cities, the growing resort to Jim Crow measures in South and North, and the mounting bitterness of Negroes because of the discriminatory treatment they suffered.

In investigating such great national problems as the role of organized labor and the most effective way for democracy to deal with powerful business aggregations, Ray Stannard Baker had shown remarkable capacity to enlarge his understanding and to grow in sympathetic appreciation of the human beings involved. This was also true of his experience in following the color line. Puzzled by the hostile response of the more aggressive black leaders to what he had written, he reexamined some of the opinions he had expressed in his book. With the passage of time he moved closer to Du Bois' philosophy of active agitation for Negro equality and in 1915 even accepted an honorary vice-presidency of the NAACP. By that time he had begun to wonder "if social equality is not, after all, the crux of the whole problem?" He continued to have faith in the promise of progress through education, economic improvement, and humanitarianism. But as the signs of danger grew during the next few years, he became appalled at "the contemptuous indifference of a large part of white America to what is going on in the depths of the volcano just below."

Following the Color Line was a pioneer work in the study of race relations in the United States. Baker's careful reporting and revealing insight make it a singularly useful account for the period it treats. Gunnar Myrdal and his associates used it as a major source in the preparation of *An American Dilemma* (1944), quoting from it more than two dozen times. In many respects it is superior to most southern travel accounts of the era, including Albert Bushnell Hart's *The Southern South* (1910), William Archer's *Through Afro-America* (1910), and Maurice S. Evans' *Black and White in the Southern States* (1915). Rupert B. Vance has described it as "the best account of race relations in the South during the period—one that reads like field notes for the future historian." [4] In its description of conditions and attitudes in the South the book often goes beyond race relations, and although not the work of a social scientist, it contributed to the conviction that the South invited disciplined sociological investigation.

Baker's volume is also significant as the most substantial contribution by any muckraker and progressive to the literature on the American Negro. It is not, strictly speaking, a muckraking book, but it does recapture some of the muckraking spirit. More important, it reflects in a superb way the assumptions and aspirations of the progressive mind which Baker typified so well. The journalist understood that the problem he was discussing was ineluctably involved in the deeper currents of American democracy, and he attempted to treat it from that perspective. He had hoped, like a good muckraker, that publicity and education would stimulate the American people to take action and gradually to set their democrary in order. But like many

---

4. Thomas D. Clark, ed., *Travels in the New South: A Bibliography*, 2 vols. (Norman, 1962), 2:18.

progressives Baker would go only so far toward greater equality. The tragedy is that even the limited reconstruction he envisaged in 1908 was largely neglected, and the progressive movement failed to come to grips with the problem.

Baker was one of the first white writers in modern America to discuss the race issue comprehensively and in a spirit of fairness. His work contributed in some measure to the forces that eventually brought the question of the Negro's status in the United States to its rightful place as a compelling national issue. But *Following the Color Line's* greatest value is as a reliable and revealing source for those interested in the course of race relations in recent American history.

8

Hoke Smith and
the New Freedom, 1913–1917

No aspect of modern American history has held a greater or more continuing interest for me than the southern politician. For the drama of southern politics has centered on the role of the region's political leaders, who have often been colorful, powerful, and intriguing. The southern politician has performed on two stages: one involving the political battles within the individual states, the other involving what Professor Key referred to as "the relations of the South as a whole with the rest of the nation." Southern congressmen have usually dominated the second of these stages. The first administration of Woodrow Wilson was an auspicious time for the congressional delegations from the southern states; a native Southerner occupied the White House, Southerners held influential positions in both houses of Congress, and the new president was committed to the enactment of a series of important reforms, many of which appealed strongly to the South.

My first study of southern politics came with the research for and writing of an M.A. thesis at the University of North Carolina entitled "Southern Congressional Leaders and the New Freedom, 1913–1917" (1947). One of these southern congressmen—Senator Hoke Smith of Georgia—became the subject of my doctoral dissertation, which was later published as *Hoke Smith and the Politics of the New South* (1958). The essay reprinted here grew out of my research for that biography and was part of a festschrift in honor of Professor Albert Ray Newsome of the University of North Carolina. It touches on the relationship between the South and the larger nation at a critical point in the evolution of American politics. In focusing on the activities of one important senator, the essay suggests the dimensions and functions of regional interests, party loyalty, Democratic factionalism, southern progressivism, and North-South stereotypes. It also says something about the eccentricities of a highly personalized politics and the impact of Woodrow Wilson's presidency on the political thinking and behavior of the South.

SOUTHERN progressives found in the Wilson administration their first real opportunity to join in the national progressive battle. Cast in responsible roles in the leadership of an administration committed to a series of definite reforms, and superbly led by the most effective Democratic leader since antebellum days, they were confronted during the four years before the nation's entry into the great European war with a mighty challenge. In one sense the challenge was not peculiar to the southern liberals but was rather a test that had to be met by all members of the national Democracy. It was absolutely necessary for the new administration to take prompt and united action in fulfilling the party's pledges if Democratic control was to be more than a fleeting episode in the long course of Republican supremacy. But southern progressives faced a particular challenge in 1913, epitomized by the simple question whether they had anything to contribute to the solution of national problems or whether they were so hedged about with sectional prejudices and particularistic notions that they would be unable to provide real leadership in the very hour of their greatest opportunity.[1]

Hoke Smith of Georgia, who was elected to the Senate in 1911, entered Congress at a propitious time in view of the recognition he had recently received as a progressive. One writer hailed him as "the most conspicuous figure in the Progressive Democracy of the

1. See Arthur S. Link, "The South and the 'New Freedom': An Interpretation," *American Scholar* 20 (Winter 1950–51): 314–24.

South," [2] while others referred to him as the "dam and sire" of the progressive movement in Georgia.[3] In 1905–6, following ten years of political retirement, Smith had begun a spectacular anticorporation and anti-Negro campaign, with the promise of numerous reforms, that was successful in overthrowing the old-line Democratic control of the state. The upheaval thus produced might have been the result, as some contemporaries contended, of the politics of the "outs" against the "ins" and of demagogic men seeking to take advantage of the passions of the time. But the Smith administration had done a good deal more than disfranchise the Negroes; it had ushered in a number of constructive reforms. It has achieved substantial advances in the state's regulation of business practices and certain modest reforms in other directions, including closer regulation of primary elections, reductions in railroad rates, and increased corporation taxes. The Smith faction had enlisted the support of many Georgians by effecting such changes as the abolition of the convict leasing system and greater appropriations for public education. Although defeated for reelection in 1908, Smith had won the governorship again in 1910 with a reform program described as the "Progressive Democracy," so called because the Smith leaders had their eyes on the progressive movement in other parts of the country. With this orientation, the Smith men found it easy to endorse Woodrow Wilson in 1912, and following the Democratic triumph, it was natural that Hoke Smith should emerge as one of the Wilson leaders in the Senate.

Characteristically, and in spite of his brief tenure in the Senate, Smith pushed forward after Wilson's election, eager to serve as a spokesman for the new administration and as a leader in the creation of its program. Because of his prestige as a former cabinet officer [4] and a widely known reform governor, because he had early iden-

2. Alexander J. McKelway, "Hoke Smith: A Progressive Democrat," *Outlook* 96 (October 1, 1910): 267–72. See also "Hoke Smith, Georgia's New Heavy-Weight Senator," *Current Literature* 51 (September 1911): 263–65; John Temple Graves, "Hoke Smith of Ga.," *Hearst's Magazine* 22 (November 1912): 46–48; New York *Times*, September 17, 1911.

3. Augusta *Chronicle*, April 3, 1914.

4. Smith had been a zealous Cleveland man in the late eighties and early nineties, using his newspaper, the Atlanta *Journal*, to rally support for Cleveland and tariff reform. So signal were the Georgian's contributions to Cleveland's nomination and election in 1892 that he was appointed to the cabinet, serving as secretary of the interior from March 1893 until September 1896.

tified himself with the Wilson movement, and because he was not the kind of man to stand on ceremony where his own interests were concerned, the Georgian assumed an active part in shaping the party plans for the implementation of the New Freedom. He was one of the progressive Democrats who attempted to reorganize the Senate committees in such a way that the progressives could dominate the important committees.[5] The result was that he received a number of good committee assignments and was appointed to the party's Senate steering committee.[6] A New York newspaper reported early in 1913 that ". . . among the new progressive senators the place [of administration spokesman] is tacitly conceded to Hoke Smith, of Georgia."[7]

During the first two years of the Wilson administration the original program of the New Freedom was virtually completed. Spurred on by their leader in the White House, the Democrats passed comprehensive tariff, currency, and antitrust legislation. Like most southern Democrats, Hoke Smith gave these measures sturdy support. While he was not an outstanding leader in the Senate's handling of this legislation, his influence in some respects was considerable. Having been associated with the tariff reform element of his party for many years, Smith was anxious to see the Democrats demonstrate their ability to enact a genuine low-tariff bill. But he was realistic enough to perceive that they would jeopardize their chances of success if their leaders insisted on radical reductions. As the Southerner wrote Woodrow Wilson in the summer of 1912, "I believe, myself, thoroughly in a tariff for revenue only, but it would be utterly impracticable to undertake . . . at this time, in good faith, to pass a tariff bill which sought to avoid anything but revenue."[8] As a member of the Finance Committee Smith devoted long hours to the work on the various tariff schedules, and he stood with Furnifold M.

5. The reorganization scheme was sometimes referred to as "Hoke Smith's Plan." Atlanta *Journal*, December 30, 1912, March 6–9, 1913; New York *Times*, January 4, 1913.

6. Smith became chairman of the Committee on Education and Labor and he was also assigned to the committees on Agriculture and Forestry, Finance, and Post Offices and Post Roads, as well as to certain minor committees. *Congressional Record*, 63 Cong., Sp. Sess., pp. 20–21. Following the death of Augustus O. Bacon, senior senator from Georgia, Smith was appointed to the committees on Judiciary and on Rules, while relinquishing his position on the Post Offices and Post Roads Committee. Ibid., 63 Cong., 2 Sess., pp. 4596, 9838.

7. New York *Herald*, quoted in Atlanta *Journal*, January 7, 1913.

8. Smith to Wilson, July 22, 1912, Woodrow Wilson Papers, Manuscript Division, Library of Congress.

Simmons in the defense of the committee's work on the Senate floor. This is not to exaggerate the Georgian's part in the passage of the Underwood-Simmons bill; it was a party measure and there were few Democratic defections. Aside from his general support of the committee's version of the bill, Smith's main concern seemed to be the needs of the South.[9]

The senator from Georgia was intensely interested in the plans for reorganizing the country's banking and currency system. He strongly supported the proposal to create as many as twelve regional banks, partly, it appears, in order that Atlanta might be selected as one of the regional banking cities, and he joined with other agrarian progressives from the South and the West in the successful demand for short-term agricultural credit.[10] He was less interested in the administration's antitrust program, which is somewhat surprising in view of his long battle against corporations and his efforts as governor to provide effective regulation of railroads and public utility companies. He supported the Federal Trade Commission bill but his major contribution to the antitrust legislation was his work on the Clayton bill as a member of the Senate Judiciary Committee. In the committee he supported the move to exempt farm organizations from the penalties of the antitrust laws.[11]

In the realm of foreign affairs Smith was a forceful administration man in 1913 and 1914. He endorsed the president's Mexican diplomacy and was one of the most outspoken defenders of the resolution repealing the Panama tolls exemption clause, despite the fact that in doing so he was forced to reverse his position of 1912.[12]

Hoke Smith's most significant service during this early period was his work for other legislation, less prominent on the administration's agenda. He had long been a propagandist for the building of a New South through scientific farming and public education, com-

9. *Cong. Record*, 63 Cong., 1 Sess., pp. 1322, 7310; Atlanta *Journal*, March 24, 25, 30, April 2–4, 1913. For Smith's efforts to force the appointment of progressives to the Finance Committee, see Edward M. House to Woodrow Wilson, November 28, 1912, Wilson Papers.

10. *Cong. Record*, 62 Cong., 3 Sess., p. 2769; 63 Cong., 1 Sess., pp. 52, 1230; 63 Cong., 2 Sess., p. 14731; Atlanta *Journal*, January 5, 1914; MS. Address (1913), Hoke Smith Collection, University of Georgia Library.

11. *Cong. Record*, 63 Cong., 2 Sess., pp. 11225, 14318, 22387; Atlanta *Journal*, June 12, 1914.

12. *Cong. Record*, 63 Cong., 2 Sess., pp. 5455, 5644–45, 7007–8, 8428–37, 10158–59; New York *Times*, March 12, April 4, June 6, 1914; Atlanta *Journal*, March 25, April 16, 1914.

plemented by the region's growing industrialization. He had participated in the educational crusade in the South during the early years of the century, making hundreds of speeches with an educational theme, donating public libraries, and serving as a member of the board of trustees of the Peabody Fund. He had followed with keen interest the work of the district agricultural and mechanical schools in Georgia, the establishment of which he had helped promote. Smith believed that there were "practical and sane ways" of helping the nation's farmers, "not in a sense of paternalism, not in a sense of taking from them their own responsibilities, but to stimulate them as individuals to a better condition . . . to carry individual responsibility and thus open the door of hope to many a struggling farmer and encourage many a tenant farmer to become the owner of the land he tills." [13] The Georgia senator had a sincere interest in agricultural and educational legislation, but he was also aware of the political benefits that could be gained from his sponsorship of such measures. As a politician he was conscious of the need to compensate in his political actions for his background as a city man and a lawyer. He was not likely to forget the predominance of farmers among his constituents, and he could not afford to forget the hold that such political enemies as Tom Watson and Joseph M. Brown held on the Georgia farmers. Thus Smith came to consider himself preeminently as a farmer's senator.

From the beginning of his Senate career the Georgian identified himself with the proposals he thought would be of value to southern farmers. He became one of the leading advocates of a bill to establish a marketing bureau in the Department of Agriculture, and he had the satisfaction of seeing large sums appropriated for the expansion of the department's marketing services. He had a part in the passage of the parcel post bill in 1912, he urged federal assistance in the construction of rural highways, and he was one of the champions of the federal warehouse bill. He assumed an important role in the enactment of the rural credits legislation, and he worked assiduously for the plan introduced by Asbury F. Lever and Ellison D. Smith providing for the regulation of cotton exchanges. [14]

13. *Cong. Record,* 64 Cong., 1 Sess., p. 7391. See also New York *Times,* September 17, 1911.

14. *Cong. Record,* 63 Cong., 1 Sess., pp. 2049–50, 2330–32, 5941; 63 Cong., 2 Sess., pp. 5078–79, 5530–34; 63 Cong., 3 Sess., pp. 2940, 5325–26; 64 Cong., 1 Sess., p. 7391; Atlanta *Journal,* March 19, 1914, January 19, 1915. See also Hoke Smith to David F. Houston, April 12, 1913, and Houston to Smith, April 14, 1913. Department of Agriculture Papers, National Archives.

But Hoke Smith's most notable contribution in the area of agricultural legislation was his sponsorship of the Smith-Lever bill, a measure providing for a federal program of agricultural extension work in cooperation with the states. The final passage of the Smith-Lever bill in the spring of 1914 marked the end of a movement of several years' duration and of a zealous two-year fight by Smith and Representative Lever.[15] Smith's part in the early preparation of the extension legislation was slight, but as Secretary of Agriculture David F. Houston said, the southern senator was "the real promoter of the bill in the Senate."[16] Smith was also the cosponsor of a complementary plan to provide for federal aid to vocational training in the secondary schools on a basis similar to that established in the Smith-Lever Act. This measure, known as the Smith-Hughes bill, was the result of the work of a presidential commission under the direction of Smith which completed its report in 1914. The Georgia senator secured the passage of the bill by the Senate in 1916, and the House passed it the following year.[17] The Smith-Lever and Smith-Hughes bills were not originally emphasized as major items in the Wilson program, but their importance was soon acknowledged, and they established a pattern of federal cooperation with the states that was often used in subsequent legislation.

The New Freedom as conceived in 1912–13 neared completion by the late summer of 1914. At that time Hoke Smith's star was at its zenith. He had just been triumphantly reelected over his longtime rival, Joseph M. Brown.[18] He had supported all of the important legislation sponsored by the Wilson administration and had taken a leading part in the enactment of the Smith-Lever bill, as well as in the passage of several other farm measures. Smith was a man who enjoyed his òwn importance. Close to the president, a powerful administration leader in the Senate, and widely praised by his constituents,

15. *Cong. Record,* 62 Cong., 3 Sess., p. 831; Atlanta *Journal,* November 13, 1912; Alfred C. True, *A History of Agricultural Extension Work in the United States, 1785–1923* (Washington, 1928), p. 108; Joseph C. Bailey, *Seaman A. Knapp: School-Master of American Agriculture* (New York, 1945), pp. 246–80.

16. Houston to Joseph P. Tumulty, May 7, 1914, Wilson Papers.

17. *Cong. Record,* 63 Cong., 1 Sess., pp. 52, 57, 2238, 9503; 64 Cong., 1 Sess., pp. 11870–78. Carroll S. Page, a Republican senator from Vermont who had sponsored a vocational education bill before Smith entered the Senate, lent strong support to the Smith-Hughes bill. In the House of Representatives Dudley M. Hughes of Georgia, the coauthor of the measure, steered the bill to its passage.

18. In the Democratic primary of August 19, 1914, Smith received over 135,000 votes to something over 69,000 for Joseph M. Brown. Atlanta *Journal,* August 19–23, 1914.

he could well feel expansive. Almost certainly he agreed with the estimate contained in a periodical article early in 1914 which stated that "probably the single new Democratic Senator who wielded the largest influence is Mr. Hoke Smith, of Georgia." [19]

But the harmonious and fruitful days of the previous two years were almost over for Smith, and certain developments had already begun which were to lead to an abrupt change in the character of his work in the Senate. The most important of these developments was the European war, which began at the very moment Smith seemed most successful. The unsettled conditions produced by the war brought a precipitous decline in the price of cotton, and the outlook for the huge crop of 1914 was gloomy indeed. A sharp recession moved through the farming regions of the South. Smith at once took the lead among southern congressmen in pressing a series of demands for direct federal aid to the cotton farmers. The cotton congressmen became increasingly urgent in their proposals, and some of the extremists, led by the Georgian, went so far as to engage in a futile Senate filibuster late in October 1914 in an effort to secure such remedial legislation as the authorization of emergency currency and the federal purchase of surplus cotton. [20]

Hoke Smith was busy day and night with these plans, which became a veritable obsession with him. For eighteen months his battle for the cotton producers occupied his major attention. If the New Freedom had ever meant a certain philosophy or a program of liberal reform to the senator, it was soon abandoned as he concentrated upon what he considered to be injustices suffered by southern farmers. He protested continually against British trade restrictions that prevented cotton from reaching the markets of northern and central Europe, he badgered the administration to be more vigorous in its defense of American rights, and he arranged for the exportation

19. Burton J. Hendrick, "The New Order in Washington," *World's Work* 27 (January 1914): 319. "As a member of the steering committee," continued Hendrick, "Mr. Smith did much in shaping the Senate's organization. He bridges the present and past as does no other Democrat in Washington."

20. Smith proposed a bill to provide for federal licensing of cotton warehouses, which the Senate passed; an amendment to the Aldrich-Vreeland Act designed to extend its application to state banks; a measure to repeal for a limited time the 10 percent tax on state bank notes; and a bill directing the purchase by the government of five million bales of cotton at ten cents per pound. *Cong. Record*, 63 Cong., 2 Sess., pp. 16915–27, 16968–73; Atlanta *Journal*, August 13, 14, September 2, 28, October 11, 12, 24, 25, 1914; New York *Times*, October 23, 24, 1914.

of cotton to neutral and belligerent countries. He became so enraged in 1915 at British infringements that he spoke threateningly of a congressional embargo. "Throughout the long period of uncertainty and upheaval," wrote a Georgia newspaperman some years later, "cotton had in the senate of the United States at least one man who never faltered in the fight for the rehabilitation of the market and the maintenance of a price giving a fair return to the southern pro-ducer,"[21] Smith soon began to differ with the Wilson administration in its attitude toward the Allies and to feel that the president and his advisers did not really appreciate the plight of the farmers. His rela-tionship with Wilson became increasingly strained, and he began to adopt a negative or wavering position on such legislation as the La Follette Seamen's bill and the administration shipping bill.

Smith seems to have miscalculated in his estimate of the support he could count on from his Georgia constituents in the cotton crusade. This is not to underestimate the angry feeling among south-ern cotton men at the British blockade. As Representative Hatton W. Sumners found on touring his Texas district in July 1915, there was "a state of general apprehension and rapidly growing resentment because of England's probable attitude towards cotton. . . ."[22] But when the price of cotton increased in spite of the British violations—partly because the British began to increase their cotton purchases in the United States—southern farmers were less willing to approve criticism of the Wilson administration, especially when such criticism was hostile to the side which most Americans believed was fighting for human rights and democracy in the European war. Smith was probably led further along in his censure of the adminis-tration than he originally intended, only to realize too late that his hasty words, which had often rung harshly in administration ears, prevented a resumption of his role as an administration spokesman. In part this appears to have been the result of a simple lack of forethought; Smith was always inclined to be overly enthusiastic about a current remedy and to lose sight of an occasional relevant factor. Moreover, he was a man of inordinate ambition with a naive but all-encompassing vanity. Perhaps he was intoxicated by the size of his overwhelming primary victory in 1914, and perhaps his prom-ises of federal aid during the early weeks of the cotton crisis, failing as they did, turned to bitter ashes in his mouth. Perhaps the constant

21. Theodore Tiller in the Atlanta *Journal,* July 14, 1919.
22. Sumners to Woodrow Wilson, July 31, 1915, Wilson Papers.

ridicule of such enemies as Tom Watson, who declared that the senator's vote was always in the president's pocket, goaded him into defiance. No doubt all of these things were involved, as well as Smith's genuine feeling that the farmers were being wronged and that the administration had failed both the farmers and their congressional defenders. In after years the senator may have regretted the fact that the cotton struggle had been followed with such single-minded purpose, in view of the manner in which it disrupted his work along other lines in the Senate, undermined old friendships, and opened the door to the attacks of his political opponents in Georgia, not to mention the irritation it caused in his relationship with the Wilson administration. But Hoke Smith was not a man to look back; if he had any compunction about the course he had taken, he kept it to himself.

Although the cotton depression in the South was the immediate cause of Smith's estrangement from the Wilson administration and of his eventual frustration as a constructive legislator, there were other factors that influenced him in his course after 1914. He began to find himself opposed to some of the administration's plans as they reflected a growing concern for social legislation in 1915 and 1916. Essentially the Georgian was a political opportunist who adhered to no well-conceived political philosophy, yet more than most of his southern contemporaries he believed in using the government, state and national, as an instrument to advance human progress. But as his fondest hopes of utilizing the government's power to relieve southern distress failed of realization, while the administration began to move more rapidly to achieve a large program of social legislation that was oriented toward urban and industrial problems, Smith drew back. He began to invoke the doctrine of state rights and to emphasize certain notions that stemmed from classical economics. This attitude did not prevent him from supporting measures with a distinctly Populist complexion as long as they were in the interest of southern farmers. But the specter of government ownership disturbed him. He opposed the Alaskan railroad bill early in 1914 and later in the year sought to restrict the Commission on Industrial Relations in its investigation.[23] He attempted to apply in limited degree the old doctrine of contributory negligence to the provisions

23. Smith felt that the bill to provide for the construction by the government of a system of railroads in Alaska was "utterly unwise," and that it allowed the president too broad and undefined authority in completing the project. *Cong. Record,* 63 Cong., 2 Sess., pp. 43–45, 2154, 2173, 2250, 3646–47, 11681–83, 11687–88.

of the employer's liability legislation, and he endeavored to limit the plan providing for a bureau of labor safety in the Department of Labor. "I think we are drifting in our philanthropic purpose to serve humanity into the danger of a failure entirely to recognize the differences between men," the Southerner declared during the debate on the employer's liability bill in 1916.[24] In 1915–16 he opposed the federal child labor bill on the ground that it was an invasion of state rights.[25]

It would be a mistake to overemphasize Smith's opposition to the expansion of governmental powers. He himself pointed out more than once that he believed in a government with broader jurisdiction than many of his Democratic colleagues in the Senate were willing to approve, and when he was seeking federal assistance for some purpose in which he was interested, he apparently gave little thought to conservative inhibitions.[26] He was not so recalcitrant as to oppose all of the administration's labor proposals, voting for instance in favor of the Adamson eight-hour-day measure despite the fact that he condemned the railroad strike that led to its passage as a "horrible blunder."[27] Nevertheless, on prohibition, woman suffrage, immigration restriction, and Negro officeholding Smith adopted positions in line with dominant southern prejudices.[28]

In 1916, with the national election approaching, Smith seemed to make a real effort to close ranks with administration forces. After a long Senate speech in January 1916 against the British trade infringements, he contented himself with an occasional protest. While he was critical of certain features of the preparedness program sponsored by President Wilson in 1916, he gave it his support. He refused to endorse the Gore resolution to prevent Americans from taking passage on armed belligerent ships.[29] He hesitated for a time in the spring of 1916 when the Senate Judiciary Committee was considering the confirmation of Louis D. Brandeis—apparently because

24. *Ibid.*, 64 Cong., 1 Sess., pp. 11518, 12166–67, 12888–89, 12896.
25. *Cong. Record*, 63 Cong., 2 Sess., pp. 11681–83, 11687–88; 64 Cong., 1 Sess., pp. 12089, 12313; Macon *Telegraph*, March 8, 1915; Atlanta *Journal*, July 24, 30, 1916; Smith to C. Strickland, July 6, 1917, Smith Collection.
26. See, for example, the Georgian's remarks in 1916 on the proposed government nitrate plant. *Cong. Record*, 64 Cong., 1 Sess., pp. 5711–12.
27. *Ibid.*, pp. 12896, 13402, 13655.
28. *Ibid.*, 63 Cong., 2 Sess., pp. 12003–12004; 64 Cong., 1 Sess., pp. 10139, 10142, 10210, 12925, 12927–28; 64 Cong., 2 Sess., pp. 1054–56, 1066.
29. *Cong. Record*, 64 Cong., 1 Sess., pp. 2683, 5164, 5227, 5355, 5358, 5578,5628; Atlanta *Journal*, March 5, 1916.

of the numerous reports of Brandeis' radicalism—but in the end he voted in the committee to confirm the appointment.[30]

The fact that by this time Smith was under heavy attack in Georgia and that his enemies there were denouncing him as a German sympathizer is another factor that helps explain the sudden moderation in the senator's attitude toward the administration. In an editorial entitled "Hoch der Hoke!" the Macon *Telegraph* called him the "high priest and prophet" of the traitorous pro-German cabal.[31] Another newspaper indignantly declared of Smith: "He is disloyal to the American people from whom he comes in that his voice has been raised only for money, never a word as to the right or wrong of this war, never a word as to any obligation on our part to set our faces against the butchery of innocents on the high seas—only that we must move heaven and earth to get our cotton into Germany."[32] Even the Atlanta *Journal*, always his champion in the past, was critical of his course. In the light of these storm warnings, Smith began to act as if his loyalty to the administration had never been in doubt. He campaigned for the party in several states in 1916, praised the New Freedom, and described Woodrow Wilson as the greatest leader who had occupied the White House in fifty years.[33] Later, early in 1917, he praised the president's diplomacy toward Germany and refused to go along with the opposition to the arming of merchant ships.[34] But Smith never regained Wilson's confidence.

The general direction of administration policies in foreign and domestic matters in 1915 and 1916 had much to do with the deterioration of the once cordial relations between Hoke Smith and Woodrow Wilson, but a new irritant caused a heightening of the tension between the two men and led to harsh words and embittered feelings.[35] Early in 1917 Smith and his colleague, Thomas W. Hardwick,

---

30. *Cong. Record*, 64 Cong., 1 Sess., pp. 6972, 9032; Atlanta *Journal*, May 22, 24, 1916; Henry Morgenthau to Woodrow Wilson, May 18, 1916, Wilson Papers.

31. Macon *Telegraph*, April 11, 1916.

32. Augusta *Chronicle*, quoted in the New York *Times*, February 5, 1916.

33. In his campaign addresses the Georgian emphasized Wilson's success in keeping the country out of war. Atlanta *Journal*, September 29, October 25, 26, 1916.

34. *Cong. Record*, 64 Cong., 1 Sess., pp. 12627–31, 12812–13, 12825; 64 Cong., 2 Sess., p. 1885; *New York Times*, January 27, 1917.

35. In earlier years there had been rumors in Georgia to the effect that Smith and other aggressive lawyers in Atlanta in the early 1880s "by their unethical methods" had been responsible for Wilson's decision to abandon the legal profession. There seems to have been no basis for such accusations, at least as far as Smith was con-

an outspoken advocate of state rights who at times exerted considerable influence over Smith, became involved in a struggle with the president and Attorney General Thomas W. Gregory over the appointment of a federal judge for the southern district of Georgia. When Wilson decided to appoint a man who had not secured the senators' endorsement, the latter were furious and sought unsuccessfully to have the president appoint another man. They claimed that Wilson's choice would be interpreted in Georgia as a victory for the anti-Smith faction and that they had not been consulted about the man selected. Wilson's nominee finally withdrew his name, but the Georgia senators were equally dissatisfied with the president's second selection and went so far as to defeat his confirmation. At this point Wilson found the conduct of Smith and Hardwick "past understanding."[36] He appointed a third man only to have this nominee treated in the same cavalier fashion. Neither side would give in, and the senators apparently felt that they would lose face if they could not name the new judge. Smith expressed regret that he "must" pursue such a course, just at the time "when I had hoped for united support of all acts of the Administration, and when I know the comfort it will give those in Georgia opposing the important measures now pending."[37] "The trouble with the Senators from Georgia," Wilson observed to John Sharp Williams, "is that they have practically taken the position that I have no right to name anyone whom they have not suggested."[38] By the summer of 1917 matters had gone too far to be repaired.

Meanwhile, Hoke Smith had launched a vociferous attack on the defense measures, including the plans submitted by the administration after the declaration of war in April 1917. As was the case in the cotton crisis, the struggle over the Georgia judgeship caused Smith to go to greater extremes in his criticism of the executive leaders than he would have gone otherwise. The conscription bill, the espionage

---

cerned. But Wilson had written an article on the Cleveland cabinet in 1893 in which he was highly critical of Smith's selection. Later, during the controversy over the Treaty of Versailles, the president told Colonel House that Smith was an "ambulance-chaser." See the Talbotton (Ga.) *New Era*, quoted in Macon *Telegraph*, July 12, 1912; Woodrow Wilson, "Mr. Cleveland's Cabinet," *Review of Reviews* 7 (April 1893): 286–97; Thomas A. Bailey, *Woodrow Wilson and the Great Betrayal* (New York, 1945), p. 13.

36. William J. Harris to Woodrow Wilson, February 12, 1917, Frank Park to Wilson, March 15, 1917, and Wilson to U. V. Whipple, May 1, 1917, Wilson Papers.

37. Smith to Woodrow Wilson, April 10, 1917, Wilson Papers.

38. Wilson to Williams, July 5, 1917, Wilson Papers.

legislation, the railroad priorities bill, and the Lever food control bill were subjected to the senator's sharp barbs. He denounced the broad delegation of powers to the president, and he voiced his distress over the loss of individual liberty portended by such legislation, particularly the threats to the southern farmer's unencumbered operation. The priorities bill amounted to "practical despotism in the United States," he declared, while adding "I am utterly opposed to legislation which adds to the unrestricted power of one man." He quibbled endlessly over the food control bill, warning Americans that "we don't want dictators."[39]

The very fact that Wilson was able to bend Congress so completely to his will seemed to encourage Smith in his rebelliousness. His sensitiveness for his own "self-respect" and for the prerogatives of the Senate was like an open wound that was constantly being irritated by President Wilson's increasing demands for additional powers.[40] For his part, Wilson had come to consider Smith "distinctly hostile" to his administration.[41] But the Georgian would not assume the role of an outright opponent, insisting that he was only helping to "perfect" hastily devised legislation. He approved the "general purposes" of the legislation, Smith said, "but in their details I have found them faulty and have aided to correct them and to protect the President as well as the public from some of their unwise detail provisions."[42] Whether because of his fetish for party regularity, because of the mounting pressure at home, or because of some other reason, the senator invariably voted in the end for the various defense measures. He would neither be an ardent advocate of administration war proposals, like Lee S. Overman of North Carolina, nor a dyed-in-the-wool opponent, like James K. Vardaman of Mississippi. According to one of his defenders, the Georgian was a senator "who thinks for himself and who votes for or against measures according to his own views of his duty to his state and his nation."[43] Neverthe-

39. *Cong, Record,* 64 Cong., 2 Sess., pp. 3258, 3347, 3643, 3645, 3714, 3738; 65 Cong., 1 Sess., pp. 837–38, 1686–87, 1784, 1789, 2438–39, 2501, 2508, 2651–53, 2965, 4627–28; New York *Times,* April 17, June 1, 1917.

40. Henry Morgenthau reported as early as May 1916 that Smith and some of the other Democratic senators had been "nursing their discontent so long that it may become chronic—." Morgenthau to Wilson, May 18, 1916, Wilson Papers.

41. Ray Stannard Baker, *Woodrow Wilson, Life and Letters,* 8 vols. (Garden City, 1927–39), 7: 113.

42. Smith to C. Strickland, July 6, 1917, Smith Collection.

43. Alexander J. McKelway to Lucian Lamar Knight, July 21, 1917, Alexander Jeffrey McKelway Papers, Manuscript Division, Library of Congress. See also *Cong. Record,* 65 Cong., 1 Sess., pp. 757–58, 1785, 2270–71, 5251–52.

less, the result was disastrous for Smith; the administration would have little to do with him, and he was called a traitor at home, despite his best efforts to demonstrate his complete loyalty during the last year of the war. Thus a pattern was set for his frustration from which he was never able to escape during his final years in the Senate.

In the beginning Smith's differences with the Wilson administration grew out of his profound disappointment over the failure of the administration to come to the active aid of the depression-ridden cotton farmers and out of personal pique that was encouraged by a number of unfortunate developments. More fundamentally, however, Smith's course in 1916–17—and during the controversial years 1919 and 1920—was the result of a deliberate effort on his part to ride out one of the frequent storms that gathered over the bitter Democratic factionalism in Georgia. He tried to follow a middle-of-the-road course between the violently anti-Wilson following of Tom Watson and the vigorously proadministration stand he himself had taken during the first years of the Wilson presidency. The trouble was that Smith's opponents, led by Clark Howell of the Atlanta *Constitution* and Governor Hugh M. Dorsey, seized upon the senator's early disagreements with Wilson in a shrewd attempt to make him out as an opponent of the president, and when Smith had gone far enough in his criticism of the administration, they rapidly maneuvered themselves into position as the true administration faction in the state. At the same time, they managed to maintain a tenuous alliance with Tom Watson. In short, Hoke Smith was outmaneuvered on the local scene by as astute a series of political moves as has occurred in one-party politics.

In profile Smith's career between 1913 and 1917 can be sharply etched. At the outset there was optimism and the promise of national leadership. For two years the Georgian worked in harmony with the new Democratic administration, lending valuable support to the original Wilson program and using his legislative skill and his remarkable energies to help secure the enactment of important agricultural legislation. Then followed a year and a half of constant agitation in the interest of the cotton producers and a widening rift between Smith and the Wilson administration. In the meantime, the southern senator was finding it difficult to support the social legislation being promoted by the president. Despite Smith's efforts to reverse his course in 1916, the patronage struggle and his sharp attacks on the administration's early war measures led to a steady impairment of his good relations with Wilson.

It would be inaccurate to attribute Smith's failure to follow Woodrow Wilson's lead after 1914 entirely to his own limitations. Circumstances seemed inexorably to conspire against him, and his political enemies in his home state never ceased in their efforts to embarrass him. If Smith was inconsistent during the Sixty-fourth Congress, so was President Wilson. But in the final analysis the senator from Georgia was unable to meet the test of responsible leadership. At times he was a strong political leader, and he proved again and again during the first two years of the administration that he could take the lead in the formulation and completion of a constructive program. An intense concern for his own vanity and some innate rebelliousness seemed to undermine his good judgment, however, and when cast on the defensive he was not able to make his criticisms—many of which had merit—in such a way as to retain the goodwill of administration leaders. In some ways the Georgian was a progressive, but his progressivism was too sectional to include much beyond agricultural and educational legislation that would benefit the South. He could scarcely conceive of the government as an active force in an urbanized and industrialized America.

In many respects Hoke Smith was one of the best qualified Democratic leaders in the Senate during the Wilson period. It was his own misfortune as well as that of his countrymen that he did not more fully achieve his earlier promise as a political leader. In a larger sense, his inability to rise to the occasion in the exercise of national leadership was characteristic of most southern progressives on the national level. For the sources of the Georgian's limitations as an outstanding Senate leader—an intense sectional preoccupation and a highly personalized and undisciplined political constituency—were equally applicable to many another southern liberal during the progressive era.

9

Ralph J. Bunche and the Making of a Documentary Classic

⟨⟩ "The Political Status of the Negro," a massive, unpublished memorandum prepared just as the New Deal came to an end, became an invaluable source for students of southern politics and the black experience in the period between the two world wars. The study was distinguished not only because it contains a wealth of firsthand testimony about contemporary racial practices and ideas in the United States but also because it was drafted by the black scholar Ralph J. Bunche and used by Gunnar Myrdal in writing *An American Dilemma*. The most substantial sections of the memorandum were published in 1973 as *The Political Status of the Negro in the Age of FDR*. The essay that follows served as the Introduction to the volume.

Bunche set out to obtain as much empirical evidence as possible about black Americans and current politics. He wanted the kind of information that would enable him to answer critical questions such as: To what extent were Negroes in the 1930s involved in political affairs? In the case of the southern states, were blacks as thoroughly excluded from politics as they had been a generation earlier when legal disfranchisement became effective? What were the principal exclusionary devices used to prevent Negro men and women from taking part in politics? Where and under what circumstances were blacks permitted to vote? What impact did the New Deal have on the political status of the Negro? Were attitudes about the place of Negroes in politics changing? And what were the prospects for a more democratic politics, particularly in the South?

When Ralph Bunche and his assistants began their search for information on American blacks and the political process, they could find almost no scholarly works on the subject, aside from a few historical monographs. Since then a number of illuminating studies have been published on various aspects of the Negro's political status in the 1930s, but we are still lacking a large-scale treatment of the topic. One aspect of the black political experience in the thirties—the ideas and activities of liberals in the field of race relations—is dealt with in Morton Sosna, *In Search of the Silent South: Southern Liberals and the Race Issue* (1977), and John B. Kirby, *Liberalism and Race: The Roosevelt Era and Black Americans* (forthcoming). Donald R. Matthews and James W. Prothro, *Negroes and the New Southern Politics* (1966), analyze the political involvement of southern blacks in the 1950s and 1960s. Their impressive work, which is based on a vast collection of systematic data, is the kind of study that Bunche would like to have done for the 1930s had he had sufficient time and resources.

L A T E in the summer of 1938 a young social economist affiliated with the University of Stockholm sailed from his native Sweden for the United States. He had embarked upon what would prove to be a momentous enterprise: to become director of "a comprehensive study of the Negro in the United States, to be undertaken in a wholly objective and dispassionate way as a social phenomenon."[1] The project resulted in the publication of *An American Dilemma: The Negro Problem and Modern Democracy* (1944)—two large volumes, containing 1,024 pages of text in 45 chapters and 462 pages of introductions, appendixes, notes, and bibliography. Its impact was immediate and far-reaching. The eminent sociologist Robert S. Lynd described it as "the most penetrating and important book on

---

1. Gunnar Myrdal, with the assistance of Richard Sterner and Arnold Rose, *An American Dilemma: The Negro Problem and Modern Democracy*, 2 vols. (New York, 1944), 1: ix.

our contemporary American civilization that has been written." Another distinguished scholar, Rupert B. Vance, has pointed out that the work represented a new trend: the impact of modern research organization developed in the United States on the tradition of the foreign observer and such famous commentaries as those of Tocqueville and Lord Bryce.

The foreign observer in this case was Gunnar Myrdal, an internationally known scholar and successor to Gustav Cassel in the chair of social economics at the University of Stockholm. Myrdal was a close observer of the American scene. He had earlier spent a year in the United States as a Fellow of the Spelman Fund, and he traveled extensively in this country during the three years which he spent working on *An American Dilemma* while on this side of the Atlantic. He wrote, and was solely responsible for, the final report. Yet the work was truly a cooperative study, authorized and financed by the Carnegie Corporation of New York, employing six top staff members to assist Myrdal, thirty-one independent workers outside of the staff, thirty-six assistants to the staff members and outside collaborators, a corps of secretaries and typists, and some fifty experts who acted as consultants. Myrdal's most important sources were forty-four monographs (comprising about 15,000 typewritten pages) which were largely prepared by authorities outside his staff. Nine of these memoranda have been published; the others are now located in the Schomburg Collection of the New York Public Library.

One of the American scholars who contributed most as a member of the Myrdal research team was a young Negro political scientist named Ralph Johnson Bunche. At the time Bunche joined the Carnegie-Myrdal project, he was a thirty-four-year-old professor at Howard University who had already demonstrated unusual ability and great promise as a student of race relations and international affairs. He had written a Ph.D. dissertation at Harvard on colonial administration in French West Africa. He had traveled and studied in Europe, Africa, and Southeast Asia under fellowships from the Rosenwald Fund and the Social Science Research Council. Bunche was a dynamic, knowledgeable, and fair-minded scholar, a man of great personal charm and *savoir-faire*, with an intuitive grasp of racial complexities in America. The possibilities of the Myrdal study excited his imagination, and he joined it enthusiastically. He helped shape the research design for the work, and as one of the half-dozen staff members, he was intimately involved in the investigation from early 1939 to the end of the summer of 1940. He was the author of four of the forty-four research monographs, the most substantial of which was "The Political Status of the Negro."[2]

Bunche's memorandum on politics was strongly influenced by his own experience as an American Negro and by his scholarly interest in such questions as Negro improvement organizations and the impact of the New Deal on black people and other disadvantaged groups. But a large part of the raw material that found its way into his lengthy memorandum came from the field notes on hundreds of interviews conducted with whites and blacks. Some of these interviews were carried out by Myrdal and Bunche, who made an automobile tour of the South in the autumn of 1939. Their reception in the Deep South during that memorable trip was not always friendly. They left one Georgia town in a hurry when the local sheriff warned: "You folks are goin' around insultin' people by askin' them fool questions? You'd better get outta town before I run you in." On another occasion they were forced to flee from an irate band of Alabamians who followed them in an automobile and fired a gun at them![3]

Most of the interviews were conducted by Bunche's assistants in the fall of 1939 and the first half of 1940. The first to begin was Wilhemina Jackson, a Howard student, who moved through the South Atlantic states from Virginia to Florida, interviewing many Negroes and some whites. Another of the interviewers was James E. Jackson, who had earlier worked in the labor movement. He traveled from Virginia to Tennessee, and then to Arkansas, Kentucky, Mississippi, Texas, Louisiana, Oklahoma, and Missouri. The third of the interviewers was George C. Stoney, a recent graduate of the University of North Carolina who had been working at the Henry Street Settlement in New York. He concentrated his field work in Alabama, Georgia, and South Carolina. Stoney, the only white member of the group, made a special point of talking with local officials. He conducted about half of all the interviews.

The interviewers were given a rough itinerary and a list of counties to visit, but once in the field they were largely dependent upon their own resources in making contacts, unearthing data, and decid-

2. Bunche's other memoranda were "Conceptions and Ideologies of the Negro Problem," "The Programs, Ideologies, Tactics, and Achievements of Negro Betterment and Interracial Organizations," and "A Brief and Tentative Analysis of Negro Leadership."

3. J. Alvin Kugelmass, *Ralph J. Bunche: Fighter for Peace* (New York, 1952), pp. 89–91.

ing whom to interview. Stoney had earlier toured the South in search of material for a series of stories he wrote for the Raleigh *News and Observer*. As an interviewer for Bunche, his technique was to visit the office of the local newspaper when he first arrived in a community, to acquaint himself with recent elections by reading extensively in the back files of the paper, and then to search out public officials, including the members of the election commission. As a result of his research, he frequently found that he had more "facts" about the local situation than the people he interviewed. He made notes during his interviews and prepared a report on each person he questioned. Stoney thought of his investigations as "county and precinct studies," and he sought to gather as much demographic data, illustrative newspaper stories, and other information as possible.[4] After finishing his interviews in Putnam County, Georgia, he added a note to Bunche: "So much attention was given to the political views of the Justices of the Peace because I want to show the kind of men who are in control of precinct politics. These men, as you can tell, have absolute power over the polls."[5]

The heart of the reports prepared by Stoney and the other interviewers was their interview notes. Stoney in particular had a remarkable talent for reproducing the language he heard, for spotting the revealing comment and the vivid expression. An open, friendly, and engaging young man, he seemed to know how to approach all manner of people, to make them feel comfortable in his presence, and to get them to talk freely. Although he remembers being threatened (as was James Jackson) on two occasions, he was never harmed. He soon discovered that when he talked with Southerners individually, they had plenty of complaints about politics and government, but they would not voice these complaints as readily or tell him the same story when he talked with them in groups. Stoney's reports were filled with interesting vignettes and the personal experiences of ordinary people. They often contained a touch of humor. In reporting on his visit to Six Mile, South Carolina, for instance, he told of his efforts to locate a Republican physician in the community. "I never found him, or any other Republican," he wrote, "though I went on a number of wild goose chases." When he entered one "dingy junk-shop of a store" in Greene County, Alabama, the young and embittered proprietor greeted him by demanding: "Who are you

4. Interview with George C. Stoney, New York City, June 9, 1971.
5. Undated field report in Stoney's possession.

looking for?'' When Stoney had explained his mission, the merchant exclaimed, ''Hell, what's there to see around here but cows and niggers?''

Since most of the field notes on these interviews are not available, it is impossible to determine how many individuals were questioned in connection with the project. A tabulation of the references in ''The Political Status of the Negro'' provides a figure of approximately 550 persons, but the total was undoubtedly much larger than that, since Bunche was selective in his use of the interview material. A breakdown of the references to interviews in the memorandum reveals that some 342 whites and 208 Negroes were questioned. The geographical distribution of persons interviewed shows Alabama with 148, Georgia with 118, South Carolina with 92, and North Carolina with 53. There were fewer interviews in Virginia, Florida, and Texas, while Mississippi, Louisiana, and Arkansas were largely ignored, as were the border states. Only a handful of interviews was carried out in northern cities.

While the interviews were in progress, Bunche spent considerable time in Myrdal's New York headquarters working on a variety of tasks. He was concerned not only with the Negro's place in politics, but also with black organizations, leadership, and ideology, and he wrote reports on all of these subjects. Formulating the various memoranda was an awesome assignment, and meeting Myrdal's deadline of September 1, 1940, for the completion of all research monographs seemed altogether impossible. ''The Political Status of the Negro''—the longest of the four Bunche memoranda—was the last to be finished, and it was completed only by dint of round-the-clock labor during the late summer of 1940. Using the limited secondary material that existed at that time and relying heavily upon the copious field notes of his assistants, Bunche dictated for hour after hour during those hectic August days.

In its original form, ''The Political Status of the Negro'' ran to 1,660 typed pages divided into 19 chapters, 3 appendixes, and a bibliography. The first part of the memorandum contains a lengthy section on the American political tradition and the historical background for the study of the Negro's political condition in modern times. Then there are chapters on the southern political process, registration procedures in the South, the white primary, and the poll tax; on Negro registration, the Negro at the southern polls, Negro voting in the Agricultural Adjustment Administration's (AAA) cotton referenda, blacks in Atlanta and in Memphis, the Negro as an issue in southern politics, and benefits derived from Negro political activity in the South; on Republican politics in the southern states; on liberalism in the South; on Negro political involvement in the North; and on black officeholders in the federal government.

The memorandum was not a finished product, as Bunche was careful to point out in the preface he wrote in 1940. It was rather "a terribly hurried, poorly integrated, and roughly written job." Frankly, the author remarked with some exasperation, the procedure he and his assistants followed had been "quite mad." Meeting rigid deadlines had been made a fetish, and the keynote had been "pell-mell, headlong, furious production." Consequently, there had been little time for reflection and analysis. The great task had been "that of attempting, within a very short period, to put together the diverse materials at hand." The Howard professor noted that little scholarly work had been done on the Negro in American politics, but he was still somewhat apologetic about the inclusion of so much primary material in the memorandum. Yet, ironically, it was his skillful use of the field notes that made his report an extraordinary document.

The subtitle that Bunche added to "The Political Status of the Negro" tells a good deal about the work's fundamental character. It reads: "With Emphasis on the South and Comparative Treatment of the 'Poor White.' " If his comprehensive consideration of southern politics, Bunche singled out three salient features of political affairs south of the Potomac: (1) the looseness and corruption of political practices; (2) the extent of the disfranchisement of both blacks and whites; and (3) the lack of effective reform movements at the grass-roots level. The memorandum gave only limited attention to Negroes in northern and midwestern politics.

The Bunche report contains voluminous testimony concerning the inefficient, unfair, and fraudulent conduct of elections in the southern states. Election officers were frequently ignorant of their duties, and they were sometimes dishonest. Registration lists were poorly kept, usually inaccurate, and often padded. The purging of the voting lists was a hit-or-miss process. There was little if any state supervision of voter registration. Enrollment for primary elections, except in the case of Negroes, was extremely informal. A member of the local enrollment committee in a South Carolina community observed that all he did was to take the enrollment book when the chairman of the party brought it to his drugstore, where the registration occurred, spread it out on his counter, and keep the pencil sharp! In most cases, the rules required that a registrant sign in person, but in practice a person was frequently allowed to sign for other members of his family and for the sick and disabled. Nevertheless, some registration boards took their jobs seriously. One registrar declared that he liked to think of registration as "a kind of quality test" and that people "ought to have certain responsibilities." But there was much evidence to support the comment of a registrar in Coffee County, Alabama: "The sentiment's against refusing to register a man [white and Democratic] unless he's plumb out crazy."

The registrar in the South, Bunche concluded, was seldom an obstacle to would-be white voters. A registration officer in Lee County, Alabama, observed, in referring to the various constitutional tests in that state: "We [have] never used any of those things against a white man. I'll just be honest with you." On the other hand, the chairman of the board of registrars in Beaufort County, South Carolina, asserted that literacy and property tests were strictly enforced in his locality. "We do that to keep down the niggers," he confessed. The tax collector of Macon County, Georgia, who registered all voters in that civil division, expressed shock at the suggestion that in other Georgia counties people were registered without having to make a personal appearance. "Good Lord!" he exclaimed. "If it was that way, I could put a couple of hundred people's names down on the books myself, pay up their poll taxes, and haul them in and get elected to anything I wanted to."

The Bunche memorandum called attention to the widespread absence of a secret ballot in southern elections. Voting booths frequently were not employed and sometimes tables were not even provided. Many voters had to have their ballots marked for them, thereby opening the door to fraud and improper interference by election officials. Such voters would often say to the clerk, after indicating their choices among a few of the candidates, "You fill in the rest." Election officers and others were able to use the numbers on ballots to check on the way people voted. In some precincts the man who wanted to sell his ballot would let one of the officials see him mark his ticket. If he marked it right, he was given a "little blue bead" (or perhaps a poker chip) which he then exchanged for the sale price. Absentee ballots were another source of election irregularities, and in some cases the candidates themselves were allowed to call for such votes.

There was a close connection between the misuse of the ballot and county (and municipal) political machines in the South. According to Bunche, "Votes are controlled and checked by registration slips, the 'chain letter' system, vote buying, poll tax payment, double voting, vote stealing, 'counting out' unfortunate candidates, employment of 'agents' to sign up voters, and many variations of these methods." When a new board of registrars assumed office in Chatham County, Georgia, in 1936, it found that the "ring" had padded the voting list with hundreds of dead and removed persons for whom it was continuing to pay poll taxes. The registrars in Jefferson County, Alabama, were said to have struck the names of two thousand deceased people in a recent purge of the voting roll. The political machines themselves were frequently beholden to powerful business interests, which also followed questionable tactics in some elections. Vote buying was so widespread as to form an integral part of the election process in much of the region. In Bibb County, Alabama, for example, the Bunche interviewer was told that between four and five hundred of the two thousand votes normally were "bought." The complaint was often heard that people had "gotten in the habit of selling their vote." Most candidates found it necessary to provide some "hauling" and "favors," and a certain amount of this kind of expenditure was considered quite proper. The really ambitious candidate, remarked one Alabama registrar, made a house-to-house canvass. He "backslaps, baby-kisses, and bites a chew off the same plug with every farmer from here to Tennessee, and, if he has enough two dollar bills, he gets elected." If there was a benign aspect to such practices, there was also an occasional note of humor in them, as the field reports showed.

Bunche and his assistants provided a great deal of evidence to support their contention that the poll tax was a serious medium for the corruption of elections. In many places the administration of the exemption clauses was very liberal, and little effort was made to apply the tax as a systematic registration and voting requirement. An officer of elections in Madison County, Alabama, stated that candidates paid the poll taxes of many voters in his area: "I seen them pay up as much as $15 for a fellow, and I say it's a good thing, too, because there's so many people just ain't got that much money— folks on the WPA and all. They wouldn't be able to vote unless somebody helped them." A clerk in the office of probate judge in the same county estimated that one-third of the votes there were "bought," many of them twice—once with poll taxes and again with the "pay-off" at the polls. The registration in Greene County, Georgia, in the spring of 1940 was the largest in the county's history. Over three thousand dollars in back poll taxes were collected, and, according to a Greensboro justice of the peace, "two-thirds of this was paid by the candidates."

Although many white Southerners were able, in one way or another, to escape the maze of suffrage qualifications and get their names on the registration lists, low voting percentages were among the most pronounced characteristics of the region's politics. A Charleston, South Carolina, party official explained the pervasive political apathy by saying, "The trouble is you got to give people something before they'll vote." Because of the one-party dominance, "they don't get nothing for the general election." Typical of many disadvantaged whites was the remark, "No, I don't vote. I don't care nothing about it. Whoever they elect, it's all right with me." Such indifference was sometimes feigned. Politics, some people asserted, "is the rottenest thing in this world. . . . It will make a liar out of you quicker'n anything I know of." On the other hand, the interviewers reported that they were occasionally told that "there's a class of white people that oughtn't to vote." While the poll taxes of some voters were paid for them by candidates and machines, a larger number failed to vote because of the tax requirement. As one humble white woman said, "My husband's talked about voting ever since I can remember. He was going to vote this time, but he couldn't get the money together in time. When he does, I'm going to make him save up for *me*, too."

Defenders of the poll tax made much of the point that the revenue from the levy went to the support of the schools. They were even more insistent in arguing that the poll tax held back a potential flood of black political power. Asked whether he thought the poll tax should be repealed, the clerk of the election commission of Hamilton County, Tennessee, expressed a view common among white Southerners:

Why? And have some big, black son-of-a-bitch sitting up in the courthouse sending white men to jail? That's what would happen if the niggers started voting heavy here. They'd have a black commissioner at City Hall— some sporting black reared back like God Almighty. No, Sir! Son, I'm not for that! I'm a Southerner and a Democrat. I was born and bred in the South, and that kind of thing ain't in the blood that runs in *my* veins.

The mayor of Chattanooga was just as emphatic: "Yea! What you want to do, repeal it and have the niggers in this town bond us to death? They'd have this town in the poorhouse in two years. They don't pay taxes, so they don't care how much you spend." Nevertheless, many Southerners expressed dissatisfaction with their local officials.

If the percentage of white Southerners on the voting lists was small by national standards, it was still magnificent when compared with the percentage of enfranchised Negroes in the region. For all his knowledge of the South, George Stoney was struck by the "complete freeze-out of Negroes" in local politics. Bunche estimated that in 1940 no more than 200,000 blacks were registered in the eleven ex-Confederate states, and that over half of those qualified were located in the three states of Virginia, North Carolina, and Tennessee. Only about 1,500 Negroes voted in the whole state of Alabama in 1936, despite the fact that some 18,000 black veterans were included in that state's blanket exemption of World War I veterans from the necessity of paying the poll tax. Whereas the registration of white people was often informal and slipshod, that of Negroes almost always involved "a harsh, hostile, and rigid application of the law and often something more than the law." A registrar in Lee County, Alabama, recalled: "We have had a good little bit of trouble with niggers. . . . Way back in 1920, when I was on the board before, we had a world of nigger women coming in to register. There was a dozen of them, I reckon, come in one registration period. We registered a few and then we stopped."

A Negro's ability to register in a particular locality in the South, Bunche wrote, was determined in large part by the attitude of the local registrars, which varied considerably. Many responsible whites in southern communities were willing to permit a token registration of the more successful blacks. This was not considered "dangerous." But most registration officials seemed to consider Negro efforts to register as "trouble." The chairman of the board of registrars in Macon County, Alabama, a woman, reported that the only "trouble" the registrars had with Negroes resulted from the efforts of orderlies at the Veterans' Hospital in Tuskegee to register. "Honestly, it's awful the way they are doing," she exclaimed. "Oh! They come in and they say they have been here two years when they haven't. They are not really intelligent nigras like the ones out at Tuskegee [Institute], you know. We have to ask them a lot of questions about the Constitution and everything to keep them out." Even with a sympathetic chairman of the registration board, Negroes customarily could not get their names on the voting list the first time they tried. There were some examples of registrars who accepted Negro applicants after hours as a favor to black friends.

The chairman of the board of registrars of Dougherty County, Georgia, claimed that there was a "good nigger vote" in his county, perhaps two or three hundred, and that they were property holders and taxpayers. Continuing in a philosophical vein, he declared:

You know, we've spent a fortune educating the niggers down here. The nigger race has come a lot farther than the white race in such a short time. You just look back at slavery times and count up. . . . It's wonderful, and it's all due to the credit of the Southern white man. The Yankees haven't done a damn thing for the niggers, and we'd be a lot better off if they'd leave us alone to handle things as we know how to.

There were only four or five Negroes on the voting roll in Coffee County, Alabama, according to the chairman of the board there. "We aren't troubled with that here," he remarked. "The people wouldn't stand for it. Now, I recognize that some niggers are capable of voting a lot more intelligently than a lot of white men who do vote. They are exceptions, of course, and I believe they've got sense enough to know why white people don't want them to vote." The fact was that the social climate and mores of the South created an atmosphere of essential intimidation for black registrants. The tax collector of Newton County, Georgia, admitted that blacks were discouraged from voting, but he asserted that he had never tried to keep a colored person from registering, provided he paid his taxes. In his words, "Negroes just don't have the nerve to come up and ask for registration. They feel that they could not and should not register." An Alabama official was brutally forthright: "There ain't a fuckin' nigger in this end of the county who'd so much as go near a ballot box."

A Negro leader in Macon County, Alabama, explained some of the difficulties his people encountered with the board of registrars:

First, they started making you get two witnesses to vouch for you—two legal voters. When we got that easy, they made us get two white witnesses. I started putting pressure on people who I trade with and they signed for them all right. Then, they started saying we had to get two white people who worked in the courthouse. Then was when we started putting pressure on candidates we'd supported. Now, they'll let us sign with about anybody. . . . They've started this year asking a lot about the Constitution.

This note of subterfuge recurs again and again in the Bunche memorandum. For example, the chairman of the Negro Voters' Club of Huntsville said that black teachers in that community had been trying to register for a long time. He described what happened: "You go up there and they might tell you the blanks have given out or it's closing time. Most of the time they just walk out on you. The law says, they say, that all three of the registrars must be there before they can register a person. This isn't so, because I've seen them register white people when only one is there, but just as soon as they see a Negro coming, one of them gets up and walks out, and that's the end of it." In another Alabama community a black applicant was told that he would have to recite the Constitution. In desperation he recited the Gettysburg Address, whereupon the registrar said, "That's right. You can go ahead and register."

A justice of the peace in Greene County, Georgia, described three Negro voters who "come in every time. They're mighty polite. . . . Always with their hats in their hands. I haven't got any kick there. . . . Naturally, they vote for the New Deal, because give a nigger a little sweetnin' and he'll vote any way." Continuing, he declared: "You can't get a nigger to chop wood or wash clothes any more. It's past history! They're working for the government." A patent medicine salesman in one Alabama community was alarmed at the thought of Negro enfranchisement. "If you don't watch out," he warned, "you're gonna have the same kind of niggers you got over in Miami. They know now, by God, they can control an election and they've got the police department scared." According to the chairman of the county board of registrars in Montgomery, "All niggers—uneducated and educated—have one idea back in their mind—that they want equality. . . . It is necessary to keep the Negro from voting, for voting would lead to social equality. The niggers are in the majority in this county and in Alabama. They would take over the power in the state. The white people are never going to give them this power."

Bunche emphasized the mood of apathy and hopelessness that characterized the Negro's political outlook in the South. He also noted the way in which white Southerners rationalized this condition. Senator Byron Patton Harrison of Mississippi gave a classic statement when he declared: "The nigra is satisfied down there from a political standpoint. In my state, the nigra has played no part in politics for forty years and has no desire to do so. We are all content to leave the situation alone as it is." Southern registration officials usually explained the absence of Negro names from the voting rolls by saying that blacks "just don't care to register." Many of these officers contended that Negroes were free to vote in all elections except the Democratic primaries. This was a dubious privilege even in places where it was a reality, in view of the overwhelming finality of the primary results.

The "what's the use?" attitude of most southern Negroes was evident in the interviews Wilhelmina Jackson conducted among black workers on Butler Island, near Darien, Georgia. One woman told her: "Yes, I register, but I do not vote. I just don't have time. You see, I always be working at voting time and all like that." A young woman: "I don't vote, but what I got to vote for?" A pulpwood worker: "Naw, I don't vote. Black man ain't got no right. Even Negroes serving on the juries are so old that they can't get out of their own way, and all they can do is 'yes' the white man." A fisherman: "No, I don't vote. I didn't pay my taxes. Tain't much use anyway."

The whites' fear of the Negro as a voter seemed to stem not so much from doubt about the black man's intentions as from fear of the way "white politicians" would manipulate Negro voters or apprehension that they might be used by labor unions, mill owners, or landlords. It was not fear "of black domination at all," in Bunche's opinion, "but a fear of white domination, in a political game in which the Negro voter is only a pawn." The tax collector of Putnam County, Georgia, remarked that "niggahs would be all right voting if the whites was what they ought to be. That was the trouble before [disfranchisement]. White fellows wouldn't leave them alone." There was also some evidence that southern politicians opposed Negro enfranchisement on the practical grounds that it would enlarge the electorate, make campaigning more expensive, and result in a less predictable outcome.

Stoney encountered some old-time politicians who enjoyed the opportunity to describe their part in the "nigger vote buying" and "nigger vote stealing" of the "old days." They liked to tell of the fights that broke out over the attempts to steal the "nigger vote," of how their Negro votes were bought with liquor and women, and of how they led the black voters along with music like the Pied Piper of Hamlin. High-jacking the other man's Negro voters was a vital part of this "progress." It was rather ludicrous, observed Bunche, for southern officials to claim that this situation made Negro disfranchisement necessary and that "clean government" in the South was the result of that disfranchisement.

The Bunche report contains some information on the way Negro votes were used by political machines in such places as San Antonio and Memphis. One informant estimated the number of "controlled Negro votes" in Hamilton County, Tennessee, at two thousand. A reporter for the Chattanooga *Times* graphically described the "system" employed by Walter Robinson, an influential black politician in that county. The chairman of the Democratic committee in Ware County, Georgia, said that two hundred Negroes had voted in a recent election in that county. As he put it, "Their so-called leaders lined them up and they voted like sheep. That is what always happens. I know every time we start to have a bond election, they go out and round up the nigras." Occasionally, even in the Deep South, white politicians would appeal for Negro support, but they were reluctant to do so openly.

Despite the fact that Negroes were almost completely disfranchised in the South at the time he prepared his memorandum, Bunche expressed the view that an increasing number of blacks in the region were showing a determination to exercise the ballot. Some Negroes were beginning to question the old "back door" methods that enabled a few members of the race to get their names on the registration lists, and these critics were demanding a more militant approach. Here and there one could find examples of greater Negro involvement in politics. An organizational drive in Macon, Georgia, added almost 200 blacks to the voting list. By 1939 approximately 2,100 Negroes were registered in Atlanta, as compared with fewer than 1,000 in 1936. The number of black registrants in Duval County, Florida, increased from fewer than 1,500 in 1936 to more than 8,000 in 1938. Negroes were taking a more active political role in a number of municipalities in the South, and some were being admitted to the Democratic primaries. One Negro worker said to an interviewer: "They's talked more politics since Mistuh Roosevelt been in than ever befo'. I been here 20 years, but since WPA, the Negro sho' has started talkin' 'bout politics."

Perhaps the most promising development, certainly in the Deep South, that seemed to point toward the political activation of the Negro was his participation in the AAA cotton referenda. As Bunche wrote, "Many thousands of Negro cotton farmers each year now go to the polls, stand in line with their neighbors, and mark their ballots independently, without protest or intimidation, in order to determine government policy toward cotton production control." An Alabama county agent reported that a larger proportion of black than white farmers voted in these referenda. As he explained, "It's the only election they get to take part in." The county agent in Greene County, Georgia, said of the Negro voters in these elections: "They look forward to it." But, he added, "I don't think half of them know what they're voting about." In retrospect, it appears that Bunche exaggerated the significance of the black man's participation in the cotton referenda. Seldom, if ever, was a Negro allowed to serve on the local committees that supervised the elections, and blacks do not seem to have had much part in the selection of the members of the committees.[6] Yet these referenda did permit many Negro farmers some part in public affairs.

There was an undercurrent of expectation, no doubt associated with the ferment of the New Deal, that seemed to promise the likelihood of future changes even in the Negro's role in southern politics. A former mayor of Charleston expressed it this way: "The nigger's going to get the vote in the South one of these days. I don't like to see it coming, but it is." Some white farmers, one Alabamian noted, had come to feel that Negroes should have "a few more rights. . . . It hasn't been so long since a lot of these big farmers in Alabama thought what mattered to a nigger, didn't matter." The chairman of the Hall County, Georgia, Republican party declared: "All over the country it's the trend to give the nigger the vote. I don't see how they can keep it out of Georgia long. It does look like they ought to get a vote somewhere, but I don't know what the black counties will do when that day comes."

Fundamentally, Ralph Bunche's interpretation of "The Political Status of the Negro" was consistent with Gunnar Myrdal's theme in *An American Dilemma*. To Myrdal, race relations in the United States represented, not a "Negro problem," but a "white man's problem." The white man had imposed a way of life on the Negro which was at variance with the "American Creed" which the white man himself espoused, and it was the responsibility of white men to formulate and effect a more adequate and morally correct treatment of Negroes. The existence of the historic ideals in the United States, Myrdal contended, had set up a great ideological conflict, in large part a psychological struggle within the individual, who recognized that racial prejudices and discriminatory practices did not conform to the generally accepted creed. Bunche seemed to be less optimistic than Myrdal about the potential power of American Negroes as a result of the split in the moral personality of whites. He gave greater weight

6. Myrdal was more cautious in his evaluation, explaining that Negroes voted because "their votes are needed." He noted that they "are seldom allowed to vote for committeemen. Even when Negroes do exercise some privileges, it seldom means that they have any real influence on the decisions" (*An American Dilemma*, 1: 259).

than Myrdal to the existence of a countercreed in the South which provided white Southerners with sanctions for their support of traditional racial attitudes and institutions. Like Myrdal, Bunche tended to exaggerate the role that labor unions might play in resolving the nation's racial dilemma, to explain racial prejudice too much in terms of class divisions, and not to foresee the extent to which impetus for future changes in the Negro's status would come from blacks in the South.

Although Bunche did not neglect ideological factors (he had a sharp word for those who contended that it mattered little to the American Negro whether the Nazis or their opponents won the struggle in Europe), he stressed economic and class conflict. "The so-called Negro problem in America," he declared, "is only incidentally a racial one. Many of its major roots go deeper than race and are themselves embedded in the fundamental problems of economic conflict and distress which afflict the entire society." Like Charles A. Beard, he saw the Civil War as essentially a clash between the growing industrial power of the North and the agrarian landholding interests of the South. He adopted a revisionist view of Reconstruction. The Democratic party in the southern states, he wrote, represented the upper and middle classes. The political South was basically an oligarchy, effectively run by large landholders, bankers, and corporations. Yet the South had never really been solid, according to the Howard political scientist. "Only the clever manipulation of the threat of black dominance has kept the underprivileged white masses and the privileged upper classes of the South from coming to a parting of the political ways." Negro disfranchisement was the one thing on which the white South was "99 and 44/100 per cent pure," and even that, as carried out in the 1890s and early 1900s, had been the subject of bitter controversy among white men.

While Bunche referred to the South as a political oligarchy, he pictured it as being decentralized, almost anarchistic. He placed great emphasis on the limited suffrage in the region and sought to show the depressing and stultifying influence of the poll tax upon white Southerners. Yet, as a result of his study, he saw some signs of change, some easing of the old white attitude of "absolute hostility toward Negro voting," some inclination on the part of white Southerners to abandon "the Negro diversion." In *An American Dilemma* Myrdal wrote: "Despite all professions to the contrary, the acceptance in principle even by the conservative white Southerners of the American Creed explains why so many exceptions are made to the rule of excluding Negroes from voting." In fact, he concluded, the "Southern franchise situation" was "highly unstable" and would be *"politically untenable for any length of time."* [7] Bunche himself was not without hope for the future democratization of the South, seeming to find some modest gains in the extent of liberal sentiment, interracial cooperation, and awareness of common economic problems in the southern states. He was cautiously optimistic about the Negro's chances of entering more fully into southern political affairs in the coming years. He also suggested the improving possibility of a more competitive party situation in the South. "The lily-white Republican movement in the South might actually be of some ultimate advantage to the Negro," he observed. "That is, if the Republican party, as a white party, can attract to itself the large number of severe critics of the New Deal in the region, it may actually be an opening wedge for a two-party system in the South." But Bunche was not misled into believing that the Negro's status would change overnight. His memorandum reveals how limited and inchoate black protest of even the mildest sort was in the southern states during the 1930s. There was no genuine reform movement that affected the mass of the people—white or black—and southern liberalism was, to Bunche, a weak reed indeed.

Even at the time it was prepared, the Bunche memorandum suffered from a number of deficiencies. The narrative was rambling and repetitious. There was little that was original in the author's commentary, which was intended to summarize existing scholarship and to point up the findings of the field investigations. Bunche pointed out, in his chapter on the historical background, that he was not attempting any "original postulations." "I don't mind 'sticking my neck out' on occasion," he wryly remarked, "but I do not care to do so recklessly and without some chance of getting it back in again." More serious was Bunche's failure to make distinctions of a subregional kind. He emphasized the point that there were many Souths, but the fact that his data were drawn so largely from the Southeast (particularly Alabama, Georgia, and South Carolina) made it difficult for him to speak authoritatively about regional patterns and internal contrasts. Bunche had planned a much more elaborate treatment, including a quantitative analysis of black voting and the factors associated with the Negro's political status in the South, but lack of time and money made it impossible to undertake any of these studies on a thoroughgoing basis. The treatment of Negro politics in

7. Myrdal, *An American Dilemma*, 1: 461, 518.

the North was even less adequate, being largely derivative and based on little empirical research. The only extensive interviewing done outside of the South and border states was Wilhelmina Jackson's investigations in Philadelphia. Bunche had hoped to carry out a statistical analysis of black voting in selected northern cities and to study several other aspects of Negro politics in the North, but lack of time and resources rendered this impossible.

Many scholars, including V. O. Key and Alexander Heard, have used "The Political Status of the Negro." These writers and others made use of the memorandum's interview material, and some of them were influenced by Bunche's interpretation of such phenomena as the South's limited suffrage, the white primary, the role of the "courthouse gang," the crucial importance of the South in Congress, and, especially, the place of the Negro in southern politics. The black man exercised very limited suffrage, wrote Bunche, but his very presence was "a dominating influence upon Southern politics." Indeed, the "nonvoting Negro remains the greatest single political influence" in the region, the "essential vehicle of Southern politics."

Bunche's massive report on the Negro in politics is a valuable historical document. It did a great deal to shape Myrdal's treatment of the subject in *An American Dilemma,* particularly the chapter entitled "Political Practices Today." The memorandum supplies us with a backdrop against which we can measure change in the Negro's political status and interpret the origins and consequences of the Second Reconstruction. The work's most enduring value, however, lies in its wealth of personal interviews and firsthand impressions of the Negro and southern politics.

The memorandum is important as a source of information about political practices in the southern states—registration procedures, the application of suffrage qualifications, the extent of white and black disfranchisement, the conduct of elections, the operation of local political machines, and the limited nature of the Negro's involvement in the political process. It offers some insight into the historical, economic, sociological, and psychological factors that accounted for these practices, as well as some understanding of the myths, stereotypes, and symbols that contemporaries often used to explain and justify them. The report is also significant because of the light it throws on the characteristics of Negro political life, on the levels of black political involvement, and on the patterns of race relations, particularly in the South. It tells us something about black political leadership during the New Deal era—about the styles and meaning of that leadership—and the nature of Negro advancement organizations. It provides some impressions of the kinds of Negroes who participated in politics, which areas of the South they inhabited, and which factors encouraged their political involvement.

Perhaps the most interesting aspects of the Bunche report as a historical source are those that disclose the attitudes of the people interviewed. These are quite revealing and all the more fascinating because they are so frequently expressed in everyday langauge. They bear on all manner of things: the ballot, the community, the government, the New Deal, local concerns, class differences, and matters of race. Racial feelings and attitudes, by the very nature of the investigation, are most prominent. The reader will find it rewarding to explore any number of questions touched on in this study. For example, what does it reveal about the differences in racial attitudes between southern whites and blacks? How wide was the range of racial attitudes in the two subcommunities? Did either whites or blacks correctly perceive the attitudes of the other race? Is there evidence of a reorientation of the Negro's thinking as a result of the economic depression and the New Deal? Is there evidence of a shift in white attitudes toward blacks during the Roosevelt era?

One has only to compare Talcott Parsons' and Kenneth B. Clark's recent study, *The Negro American* (1966), with Myrdal's *An American Dilemma* to realize how extensive the changes have been during the last two decades, both in the Negro's place in American society and in the scholarly methods of analyzing racial and minority problems. For all its information and illumination, *An American Dilemma* has become outdated as an approach to the "Negro problem." Today it is essentially a historical document. This is preeminently true of Ralph Bunche's memorandum on Negro politics. As a historical document, "The Political Status of the Negro" can be read with much profit, not only for what it tells us about election procedures, political practices, and black proscription, particularly in the South, but also for what it reveals about the lives of ordinary Americans in the era of Franklin D. Roosevelt—their conditions, habits, prejudices, myths, and aspirations. Before the opinion survey had become a well-established technique of the social scientist, the interviews and personal observations of Bunche and his assistants provided the basic ingredients for a unique source in understanding more fully the nation's most tragic domestic failing. Thus the memorandum is an important contribution to the new literature on the historical experience of black Americans, not least because of the perspective it offers on the Negro revolution of our own time.

10

The Regional Imagination:
Social Scientists and the American South

Although history has been the discipline most fully involved in the scholarly study of society in the South, the region's character and culture have not been neglected by other fields of systematic inquiry. The social sciences, particularly sociology, political science, and economics, have made notable contributions to the collection of empirical data about the South and to the interpretation of southern behavior and thought. Social scientists have frequently used the region as a social laboratory; they formulated the concept of regionalism as a tool of analysis; and they brought a comparative perspective to their investigations, especially in relating the southern states to the rest of the country. One has only to cite the names of Howard W. Odum, Rupert B. Vance, Charles S. Johnson, and V. O. Key to be reminded of the original and illuminating works on the South written by social scientists. For the historian of the twentieth-century South, regional studies by these and other scholars in the social sciences are absolutely indispensable.

The paper that follows, presented as the presidential address at the annual meeting of the Southern Historical Association in 1967, gives some account of the development of the various social sciences in the South and their use of the region as a focus and mode of scholarly analysis. The essay suggests that the emergence of the social sciences in the South is important not only because of the materials and methods they have produced for regional study but also because their growth represents a significant chapter in southern intellectual history. Their development was closely related to the deeper currents of social change in the South. Some of these themes are discussed at greater length in George B. Tindall's *The Emergence of the New South, 1913–1945* (1967).

O N E of the distinguishing features of modern American life is the influential role of scholarship and research, including the study of behavior in the social system commonly referred to as the social sciences. A second and generally unrelated aspect of the recent cultural scene in the United States is the continued manifestation of regional distinctions and interests. Despite the powerful sweep of cultural uniformity and increasing economic and political centralization, regionalism in America has survived and in some respects flourished. In the modern American mind the regional imagination has expressed itself most compellingly in the South, both in the attitude of the region's own inhabitants and in the image it evokes in other parts of the country. The development of the social sciences in the South was closely related to the processes of social change in the region, but the growth of the social studies in turn profoundly influenced the course of southern regionalism in the twentieth century. This is a phenomenon of considerable importance, not only because it makes up a significant chapter in the intellectual history of region and nation but also because it has produced a large body of materials and concepts of great potential value to the historian.

In the first two decades of the twentieth century, a period of national self-examination and social reform, the American South began to emerge into a new regional focus and its intellectual life experienced a slow but perceptible quickening. The most notable evidence of this development was the appearance in the late nineteenth and early twentieth centuries of a group of professionally trained historians.[1] The newer social studies, on the other hand, were just beginning to define themselves and scarcely existed as specialized disciplines. Most colleges and universities in the South

---

1. Wendell Holmes Stephenson, *The South Lives in History: Southern Historians and Their Legacy* (Baton Rouge, 1955).

were financially impoverished, they were still dominated by a traditional outlook, and there was as yet little appreciation of the social
potentiality of higher education. Although several nineteenth-
century Southerners, including George Tucker, George Fitzhugh,
and James D. B. De Bow, concerned themselves with the sociology
and political economy of their region, their writings contributed little
to the academic growth of the social sciences.[2] The sociologist
Thomas J. Woofter, Jr., later recalled that when he entered the University of Georgia in 1908 the only social science offered, other than
history, was a half-year course in elementary economics.[3] Where the
new social science disciplines were taught at all, they were usually
offered in combination, generally with history.[4] The oldest surviving
scholarly organization in the social sciences, the Southern Society for
Philosophy and Psychology, was established in 1904, but its founder
was a professor of philosophy and education, and the society seems
to have been dominated by philosophers during its early years.[5]
Here and there separate departments in the emerging social sciences
began to appear during the early 1900s, but there was little graduate
work in these disciplines before 1920.[6]

Nevertheless, some first steps were taken in the organizing of
research in the new disciplines. Beginning in the years before World
War I a series of "economic and social studies" made on a county-
by-county basis emanated from several southern state universities,
notably those of Virginia and the Carolinas. Perhaps the most prominent exponent of this research was Professor Eugene C. Branson,
first at the Georgia Normal School in Athens and later at the Univer-

2. L. L. Bernard, "The Historic Pattern of Sociology in the South," *Social Forces* 16
(October 1937): 1–12.

3. Woofter, *Southern Race Progress: The Wavering Color Line* (Washington, 1957),
p. 20.

4. For a discussion of the context in which history and the other social sciences
developed in this period, see Frederick W. Moore, "The Status of History in Southern
Colleges," *South Atlantic Quarterly* 2 (April 1903): 169–71; and Joseph J. Mathews, "The
Study of History in the South," *Journal of Southern History* 31 (February 1965): 3–9.

5. Marjorie Harris and Earl A. Alluisi, "The Southern Society in Retrospect: An
Abbreviated History of the First Sixty Years of the Southern Society for Philosophy
and Psychology, 1904–1964," *Perceptual and Motor Skills* 18 (June 1964): 665–70.

6. A total of only ten Ph.D. degrees in the social sciences was awarded in all of the
ex-Confederate states during the years 1900–1920; nine of these were in history. Mary
Bynum Pierson, *Graduate Work in the South* (Chapel Hill, 1947), pp. 228–40. Except
where otherwise noted, the South is defined in this paper as the former Confederate
states plus Kentucky and Oklahoma.

sity of North Carolina, where he headed the Department of Rural Social Economics and contributed significantly to the extension program being organized by that institution.[7] Meanwhile, the colleges of agriculture and agricultural experiment stations in the South were broadening their research to include such questions as agricultural marketing, land tenure, and rural credit systems.[8]

Another beginning was made in the study of race relations. As one sociologist pointed out a few years ago, "Robert E. Park and William I. Thomas, fathers of sociological research on racial and ethnic problems, held their first discussions on the dusty roads around Tuskegee just over fifty years ago."[9] By that time the Negro bibliographer Monroe N. Work had developed the Records and Research Department at Tuskegee, and in 1912 the department produced the first edition of *The Negro Year Book*. The first scientific study of the Negro in the South had begun fifteen years earlier when W. E. Burghardt Du Bois, a young Negro scholar with a Harvard Ph.D., went to Atlanta University to supervise the sociology program and to direct a series of conferences on Negro problems. Du Bois directed the preparation of sixteen monographs between 1897 and 1914, and while these studies were uneven in quality and lacking in systematic theory, they represented an attempt "to traverse the society," to employ such empirical techniques as the schedule, questionnaire, and interview.[10] Work in sociology and race relations was also introduced at Fisk University and a few other black colleges before World War I. Meanwhile, there were other signs of more objective study of race relations in the South: the publication of Willis Duke Weatherford's textbook on *Negro Life in the South* (1910), the scholarships and special studies sponsored by the Phelps-Stokes Fund, the organization of the University Commission on Southern

7. Edmund deS. Brunner, *The Growth of a Science: A Half-Century of Rural Sociological Research in the United States* (New York, [1957]), pp. 7–8; Louis R. Wilson, *The University of North Carolina, 1900–1930: The Making of a Modern University* (Chapel Hill, 1957), pp. 207–21.

8. See, for example, John K. Bettersworth, *People's College: A History of Mississippi State* (University, Ala., 1953), pp. 246–48, and Charles Gano Talbert, *The University of Kentucky: The Maturing Years* (Lexington, 1965), pp. 24–25.

9. Everett C. Hughes, "The Sociological Point of View," in *The Deep South in Transformation: A Symposium*, ed. Robert B. Highsaw (University, Ala., 1964), p. 75.

10. Basil Joseph Mathews, *Booker T. Washington: Educator and Interracial Interpreter* (Cambridge, 1948), pp. 105, 148–49; Elliott M. Rudwick, *W. E. B. Du Bois: A Study in Minority Group Leadership* (Philadelphia, 1960), pp. 34–36, 39–53.

Race Questions, and the launching of the Association for the Study of Negro Life and History.[11]

During the first decade and a half of this century the South was the scene of a series of uplift campaigns in such areas as public education, agricultural reform, and public health.[12] These crusades, in which northern philanthropists cooperated with southern leaders, did a good deal to heighten the regional consciousness of the South and to bring the region into national view. The climax of this reform came with the work of the Southern Sociological Congress during the years 1912–20. In its annual meetings and various campaigns the congress brought together a dedicated group of ministers, educators, social workers, and others who sought to study, discuss, and improve social conditions in the southern states. In the beginning they thought of the congress as an organization of specialists engaged in the scientific study of southern problems, but they interpreted sociology to mean social reform and the movement soon came to be characterized by an inspirational emphasis.[13]

The social sciences were beginning to establish their separate identities in the South by 1920, and a modest start had been made in research in a few fields by that time, but it was nevertheless true that they had as yet produced little in the way of regional literature. Among the social sciences only history had contributed significantly in this respect. Less scholarly works included many travel accounts and journalistic reports, some of which helped create the image of the "backward South."[14]

The 1920s marked a new phase in the development of the social sciences in the South, in the evolution of regional awareness, and in the convergence of the academic social studies and the analysis of the

11. Wilma Dykeman, *Phophet of Plenty: The First Ninety Years of W. D. Weatherford* (Knoxville, 1966), pp. 45, 69; George B. Tindall, "Southern Negroes Since Reconstruction: Dissolving the Static Image," in *Writing Southern History: Essays in Historiography in Honor of Fletcher M. Green*, ed. Arthur S. Link and Rembert W. Patrick (Baton Rouge, 1965), pp. 340–44; James Hardy Dillard et al., *Twenty Year Report of the Phelps-Stokes Fund, 1911–1931* (New York, 1932), pp. 10–13.

12. C. Vann Woodward, *Origins of the New South, 1877–1913* ([Baton Rouge], 1951), pp. 396–428.

13. E. Charles Chatfield, "The Southern Sociological Congress: Organization of Uplift," *Tennessee Historical Quarterly* 19 (December 1960): 328–47; and Chatfield, "The Southern Sociological Congress: Rationale of Uplift," ibid. 20 (March 1961): 51–64.

14. See Thomas D. Clark, ed., *Travels in the New South: A Bibliography*, vol. 2: *The Twentieth-Century South, 1900–1955: An Era of Change, Depression, and Emergence* (Norman, Okla., 1962).

region's society and culture. The milieu was now more favorable to the growth of the social sciences. World War I had broadened southern horizons, raised economic expectations, and widened the meaning of social welfare. The war and its aftermath also led to a new and more comprehensive interracial movement. During the 1920s the public service concept of government became firmly established in the South; state councils of social agencies and schools of public welfare and of social work were created; the professionalization of educators, social workers, and welfare specialists gained momentum; and the first modern universities began to emerge in the region.[15] In an era when the social science movement was experiencing vigorous growth in the United States and in which those disciplines were coming to be viewed as distinctive in method and purpose, southern social scientists caught some of the *élan* of the new approaches to the study of human behavior. They shared in the vision of utopian possibilities being opened up by the use of organized, collaborative research and scientific investigation. Their progress and their rationale, like that of other American social scientists, revealed the interrelation and the interdependence of organized academic research, the academic society, and the philanthropic foundation.[16]

The social sciences became more prevalent and more clearly defined in southern colleges and universities.[17] Graduate departments as distinct organizations made their appearance, and half a dozen southern universities awarded Ph.D. degrees in the social sciences

15. George Brown Tindall, *The Emergence of the New South, 1913–1945* ([Baton Rouge], 1967), pp. 61–69, 219–84; and Tindall, "Business Progressivism: Southern Politics in the Twenties," *South Atlantic Quarterly* 62 (Winter 1963): 92–106. The early volumes of the *Journal of Social Forces* (1922–) provide abundant evidence of these trends.

16. Henry F. May, "Shifting Perspectives on the 1920's," *Mississippi Valley Historical Review* 43 (December 1956): 407–11; John Higham, "The Schism in American Scholarship," *American Historical Review* 72 (October 1966): 13–15; Barry Dean Karl, *Executive Reorganization and Reform in the New Deal: The Genesis of Administrative Management, 1900–1939* (Cambridge, 1963), pp. 39–51.

17. An inquiry addressed to college teachers in the social sciences by the Southern Regional Committee of the Social Science Research Council in 1930 brought 553 replies (53.2 percent of those polled), with this breakdown among disciplines: 41.6 percent in history and political science, 26.2 percent in economics, 16.4 percent in sociology, and 15.8 percent unclassified. Psychology was not included. See Benjamin B. Kendrick, "Research by Southern Social Science Teachers," *Social Forces* 9 (March 1931): 362–69.

during the 1920s, with sociology and economics beginning to challenge history's dominance.[18] Institutes for academic study of social problems were established at the Universities of North Carolina, Virginia, and Texas. Departments and schools of business administration, which began to appear in southern colleges and universities during the prewar period, increased rapidly in the 1920s. By 1930 there were nine bureaus of economic and business research in the region.[19] Several new journals and organizations reflected the development of the social sciences: the *Southwestern Political Science Quarterly* (1920), the *Journal of Social Forces* (1922), the Southern Economic Association (1928), and the Southern Political Science Association (1929).

Among southern educational institutions the University of North Carolina made the most impressive gains. During the presidency of Harry Woodburn Chase (1919–30), North Carolina became the leading university in the region, "the Wisconsin of the South," according to some contemporaries. Chase's innovations included the creation of schools of commerce and public welfare, the development of a scientific department of psychology, the reorganization of the graduate school, the establishment of the University of North Carolina Press, and the founding of the Institute for Research in Social Science.[20] The institute was to become the single most important academic agency for the promotion of southern regionalism in the social sciences. As the historian of the modern University has written, "It immediately brought the social and economic problems of the State and region under careful survey, and through its publications, it greatly extended interest in and understanding of State and Southern social problems."[21]

A powerful stimulus to the creation of research facilities at the University of North Carolina and other southern institutions was the support of the great foundations, which were shifting their emphasis

18. The University of North Carolina led southern institutions in the number of Ph.D. degrees awarded in the social sciences with thirty-one during the decade. The University of Virginia granted eleven, followed by the University of Texas with ten. Pierson, *Graduate Work in the South*, pp. 228–40.

19. Walter J. Matherly, *Business Education in the Changing South* (Chapel Hill, 1939), pp. 72–76, 210–12.

20. Wilson, *University of North Carolina*, pp. 305–598; Howard W. Odum and Katharine Jocher, "Permanent Institutes," in *The Graduate School: Research and Publications*, ed. Edgar W. Knight and Agatha Boyd Adams (Chapel Hill, 1946), pp. 155–61.

21. Wilson, *University of North Carolina*, p. 467.

from reform and the practical solution of social problems to a program of scientific inquiry and long-range research.[22] A new era in the history of educational philanthropy for Negroes got under way about 1920 with more emphasis on higher education and specialized fields. By the end of the decade this trend culminated in the plan formulated by the General Education Board and the Julius Rosenwald Fund to develop four university centers for Negroes in the South.[23] The social sciences benefited from this foundation support. Empirical investigations into the conditions of Negro life and specialized studies of regional problems were also sponsored by the Commission on Interracial Cooperation and the Social Science Research Council.[24]

Sociological studies of Negro life constituted one area in which southern scholars contributed to better work in the social sciences during the 1920s; another was the field of rural sociological research. Because federal funds were available to the state colleges of agriculture for this kind of research, especially after the passage of the Purnell Act of 1924, many studies of farm tenancy, of rural communities, and of population shifts were undertaken in this period. The rural sociologist Carl C. Taylor of North Carolina State College was probably the outstanding southern scholar involved in this type of research.[25]

As the 1920s came to an end the new social science institutes and university presses were turning out monographs on a variety of state and regional problems: public welfare, labor, mill villages, prisons, income and wages, and rural life. In 1929 Rupert B. Vance's *Human Factors in Cotton Culture*, an early product of the emerging regional school in Chapel Hill, was published by the University of North Carolina Press. By 1930 that press had published eighty-eight books, about half of which were devoted to specific southern problems.[26]

But the research of social scientists in the South was still in its

22. Pierson, *Graduate Work in the South*, pp. 92–93; Tindall, *Emergence of the New South*, pp. 262–66.

23. Raymond B. Fosdick, *Adventure in Giving: The Story of the General Education Board, a Foundation Established by John D. Rockefeller* (New York and Evanston, 1962), pp. 188–211.

24. Social Science Research Council, *Third Annual Report, 1926–1927* (New York, 1927), p. 29; *Fourth Annual Report, 1927–1928* (New York, 1928), pp. 23–24; *Fifth Annual Report, 1928–1929* (New York, 1929), pp. 12–13.

25. Brunner, *Growth of a Science*, pp. 10–14, 28, 57, 115–16.

26. Wilson, *University of North Carolina*, pp. 496, 498.

early stages. No major work had yet been published, and no commanding figure had arisen to give regional direction to the social sciences. Regional visibility had been sharpened, however, by certain other developments. One was what George B. Tindall has described as the image of the "benighted South" embodied in the wave of criticism from outside the region that was directed at such things as the Ku Klux Klan, religious fundamentalism, and cultural backwardness.[27] "It is difficult now," Gerald W. Johnson wrote in 1924, "to find on the news stands a serious magazine without an article on some phase of life below the Potomac, or a discussion of one idea or another that has come out of the South."[28] Scarcely less important was the revival of southern letters, the emergence of a talented group of self-conscious writers who began to produce a distinctive regional literature.[29] They were preparing the way for the broader regionalism of the 1930s.

The Great Depression ushered in a remarkable era in the course of modern southern regionalism. Two new views of regional life emerged, the agrarianism associated with Nashville and the regionalism centered in Chapel Hill. The national emergency released a wave of reform energies and led to the forging of new social machinery. The work of the social scientists suddenly acquired unprecedented significance in a society threatened with collapse. In this setting the plight of the depressed South assumed the character of a great national problem and offered an opportunity for social planning. New Deal agencies and philanthropic foundations promoted scholarly investigations below the Potomac.[30] The South had entered what the North Carolina journalist William T. Polk described as "the Golden Age of the Gadflies. Great swarms of them hovered all over the region from Virginia to Texas," he wrote; "the South, like the white heifer, Io, who in human form incurred Hera's wrath as Zeus' mistress, bounded wildly before their stings, but mainly along the road of progress." The two main species of these gadflies, re-

---

27. Tindall, "The Benighted South: Origins of a Modern Image," *Virginia Quarterly Review* 40 (Spring 1964): 281–94.

28. Quoted, ibid., p. 284.

29. C. Hugh Holman, "A Cycle of Change in Southern Literature," in *The South in Continuity and Change*, ed. John C. McKinney and Edgar T. Thompson (Durham, 1965), pp. 392–97.

30. For an excellent discussion of the milieu in which these views developed, see Tindall, *Emergence of the New South*, pp. 575–606.

marked Polk, were "the sociological-research gadfly and the literary gadfly."[31]

The academic facilities for the training of scholars and the organizing of research in the early 1930s were not very strong even in the few places in the South where they existed at all. In 1932 Wilson Gee of the University of Virginia published a report entitled *Research Barriers in the South*. Gee's statistics revealed that southern professors carried a 30 percent heavier teaching load and received 33⅓ percent less salary than their counterparts in other regions. According to the Virginia professor, "a steady stream of the best in intellectual and leadership qualities has been pouring from out the borders of the South toward superior advantages elsewhere. . . ."[32] Gee emphasized the central importance of strong graduate schools in reversing this trend. A report on graduate instruction issued in 1934 by the American Council on Education listed only six institutions in the former Confederate states as having any graduate departments that were "adequate" for doctoral work.[33] "The typical graduate school of the region," wrote a southern political scientist about this time, "seems to be a collection of courses for permitting members and prospective members of the teaching profession to get a master's degree with a view to the improvement of salary and status."[34]

Yet marked progress was made in the development of graduate work in the social sciences. Duke University and the University of Texas joined North Carolina in leading southern institutions in this area, followed by Virginia, Vanderbilt, Peabody, and Louisiana State. By the mid-1940s a generation of Ph.D.'s from these and a few other universities in the region had been trained in such new disciplines as sociology and psychology.[35] Meanwhile, social science departments in several Negro institutions and in the land-grant col-

31. Polk, *Southern Accent: From Uncle Remus to Oak Ridge* (New York, 1953), p. 219.

32. Gee, *Research Barriers in the South* (New York and London, 1932), pp. 79–81, 166 [quote on page 166]; and Gee, "The 'Drag' of Talent out of the South," *Social Forces* 15 (March 1937): 343–46.

33. The University of Texas led the southern institutions with twelve "adequate" departments, followed by the University of North Carolina with eleven. Pierson, *Graduate Work in the South*, pp. 179–80.

34. H. Clarence Nixon, "Colleges and Universities," in *Culture in the South*, ed. W. T. Couch (Chapel Hill, 1934), p. 235.

35. Universities in the eleven ex-Confederate states during the period 1931–45 awarded approximately 195 Ph.D. degrees in history, 120 in economics, 75 in psychology, 60 in sociology, 35 in political science, and 12 in geography. Pierson, *Graduate Work in the South*, pp. 228–40.

leges were becoming more firmly established. The research institutes at North Carolina, Virginia, and Texas had become vigorous training and research agencies. In 1940 Vanderbilt established an Institute of Research and Training in the Social Sciences, and by that time bureaus of government research and of public administration were appearing in various southern universities.[36] Several additional university presses were created by the end of World War II. New academic societies and journals appeared, including the Southern Historical Association (1934), the Southern Sociological Society (1935), the *Southern Economic Journal* (1933), the *Journal of Southern History* (1935), and the *Journal of Politics* (1939).

The growing interest in fundamental research exhibited by the large foundations during the 1920s was even more evident in the 1930s. It is fair to say that virtually every important project in social science research in southern colleges and universities was directly supported by such grants. The General Education Board diverted more of its large resources to the needs of higher education in the South and in the late 1930s initiated a program to encourage the economic and social development of the region. The GEB and the Rosenwald Fund focused greater attention on black colleges and awarded hundreds of fellowships for advanced study to Southerners of both races.[37] The Social Science Research Council, with Rosenwald money, awarded sixty-three Southern Fellowships in the Social Sciences during the years 1930–33. The council also made a series of special grants-in-aid of research to southern faculty members in the social sciences during the 1930s and 1940s.[38] In 1929 the SSRC created a Southern Regional Committee which continued in existence for eighteen years. The committee investigated the status of the social sciences in the region and sought to stimulate academic research by sponsoring annual conferences and special studies of southern topics.[39]

An informal but powerful directorate emerged during this

36. Edith Webb Williams, *Research in Southern Regional Development* (Richmond, 1948), pp. 88–89, 100–102.

37. Fosdick, *Adventure in Giving,* pp. 266–97; Edwin R. Embree, *Julius Rosenwald Fund: Review of Two Decades, 1917–1936* (Chicago, 1936), pp. 27–35, 47; Tindall, *Emergence of the New South,* pp. 499–504; Pierson, *Graduate Work in the South,* p. 94.

38. Social Science Research Council, *Fifth Annual Report, 1928–1929,* p. 28; *Fellows of the Social Science Research Council, 1925–1939* (New York, n.d.), pp. xxiii–xxiv.

39. See the annual reports of the SSRC, 1929–1947, and *Problems of the Cotton Economy: Proceedings of the Southern Social Science Research Conference, New Orleans, March 8 and 9, 1935* (Dallas, 1936).

period to establish lines of communication and understanding between the academic community in the South and the organizations interested in regional reform. The key figures were the triumvirate of Will W. Alexander, whose Commission on Interracial Cooperation became a clearing house for southern information and cooperation in race relations; Edwin R. Embree, president of the Rosenwald Fund; and Charles S. Johnson of Fisk University. These men were deeply involved in the plans to create Negro university centers in the South, in several of the fellowship programs, and in many of the special studies and reports sponsored by the Rosenwald Fund and other foundations. They organized, with support from the Rockefeller Foundation, a large-scale investigation of the South's rural economy in the mid-1930s that became the basis for their famous report in 1935, *The Collapse of Cotton Tenancy: A Summary of Field Studies & Statistical Surveys, 1933–35.*[40]

Charles Spurgeon Johnson was the leader in making Fisk University the major Negro center for social research in the South and one of the outstanding research institutions in the entire field of race relations. Born in Bristol, Virginia, in 1893, Johnson studied sociology at the University of Chicago, where he was greatly influenced by Robert E. Park. After working with the Chicago Commission on Race Relations during the years 1919–21, he joined the National Urban League as director of research. In 1928 he was brought to Fisk to direct the social sciences, which had just been reorganized with foundation help. An able organizer and promoter, Johnson secured outside financial support, brought in scholarly talent, and made his department a research center of real importance during the 1930s. The department published twenty-three books from 1928 to 1940 and carried out a variety of useful surveys. In 1944 Johnson expanded the program at Fisk by inaugurating the Annual Institute of Race Relations. The Fisk sociologists were concerned with the immediate aspects of southern life, but they also demonstrated an interest in the comparative use of experience outside the South in their approach to the regional society.[41]

40. Edwin R. Embree and Julia Waxman, *Investment in People: The Story of the Julius Rosenwald Fund* (New York, 1949), pp. 73–74, 202–203; Wilma Dykeman and James Stokely, *Seeds of Southern Change: The Life of Will Alexander* (Chicago, 1962), pp. 164, 170–74, 185, 199–200, 214, 224; interview with Rupert B. Vance, July 11, 1967.

41. Edwin R. Embree, *13 Against the Odds* (New York, 1944), pp. 47–70; Joe M. Richardson, "A History of Fisk University" (unpublished manuscript in possession of its author), ch. 11; Edgar T. Thompson, "Sociology and Sociological Research in the South," *Social Forces* 23 (March 1945): 364–65; interview with Lewis W. Jones, July 3, 1967.

Johnson was also a productive scholar. His studies of Negro life in the black belt and of rural education, both based on extensive sociological field work, were significant contributions.[42] One of his books, *Growing up in the Black Belt: Negro Youth in the Rural South* (1941), was part of a large-scale investigation of Negro youth in the late 1930s.[43] Scholarly investigations of Negro conditions and race relations were also being undertaken in other southern institutions and by such northern social scientists as John Dollard and Hortense Powdermaker. Among southern white scholars, Thomas J. Woofter contributed in several books to the development of greater sophistication in studies of race in the South.[44] It was natural for Gunnar Myrdal, in making his monumental study of the problem the Negro presents to American democracy, to turn for assistance to these and other southern social scientists. Myrdal's classic work was in considerable part a "southern study," not only because much of its concern was with that region but also because a large number of southern scholars contributed to the extensive research on which the study rested.[45]

While Charles S. Johnson was developing a center for sociological research in the area of Negro life and race relations, another research entrepreneur, Howard W. Odum, was involved in a more comprehensive program of regional scholarship in the North Carolina village of Chapel Hill. More than any other single person he was "the father of the systematic scientific study of Southern society."[46] A man of prodigious energy, Odum was a creative organizer, a dreamer who was eminently practical. He was a native of Georgia (born in 1884) and a graduate of Emory College. Early in his career he developed an interest in Negro life and folklore, and as a graduate student at Clark University and at Columbia he encoun-

---

42. See, for example, Johnson, *The Shadow of the Plantation* (Chicago, 1934); and Johnson et al., *Statistical Atlas of Southern Counties: Listing and Analysis of Socio-Economic Indices of 1104 Southern Counties* (Chapel Hill, 1941).

43. These studies, sponsored by the American Youth Commission, were financed by the General Education Board. Fosdick, *Adventure in Giving*, pp. 244–46.

44. Few social scientists were associated with a wider array of organizations and research projects concerned with the South than Woofter. They included the Phelps-Stokes Fund, the Commission on Interracial Cooperation, the University of North Carolina, several New Deal agencies, and Gunnar Myrdal's *An American Dilemma*. See Woofter, *Southern Race Progress: The Wavering Color Line* (Washington, 1957).

45. Myrdal, *An American Dilemma: The Negro Problem and Modern Democracy*, 2 vols. (New York and London, 1944).

46. George B. Tindall, "The Significance of Howard W. Odum to Southern History: A Preliminary Estimate," *Journal of Southern History* 24 (August 1958): 303–304.

tered the new social sciences. He was also influenced by the southern education crusade and the nascent social welfare movement in the South during the second decade of this century as well as by his work with the Southern Division of the American Red Cross during World War I. In 1920 Harry W. Chase persuaded him to leave his position at Emory and come to the University of North Carolina as head of the Department of Sociology and director of the new School of Public Welfare. He immediately became the central figure in the development of the social sciences at North Carolina, launching summer institutes and special programs in public welfare and social work, establishing the *Journal of Social Forces,* taking the lead in organizing the Institute for Research in Social Science, and assembling a strong staff of assistants.[47]

From the beginning of his work in Chapel Hill, Odum was deeply interested in state and regional study. The *Journal of Social Forces,* while concerned with many aspects of sociology, emphasized southern issues.[48] Under Odum the Institute for Research in Social Science symbolized the new trend toward planned and cooperative research. The South became a great regional laboratory for the institute, and its elaborately organized workshop reminded one of "the sort of room . . . in which a general's staff might plan its war."[49] By the late 1920s Odum had planned a comprehensive group of southern studies, and during the following decade an outpouring of monographs on Negro life, regional portraiture, and practical social problems issued from Chapel Hill.[50] Many of these books were published by the University of North Carolina Press, which itself became a powerful force in the emergence of a regional social science literature.[51]

Howard W. Odum was more than a successful organizer of research. He was also a scholar, and he published some twenty books

47. Wilson, *University of North Carolina,* pp. 447–50, 462–68.

48. When the Southern Sociological Society was organized in 1935, *Social Forces* (as it was called after 1925) became the official magazine of the organization.

49. Jonathan Daniels, *Tar Heels: A Portrait of North Carolina* (New York, 1941), p. 274. See also Odum and Jocher, "Permanent Institutes," pp. 160–65.

50. "Institute for Research in Social Science: Publications and Manuscripts (Arranged Chronologically)," *Social Forces* 23 (March 1945): 309–28.

51. By the end of 1945 the press had published about 500 titles, over 175 of which dealt with southern topics. See W. T. Couch, "The University Press," in *The Graduate School,* pp. 175–86; Couch, "Twenty Years of Southern Publishing," *Virginia Quarterly Review* 26 (Spring 1950): 171–85; and Lambert Davis, "North Carolina and Its University Press," *North Carolina Historical Review* 43 (April 1966): 149–56.

and two hundred articles during his career. In his intellectual development the North Carolina sociologist moved from the Negro and his folksongs to folk society and folk sociology, from race relations and the South to regionalism and regional-national planning, from folkways to what he called technicways and state ways, from social values to social action.[52] Regionalism became his intellectual preoccupation about 1930, but his ideas were taking shape during the 1920s as he began to formulate social research within a regional framework. During the early 1930s Odum was a member of the President's Research Committee on Social Trends, and his experience in that committee's task of inventorying the nation's social resources and trends undoubtedly contributed to the crystallization of his regional thought. In 1931 the General Education Board made a grant to the Social Science Research Council for a southern regional study. Odum was the obvious person to conduct the study, and in 1932 the SSRC put the project under his direction, with the Southern Regional Committee in an advisory role.[53] The result was Odum's epochal *Southern Regions of the United States* (1936), a huge inventory incorporating over seven hundred indices. The study was a tour de force in the use of cultural-statistical data, and it became a bible for the regionalists.

Regionalism to Odum was a tool of analysis, an instrument for the effective synthesizing of the social sciences and to some extent of other subjects. It was also a way to study the whole of society, for Odum emphasized what he described as the "folk-regional society," a gestalt "in which all factors are sought out and interpreted in their proper perspective."[54] Regionalism, moreover, was a framework for social planning and social action. The South, in Professor Vance's phrase, was thus both "a case for analysis and a cause for social action."[55] Odum distinguished between a "national-regional" approach, which looked toward integration of the region in the nation,

52. Katharine Jocher et al., eds., *Folk, Region, and Society: Selected Papers of Howard W. Odum* (Chapel Hill, 1964), p. v.

53. Tindall, "The Significance of Howard W. Odum to Southern History," pp. 285–307; Rupert B. Vance and Katharine Jocher, "Howard W. Odum," *Social Forces* 33 (March 1955): 203–17; "From Community Studies to Regionalism," *Social Forces* 23 (March 1945): 245–58.

54. "From Community Studies to Regionalism," p. 253; George L. Simpson, Jr., "Howard W. Odum and American Regionalism," *Social Forces* 34 (December 1955): 101–106.

55. Jocher et al., *Folk, Region, and Society*, p. 109.

and a "sectional-local" perspective, which he associated with conflict and an exaggerated parochialism.[56] Other southern social scientists contributed to the theory of regionalism, but none with the clarity and force of Odum's young colleague and protégé, Rupert B. Vance. In *Human Geography of the South: A Study in Regional Resources and Human Adequacy* (1932), he provided a valuable classification of the South's cultural areas and stated some of the requirements of the new regionalism. His later volume, *All These People: The Nation's Human Resources in the South* (1945), made skillful use of regional and population theory and extended the analysis published in *Southern Regions*.

The studies that came from Chapel Hill in the 1930s and 1940s were a potent factor in the stimulation of the regional imagination. They made a strong impression upon social scientists, but their impact was not limited to the scholarly world. When Jonathan Daniels visited the office of a country lawyer in Marked Tree, Arkansas, during his tour of the South in 1937, he noticed not only law books but many works on southern problems published by the University of North Carolina Press. The lawyer eagerly queried Daniels about Odum, Vance, and other regional sociologists, and turning to his book shelves, declared: "I've got 'em all. That's a great University at Chapel Hill."[57] The regionalism of the 1930s marked a milestone in the development of the social sciences in the South, and it produced a body of writing that did a great deal to illuminate southern life, to heighten regional awareness, and to help the nation rediscover the South. "Regionalism," remarks Professor George B. Tindall, "quickened a generation of social scientists with its vision of the 'problem South,' a region with obvious deficiencies but with potentialities that demanded constructive study and planning."[58]

Regional literature in the 1930s encompassed an extraordinary variety of publications. The concept of the South's "colonial economy" found expression in such volumes as Walter Prescott Webb's *Divided We Stand: The Crisis of a Frontierless Democracy* (1937). The search for the southern identity led to the publication of W. T. Couch's *Culture in the South* (1934) and other books. Several

56. In *American Regionalism: A Cultural-Historical Approach to National Integration* (New York, 1938), Odum and Harry Estill Moore applied the regional concept to the whole nation, with a sixfold delineation of the United States.

57. Daniels, *A Southerner Discovers the South* (New York, 1938), pp. 137–40; quote on page 140.

58. Tindall, *Emergence of the New South*, pp. 583–88; quote on page 588.

notable studies dealt with rural life, including Thomas J. Woofter's *Landlord and Tenant on the Cotton Plantation* (1936) and Arthur F. Raper's *Preface to Peasantry: A Tale of Two Black Counties* (1936). Journalists wrote works of social exploration cast in a regional framework, while other popular writers produced a stream of state interpretations, travel accounts, and reminiscences.[59] The WPA Writers' Project and the Farm Security Administration's photographers added their contributions to the regional literature. All the while a dynamic movement among southern historians was creating a new regional historiography, and the literary renascence that began in the 1920s was becoming the most famous of all regional expressions.

The Tennessee Valley Authority, set up in 1933, obviously has been an influential factor in the recent history of the South. It has contributed to the popularization of the regional concept and to its identification with the South. The agency promoted the scholarly study of regional problems and itself became the subject of numerous analyses by social scientists. Its regional-studies staff became a center for the assembly and analysis of information on economic and social trends in the area. Research was an essential element in the TVA's approach, for planning and research were involved in virtually every aspect of the authority's relationship with governmental units in the valley.[60] In 1934 and 1935 the agency worked out arrangements with the land-grant colleges and state departments of education for a series of social and economic studies. Discovering that it needed to know a great deal about state and local governments in the valley, TVA developed a cooperative research program that involved academic people in the various states and produced numerous studies. Similar arrangements resulted in archaeological investigations and social surveys. The authority subsidized and in other ways encouraged the establishment of bureaus of public administration in the southern universities; it also played a major part in the development of state and local planning commissions in the region. From all these activities there developed a pattern of cooperative

---

59. Examples of such regional portrayal are Daniels, *A Southerner Discovers the South,* and J. Saunders Redding, *No Day of Triumph* (New York, 1942).

60. Joseph M. Ray, "The Influence of the Tennessee Valley Authority on Government in the South," *American Political Science Review* 43 (October 1949): 922–32; C. Herman Pritchett, *The Tennessee Valley Authority: A Study in Public Administration* (Chapel Hill, 1943), pp. 126–36; Gordon R. Clapp, *The TVA: An Approach to the Development of a Region* (Chicago, 1955), pp. 79–81.

research that nourished the growth of the social sciences and influenced their orientation.[61]

One of the agencies with which the Tennessee Valley Authority worked closely was the Bureau of Public Administration at the University of Alabama. The Alabama bureau played a key role in the early organization of southern research in political and administrative affairs. Growing out of an Institute of Public Administration organized at the university in 1937, the bureau quickly became the regional leader in the embryonic field of public administration.[62] The person who contributed most to the emergence of the bureau as a regional center was its first director, Roscoe C. Martin. A native of Texas, Martin had received a Ph.D. degree in political science from the University of Chicago and was the author of *The People's Party in Texas* (1933). During the years 1933–37 he had rehabilitated and directed the Bureau of Municipal Research at the University of Texas. A keen student of state and local politics, Martin was, in Alexander Heard's words, a "research entrepreneur nonpareil."[63] He brought a new vitality to political science in the South, gave a regional scope to the study of political behavior there, and tried to bridge the gap between his discipline and the other social sciences.

During its early years the bureau emphasized research and service related to governmental units and organizations in Alabama. A number of valuable monographs resulted, dealing with county and municipal government, state administration, and the legislative process.[64] Two case studies of Alabama counties by Karl A. Bosworth, based on intensive research and field investigations, were remark-

61. Lawrence L. Durisch, "TVA and State and Local Government," in *TVA: The First Twenty Years: A Staff Report*, ed. Roscoe C. Martin ([University, Ala.], 1956), pp. 232–43; William E. Cole, "Personality and Cultural Research in the Tennessee Valley," *Social Forces* 13 (May 1935): 521–27; Clarence Lewis Hodge, *The Tennessee Valley Authority: A National Experiment in Regionalism* (Washington, 1938), pp. 98, 156–57.

62. Rowland Egger and Weldon Cooper, *Research, Education, and Regionalism: The Bureau of Public Administration of the University of Alabama, 1938–1948* (University, Ala., 1949). See also Chester Bain, "Bureau of Public Administration, University of Virginia," University of Virginia *News Letter* 33 (June 1, 1957).

63. Heard, *A Two-Party South?* (Chapel Hill, 1952), p. ix; interview with Heard, July 17, 1967.

64. For examples, see Weldon Cooper, *Municipal Government and Administration in Alabama* (University, Ala., 1940); Roscoe C. Martin, *The Growth of State Administration in Alabama* (University, Ala., 1942); Malcolm C. Moos, *State Penal Administration in Alabama* (University, Ala., 1942); and Hallie Farmer, *The Legislative Process in Alabama* (University, Ala., 1949). By 1967 the bureau had published more than seventy books and monographs. Robert B. Highsaw to the writer, July 20, 1967.

ably successful in illuminating the relationship between politics and social structure.[65] Beginning in 1943, the Alabama bureau gave increasing attention to regional research and training, becoming a vehicle for the organization and management of a series of research and educational undertakings involving interstate and interinstitutional cooperation. This regional focus resulted in part from the General Education Board's willingness to support comprehensive research programs in the South. But there were additional factors, including the TVA and other regional organizations, the southern campaign against the existing freight-rate structure, and the example of the Chapel Hill regionalists.[66] In any case, the bureau initiated and carried through several important regional research projects during the 1940s: studies of subsistence homesteads and federal rural housing;[67] a cooperative survey of the administration of natural resources in the Southeast;[68] a cooperative appraisal of technical services available to state and local officials in the region; a study of the electoral process in the South; and a regional training program in public administration. These programs promoted collaborative research in governmental affairs, led directly to the establishment of bureaus of public administration in several other states, and generally contributed to the development of political science in the South. The bureaus of public administration in other southern universities soon began to bring out studies dealing with a wide variety of administrative problems and political behavior at the state and local levels.

The most distinguished of the Alabama bureau's regional undertakings was the project that produced V. O. Key's *Southern Politics in State and Nation* (1949), probably the preeminent regional study of politics in America. The work was first conceived in the fertile mind of Roscoe C. Martin, who about 1944 began to think in terms of a thoroughgoing study of the poll tax in the South. He gradually came to believe that a full-scale exploration of the entire one-party system

65. Bosworth, *Black Belt County: Rural Government in the Cotton Country of Alabama* (University, Ala., 1941); and Bosworth, *Tennessee Valley County: Rural Government in the Hill Country of Alabama* (University, Ala., 1941).

66. Egger and Cooper, *Research, Education, and Regionalism*, pp. 41–42.

67. Paul W. Wager, *One Foot on the Soil: A Study of Subsistence Homesteads in Alabama* (University, Ala., 1945); Rupert B. Vance and Gordon W. Blackwell, *New Farm Homes for Old: A Study of Rural Public Housing in the South* (University, Ala., 1946).

68. Six state studies prepared by scholars in the six cooperating universities were published in 1947 and 1948. For a synthesis of these studies, see Lawrence L. Durisch and Hershal L. Macon, *Upon Its Own Resources: Conservation and State Administration* (University, Ala., 1951).

was needed. In order to understand political behavior in Alabama or the Tennessee Valley or the larger South, Martin decided, it would be necessary to study a broad area and to explain the regional unity that characterized southern politics. Having formulated the general research scheme, the Alabama political scientist then secured financial backing from the Rockefeller Foundation and persuaded V. O. Key, Jr., of Johns Hopkins University to direct the project. Like Martin, Key was a Texan who had earned a Ph.D. degree at the University of Chicago. He had already demonstrated the talent that was to make him one of the nation's leading political scientists. Work on the project began in the fall of 1946. A large body of research materials was collected in Tuscaloosa, and 538 persons of significance were interviewed in the ex-Confederate states.[69] The enterprise was nothing if not ambitious. Key and his assistants found it necessary to develop new methods of analysis to accomplish their purpose. They sought to produce an accurate and comprehensive analysis of southern politics, to reach a nontechnical audience with their results, and, as Key noted in 1947, to "come out ultimately with a report that would constitute something of a contribution to the literature of political science. . . ."[70]

Southern Politics was a remarkable accomplishment in social science research, an authoritative analysis of political institutions and behavior in the American South, and, as C. Vann Woodward said in a review, "one of the major myth-dispellers of Southern scholarship."[71] While it emphasized the historic role of the black belts in perpetuating southern sectionalism, the book also disproved the old notion that all southern states fell within the same pattern. The study influenced political scientists in and out of the South. The volume demonstrated that it was possible to use new data, new approaches, and new techniques in working on an old subject.[72]

69. Alexander Heard did the interviewing in nine states, and Donald S. Strong in two. See Heard, "Interviewing Southern Politicians," *American Political Science Review* 44 (December 1950): 886–96; and Egger and Cooper, *Research, Education, and Regionalism*, pp. 47, 94–101.

70. Egger and Cooper, *Research, Education, and Regionalism*, pp. 96–97.

71. *Yale Review* 39 (Winter 1950): 375.

72. Two by-products of the Key project were Alexander Heard, *A Two-Party South?*; and Heard and Donald S. Strong, *Southern Primaries and Elections, 1920–1949* (University, Ala., 1950).

The work of the bureaus of public administration, the regional leadership of the University of Alabama, and the influence of *Southern Politics* all contributed to the growth of academic research in political science in the South. Separate departments of political science became more common after World War II, the Southern Political Science Association became a stróng organization, and the *Journal of Politics* grew into an outstanding quarterly. Yet in many southern institutions political science remained weak, overshadowed by other disciplines and frequently taught by other social scientists.[73] Sociology, often in combination with anthropology, continued its development as a distinct academic subject, but it, too, was inadequately supported in many southern colleges. A survey of sociology in the South undertaken by the Southern Sociological Society in the early 1960s indicated progress in the postwar years but revealed "a deep and genuine concern" among sociologists about the "quality" of the work in sociology in the region.[74] History and economics retained their position as the most fully developed of the social sciences on the southern academic scene, but psychology experienced the most rapid growth following the war. Separate departments of psychology were established in many institutions, and in 1954 the Southeastern Psychological Association was organized.[75] Geography emerged more clearly as a social science, escaping from its traditionally close confines with geology and stressing cultural phenomena. Strong departments were developed in a few southern universities, and the Southeastern Division of the Association of American Geographers, organized about 1946, became the most vigorous regional geographical society in the country.[76]

Advanced study in the social sciences has made significant gains since 1945. Strong Ph.D. programs have been developed in most of these disciplines, and a slow increase has taken place in the percent-

73. Robert S. Rankin, *Political Science in the South* (University, Ala., 1946); Alexander Heard, "Southern Political Science: Some Notes on Progress and Need," *Journal of Politics* 25 (February 1963): 3–13.

74. Lee M. Brooks and Alvin L. Bertrand, *History of the Southern Sociological Society* (University, Ala., 1962), pp. 70–72 and *passim*.

75. Harris and Alluisi, "The Southern Society in Retrospect," p. 677; interview with Leland E. Thune, July 21, 1967.

76. Merle C. Prunty, Jr., to the author, August 17, 1967; interview with J. Russell Whitaker, June 30, 1967.

age of the nation's Ph.D. degrees awarded in the South.[77] But much of this progress was concentrated in a few states.[78] The South continued to fall below the national averages in almost every measure of academic achievement in the social studies, and the region failed to develop a great university of really top rank. Nevertheless, "research" had become a magic word in the South, in part because of the growing belief that it was essential to economic development. State research commissions and research centers spread over the region. By the mid-1960s there were at least 800 separate nonprofit research agencies in the southern states, and about 160 of these were primarily concerned with the social sciences.[79] The cooperative programs sponsored by the Southern Regional Education Board, organized in 1948 by the Southern Governors' Conference, stimulated scholarly activity in such fields as political science, psychology, and city planning.[80] The university press movement gathered momentum in the South during the 1950s, and today fifteen of the sixty-eight members of the Association of American University Presses are located in the South. The large foundations also continued to play a major role in the promotion of social science investigations in the southern states, and the federal government, increasingly involved

77. In 1961–62 the fifteen states that cooperated through the Southern Regional Education Board awarded 14.4 percent of the nation's Ph.D. degrees in the social sciences. These states contained about 30 percent of the American population. E. F. Schietinger, *Fact Book on Higher Education in the South, 1965* (Atlanta, 1965), p. 54. The number of Ph.D. degrees awarded by southern institutions between 1947 and 1963 was approximately 1,050 in psychology, 661 in history, 405 in economics (622 if business is included), 246 in sociology, 206 in political science, 54 in geography, and 4 in anthropology. These figures are based on the U.S. Office of Education, *Earned Degrees Conferred by Higher Educational Institutions: Circular*, nos. 247 (1948), 262 (1949), 282 (1950), 333 (1952), 360 (1952), 777 (1965); and Allan M. Cartter, ed., *American Universities and Colleges*, 9th ed. (Washington, 1964).

78. Among southern states North Carolina awarded the most Ph.D. degrees in the social sciences during the period 1947–63, a total of 713. Texas came next with 639, followed by Louisiana and Tennessee with 281 each. See sources cited in note 77.

79. The number of social science research centers in the region ranged from three in Arkansas to thirty-three in Texas. North Carolina had twenty-five, Louisiana twenty, Tennessee fifteen, and Georgia eleven. Archie M. Palmer and Anthony T. Kruzas, eds, *Research Centers Directory*, 2nd ed. (Detroit, 1965), and supplements to May 1966. See also Cameron Fincher, *Research in the South: An Appraisal of Current Efforts*, Georgia State School of Arts and Sciences, *Research Papers*, no. 5 (Atlanta, 1964).

80. Redding S. Sugg, Jr., and George Hilton Jones, *The Southern Regional Education Board: Ten Years of Regional Cooperation in Higher Education* (Baton Rouge, 1960).

in the financing of higher education, became an important new factor in advancing all branches of scholarship in the region.

Except for historians, economists have exhibited the most interest in regional research during the past two decades. Although the academic study of economics and business developed relatively early in the South, those fields came to regionalism late. Specialized studies of state and regional problems by economists were published in earlier years, of course, and the Southern Economic Association focused a good deal of attention on the South. The editors of the *Southern Economic Journal* disclaimed a "belief in the existence of a distinctively Southern economics," but they hoped to encourage economic research that was "requisite to the amelioration of the South's difficulties." The *Journal* steadily broadened its scope, but it published many articles on southern subjects during the 1930s and 1940s.[81] No regional center in economics came into being during this period, however, and no major regional analysis by a southern economist was published until after World War II.

Still, the economic plight of the South provided the background for much of the regional scholarship in the 1930s, and that work helped to generate the idea of the "colonial economy" and to encourage an instrumentalist approach to the study of the southern economy. During the late thirties Odum had drawn up plans for a Council on Southern Economic Development as a means of implementing regionalism. Economic development, in fact, was a basic part of the regionalists' rationale. "As 'one of Howard W. Odum's boys,' " Rupert B. Vance later recalled, "I was accustomed to delivering occasional homilies throughout the South advocating economic development."[82] Another factor that promoted the "growth psychology" was the work of the planning commissions. All the southern states established such commissions between 1933 and 1938, and they began to busy themselves with the task of inventorying resources and collecting basic data. The National Resources Planning

81. *Southern Economic Journal* 1 (October 1933): 2; 2 (January 1936): 2; Walter J. Matherly, "The History of the Southern Economic Association, 1927–1939," ibid. 7 (October 1940): 232; Sylvia Wrobel, "History of the University of North Carolina School of Business Administration" (unpublished manuscript in possession of its author).

82. Vance, "Beyond the Fleshpots: The Coming Cultural Crisis in the South," *Virginia Quarterly Review* 41 (Spring 1965): 219. See also George B. Tindall, "The 'Colonial Economy' and the Growth Psychology: The South in the 1930's," *South Atlantic Quarterly* 64 (Autumn 1965): 465–77.

Board meanwhile sponsored a series of regional conferences which culminated in the formation of the Southeastern Regional Planning Committee in 1940. That committee completed a report in 1942 which reflected the regional planning and economic development implicit in the work of the Chapel Hill regionalists.[83] Such diverse groups as the Southern Research Institute and the Southeastern Regional Association of University Bureaus of Business Research also reflected faith in economic development.

While this was occurring, a turning point was reached in the analysis of southern economic problems. Early in 1946 the National Planning Association initiated steps that led to the formation of a Committee of the South made up of Southerners active in various fields concerned with regional development. The purpose was to make "an adequate study of economic conditions of the South, expertly conducted."[84] Calvin B. Hoover of Duke University became director of the committee's research, and several regional economic studies were undertaken. Two of the most important were *Economic Resources and Policies of the South* (1951) by Hoover and Benjamin U. Ratchford[85] and *Why Industry Moves South* (1949) by Glenn McLaughlin and Stefan Robock. The Hoover and Ratchford volume was a comprehensive guide to the region's economy which provided a valuable picture of an older agrarian economy slowly coming into economic maturity. The work by McLaughlin and Robock stimulated a great deal of further research by southern economists. In general, the economists associated with the Committee of the South rejected the "colonial-imperialistic conspiracy" of the prewar period.[86]

83. John V. Van Sickle, *Planning for the South: An Inquiry into the Economics of Regionalism* (Nashville, 1943); Albert Lepawsky, "Government Planning in the South," *Journal of Politics* 10 (August 1948): 536–67; Lepawsky, *State Planning and Economic Development in the South* (n.p., 1949); Lawrence Logan Durisch, "Southern Regional Planning and Development," *Journal of Politics* 26 (February 1964): 41–59.

84. Williams, *Research in Southern Regional Development*, p. 37; Clarence H. Danhof, "Four Decades of Thought on the South's Economic Problems," in *Essays in Southern Economic Development*, ed. Melvin L. Greenhut and W. Tate Whitman (Chapel Hill, 1964), p. 55.

85. See by the same authors, *The Impact of Federal Policies on the Economy of the South: A Report Prepared for the Council of Economic Advisers on Behalf of the NPA Committee of the South* (Washington, 1949).

86. One of the committee volumes, George W. Stocking's *Basing Point Pricing and Regional Development: A Case Study of the Iron and Steel Industry* (Chapel Hill, 1954), did emphasize the restrictive effects of northeastern policies on the South. See Danhof, "Four Decades of Thought on the South's Economic Problems," pp. 7–68; and B. U. Ratchford, "Economic Development in the South," *South Atlantic Quarterly* 64 (Autumn 1965): 496–505.

More recently southern economists have explored other approaches to regional analysis. The Inter-University Committee for Economic Research on the South, formed in 1958, has produced several studies, including a wide-ranging symposium on the regional economy.[87] Some economists of the South have shown an interest in the relevance of economic ideas on problems of underdeveloped countries. Anthony M. Tang's *Economic Development in the Southern Piedmont, 1860–1950: Its Impact on Agriculture* (1958) illuminated the way in which urbanization, industrialization, and agricultural immobility affected different areas in the Piedmont South. Economists and rural sociologists have made empirical studies of the process of farm mechanization, of its economic and social consequences, and of the increasing industrialization of rural and small-town areas in the South.[88] Other scholars have begun to study the economic effects of racial discrimination and of cultural factors.[89] In *Southern Tradition and Regional Progress* (1960) William H. Nicholls argued that the region's lag in per capita incomes results from its relatively slow rate of industrial-urban development and that this retarded growth is largely attributable to the longtime adherence to a set of cultural values inconsistent with rapid industrial development.

A few other regional studies made during the last quarter century should be mentioned. One of the most important was the Regional Land Tenure Research Project, a cooperative undertaking carried out during the years 1941–46 by the departments of agricultural economics and rural sociology in the land-grant colleges of Arkansas, Louisiana, Mississippi, Oklahoma, and Texas. The project was designed to study the social and economic aspects of land tenure in the Southwest and to develop a plan for regional research coopera-

87. Melvin L. Greenhut and W. Tate Whitman, eds., *Essays in Southern Economic Development* (Chapel Hill, 1964). Another study sponsored by the Inter-University Committee is Marshall R. Colberg, *Human Capital in Southern Development, 1939–1963* (Chapel Hill, 1965).

88. See John Leonard Fulmer, *Agricultural Progress in the Cotton Belt Since 1920* (Chapel Hill, 1950); James H. Street, *The New Revolution in the Cotton Economy: Mechanization and Its Consequences* (Chapel Hill, 1957); and, for numerous examples of postwar research in rural sociology, Brunner, *Growth of a Science*, pp 42–55, 93–96, 106–9, 125–27.

89. Examples of current economic research are given in Marshall R. Colberg, "Southern Economic Development: Some Research Accomplishments and Gaps," in *Perspectives on the South: Agenda for Research*, ed. Edgar T. Thompson (Durham, 1967), pp. 17–32.

tion. It resulted in several state reports and a large regional study.[90] In the late 1950s a project known as the Southern Appalachian Studies, with a generous grant from the Ford Foundation and the assistance of many social scientists and other scholars, completed the most comprehensive survey ever made of an area that had been bypassed by many of the modern currents of economic and social change.[91] A third example is provided by Alfred O. Hero's *The Southerner and World Affairs* (1965), an impressive study of southern attitudes toward American international involvement since the mid-1930s. A political scientist with training in psychology, Hero made ingenious use of behavioral and quantitative methods; he employed public-opinion surveys, personal interviews, and content analysis of selected newspapers, and he assimilated an enormous amount of scholarly literature.[92]

The period since World War II also brought a new interest in community studies as an approach to the analysis and characterization of regional culture. During the thirties three well-known studies of Mississippi communities, by John Dollard, Hortense Powdermaker, Allison Davis, and others, provided greater knowledge of the South's social structure and of social classes within castes.[93] In the late 1940s John Gillin, working through the University of North Carolina Institute for Research in Social Science, launched a series of anthropological field studies of modern southern culture. Morton Rubin's *Plantation County* (1951), Hylan Lewis' *Blackways of Kent* (1955), and John Kenneth Morland's *Millways of Kent* (1958) were part of a plan for the study of five counties representative of different

90. Harold C. Hoffsommer, *Regional Research Cooperation: A Statement of Regional Research Procedures as Developed by the Regional Land Tenure Research Project* (Chapel Hill, 1949); and Hoffsommer, ed., *The Social and Economic Significance of Land Tenure in the Southwestern States: A Report of the Regional Land Tenure Research Project* (Chapel Hill, 1950).

91. Thomas R. Ford, ed., *The Southern Appalachian Region: A Survey* (Lexington, 1962).

92. See also the complementary volume by Charles O. Lerche, *The Uncertain South: Its Changing Patterns of Politics in Foreign Policy* (Chicago, 1964).

93. John Dollard, *Caste and Class in a Southern Town* (New Haven, 1937); Hortense Powdermaker, *After Freedom: A Cultural Study in the Deep South* (New York, 1939); Allison Davis, Burleigh B. Gardner, and Mary R. Gardner, *Deep South: A Social Anthropological Study of Caste and Class* (Chicago, 1941). See also Maurice R. Stein, *The Eclipse of Community: An Interpretation of American Studies* (Princeton, 1960), pp. 153–74; and Hortense Powdermaker, *Stranger and Friend: The Way of an Anthropologist* (New York, 1966), pp. 129–205.

regional subcultures. Employing a theoretical framework of culture provided by Gillin,[94] these social anthropologists used the technique of participant observation, supplemented by interview schedules, statistical data, Rorschach tests, and questionnaires. These and a few similar studies led one anthropologist to conclude that "The South offers a laboratory in which theories of culture can be tested."[95]

At the time of his death in 1954 Howard W. Odum was hard at work on a book he planned to call *Mid-Century South: The New Southern Regions of the United States*. The book was designed to bring *Southern Regions* up to date; its major theme was to be regional change since 1930.[96] The regional assessment Odum hoped to write was never completed, and it is significant that the postwar period has witnessed relatively little formal academic concern with regionalism. No single university, except perhaps in the field of history, has emerged during the last two decades as a regional center for the social study of the South. The Duke University Center for Southern Studies in the Social Sciences and the Humanities, which was established in 1965, has sponsored some useful conferences and scholarly surveys of a regional nature;[97] but it is too early to tell how successful the center will be in organizing and promoting southern studies.

By mid-century sociologists in the South had begun to turn away from regionalism. Harry E. Moore, one of Odum's collaborators, has since conceded that regionalism, "something of a hangover from the brave young days of General Sociology," has gone out of fashion.[98] The trend toward the convergence of regional and national status, Vance noted in 1960, "has dulled the edge of regional claims and

94. John Gillin, *The Ways of Men: An Introduction to Anthropology* (New York, 1948); and Gillin, "National and Regional Cultural Values in the United States," *Social Forces* 34 (December 1955): 107–13.

95. J. Kenneth Morland, "Anthropology and the Study of Culture, Society, and Community in the South," in *Perspectives on the South*, p. 139. Other examples of community studies are Marion Pearsall, *Little Smoky Ridge: The Natural History of a Southern Appalachian Neighborhood* (University, Ala., 1959); Solon T. Kimball and Marion Pearsall, *The Talladega Story: A Study in Community Process* (University, Ala., 1954); and Elmora Messer Matthews, *Neighbor and Kin: Life in a Tennessee Ridge Community* (Nashville, 1965).

96. Simpson, "Howard W. Odum and American Regionalism," p. 101.

97. McKinney and Thompson, *The South in Continuity and Change;* Thompson, *Perspectives on the South;* interview with Edgar T. Thompson, July 12, 1967.

98. Quoted in Marshall W. Fishwick, *Sleeping Beauty and Her Suitors: The South in the Sixties* (Macon, Ga., 1961), p. 54.

reduced the drive of regionalism as a social movement."[99] Southern sociologists did not, of course, abandon the study of southern society. The quickening pace of urbanization, for example, stimulated urban sociology in the South.[100] But this scholarship was frequently devoid of any explicit regional framework. Such a volume as Floyd Hunter's important study of top-level decision makers in Atlanta was not in any fundamental sense a regional study.[101]

Sociologists in and out of the South were attracted to the study of revolutionary changes in race relations following World War II. They made some significant investigations of white and black attitudes toward school desegregation in the South and were joined by a few psychologists and psychiatrists.[102] Sociologists and political scientists produced a series of community studies focusing on Negro leadership and organization in southern cities.[103] Donald R. Matthews and James W. Prothro, in *Negroes and the New Southern Politics* (1966), reported the results of a six-year study of Negro political participation and its consequences in the region. Using aggregate data, survey research, and high-speed computers, these political scientists collected and analyzed a large body of systematic data on the Negro's political behavior.[104] Most of this research was shaped in some measure by a consciousness of southern distinctiveness. Agencies like the Southern Regional Council also encouraged a regional view by

99. Rupert B. Vance, "The Sociological Implications of Southern Regionalism," *Journal of Southern History* 26 (February 1960): 47.

100. See, for example, Rupert B. Vance and Nicholas J. Demerath, eds., *The Urban South* (Chapel Hill, 1954).

101. Hunter, *Community Power Structure: A Study of Decision Makers* (Chapel Hill, 1953).

102. For examples, see Melvin M. Tumin et al., *Desegregation: Resistance and Readiness* (Princeton, 1958); James W. Vander Zanden, *Race Relations in Transition: The Segregation Crisis in the South* (New York, 1965); Thomas F. Pettigrew, *A Profile of the Negro American* (Princeton, 1964); and Robert Coles, *Children of Crisis: A Study of Courage and Fear* (Boston, 1967).

103. M. Elaine Burgess, *Negro Leadership in a Southern City* (Chapel Hill, 1962); Daniel C. Thompson, *The Negro Leadership Class* (Englewood Cliffs, N.J., 1963); Lewis M. Killian and Charles Grigg, *Racial Crisis in America: Leadership in Conflict* (Englewood Cliffs, N.J., 1964); Everett Carll Ladd, Jr., *Negro Political Leadership in the South* (Ithaca, 1966).

104. Research themes and needs in the study of race relations are dealt with in Donald R. Matthews, "Political Science Research on Race Relations," an unpublished paper provided the writer by Professor Matthews. See also Elizabeth W. Miller, comp., *The Negro in America: A Bibliography* (Cambridge, 1966).

concentrating on the investigation of race relations in the South.[105] Nevertheless, the southern experience became increasingly less unique, and the deregionalization of scholarly study of the Negro and race relations was an important new emphasis, clearly revealed in the difference between Myrdal's *An American Dilemma* (1944) and the work edited by Talcott Parsons and Kenneth B. Clark in *The Negro American* (1966).

In addition to their investigations of the Negro's new role in southern politics, political scientists have begun to give attention to the region's emerging Republicanism and to such problems as malapportionment.[106] The extent of this scholarly investigation of southern politics is suggested by recent evaluations of the regional political scene edited by Allan P. Sindler and Avery Leiserson.[107] Yet political science never became as preoccupied with regional studies as did certain other disciplines, in some measure because the federal structure of government decreed other categories that served to delineate and organize political research.

As the social sciences became stronger in the South, they increasingly reflected the theoretical premises and methodological approaches developed among the various disciplines in the leading universities and national academic societies. Thus, after World War II southern social scientists tended to become more "behavioral" and more "scientific" in their research orientation. As one scholar recently said, when discussing the evolution of geography in the South, "the old descriptive applications have more and more been supplemented by field-based and/or quantitative-based studies in regional characteristics."[108] The regional concept seemed less useful than it once had, even though regional and subregional materials were used as a matter of course in many social science investigations. "Today," Edgar T. Thompson writes, "the tendency is to study behavior in the social system we call the South as representative of

105. William Clifton Allred, Jr., "The Southern Regional Council, 1943–1961" (M.A. thesis, Emory University, 1966); interview with Paul Anthony, July 7, 1967.

106. See Donald S. Strong, *Urban Republicanism in the South* (University, Ala., 1960); Bernard Cosman, *Five States for Goldwater: Continuity and Change in Southern Presidential Voting Patterns* (University, Ala., 1966); and William C. Havard and Loren P. Beth, *The Politics of Mis-Representation: Rural-Urban Conflict in the Florida Legislature* ([Baton Rouge], 1962).

107. Sindler, *Change in the Contemporary South* (Durham, 1963); Leiserson, *The American South in the 1960's* (New York and London, 1964).

108. Merle C. Prunty, Jr., to the author, August 17, 1967.

human nature and social process generally. Southern social scientists can now be more detached about the phenomena they study in this area because they are more attached to a larger human unity."[109]

Meanwhile, the old distinction between fundamental and applied research became less sharp, and many social scientists in the South, as elsewhere, took on the character of service intellectuals, devoting themselves to studies sponsored and sometimes designed by municipalities, states, foundations, and private organizations.[110] The region provided the setting for much of this research, but frequently it had little or no bearing on the methods used or the results obtained. Even so, regionalism continues to influence the social sciences in the South, and vice versa. The South remains something of a cultural and economic entity, it still provides a sociological laboratory for scholarly investigations, and southern social scientists in some degree retain their regional identity.[111]

"It is certainly no accident," wrote Gunnar Myrdal in 1944, "that a 'regional approach' in social science has been stressed in the South."[112] In the South from the very beginning the new disciplines concerned with social behavior developed not only in response to the intellectual and professional currents from outside the section, but also as a natural consequence of the process of social change. The early identification of social problems, the commitment to planning, the use of economics as a tool to advance regional development, the broadening analysis of southern politics, and the growing appreciation of the importance of regional and subregional cultural distinctions were all related to social changes that swept over the South or that seemed imminent. After they began to mature and to produce leaders, organizations, and university centers, the social sciences in the South became an influential factor in regional life in their own right. When the relationship between scholar and region was closest, during the 1930s and 1940s, regionalism became an ism in the hands

109. Thompson, "The South in Old and New Contexts," in *The South in Continuity and Change*, p. 480.

110. A spectacular example of the use of science and social science is provided by I. A. Newby in *Challenge to the Court: Social Scientists and the Defense of Segregation, 1954–1966* (Baton Rouge, 1967).

111. A survey of southern sociologists in 1959 revealed that almost half the respondents judged sociology in the South to be "different" from sociology in other parts of the country. Brooks and Bertrand, *History of the Southern Sociological Society*, p. 67.

112. Myrdal, *An American Dilemma*, 1: 70.

of the academicians—a body of doctrine and a social movement. This kind of instrumental regionalism never enlisted the support of all social scientists in the South, and by mid-century its vogue had largely passed. By that time the various disciplines in the social sciences had become well established in the region, even though they lagged behind their counterparts in some areas of the country. The development of the social sciences in the southern states is a significant aspect of the region's history in the twentieth century.

As the first of the modern social sciences to develop in the South and one of the most vigorous in our own time, the historical profession has been a part of this regional pattern. Southern historians, like the social scientists, have responded to the pressure of their culture, as well as to forces from outside the region. They have produced a large and valuable corpus of historical literature on the southern part of the United States. As historians of the South we are familiar, in varying degrees, with the immense collection of regional data and analysis touched upon in this paper—ranging from the classics by Odum, Vance, Key, and Myrdal to dull monographs and to reports that contain little of value. But have we made effective use of this monumental body of materials in our research and teaching? Are we aware of the interpretations advanced by these social scientists and of the questions they have raised? Have we seriously concerned ourselves with what sociologists and anthropologists have said about the social structure of class in the South? Do we know about the economists' identification of forces that encourage or inhibit economic growth in the region and about other social science concepts relating to social change, personality development, and the like? "The history of the South," observes David M. Potter in a cogent discussion of this point, "is more suffused with these interdisciplinary questions than, perhaps, most other fields of history. . . ."[113] There is some evidence that historians and other social scientists in the United States are approaching their work in a broader context of mutual benefit and cooperation. Those who are interested in the South and its history should participate in this approach.

Regionalism in modern America, as we know, is a phenomenon that finds its most forceful manifestation in the South. Southerners and other Americans have created a large body of myth about the

---

113. Potter, "Depletion and Renewal in Southern History," in *Perspectives on the South*, p. 89.

South; the analysis of this mythology can tell us a good deal about the inhabitants of the region and of the whole country. But the social scientists have added a new dimension to the regional imagination, a creative imagination that presents southern reality more fully than the mythology or even the perceptions growing out of experience itself. In a variety of ways, sometimes in epochal studies, fresh approaches, and lively prose, they have provided an extraordinary demonstration of ways in which society can be studied within a spatial framework. In the process, they have broadened our horizons and deepened our understanding of human behavior in the nation's most clearly identifiable but most enigmatic region.

11

The Little Rock School Crisis: Negro Rights and the Struggle for an Integrated America

Little Rock, Clinton, Mansfield, Prince Edward County, New Orleans, Ole Miss, and a dozen other southern place names are like individually colored beads on a string in the painful struggle over the desegregation of the South's public schools. These names also symbolize the mounting opposition of white Southerners to the Supreme Court's desegregation decisions, the recrudescence of extreme racial feeling in the white South, and the rise of massive resistance in southern politics. None of these episodes is more revealing to the historian than the Little Rock crisis. That encounter called forth almost all the traditional factors associated with the South's political sectionalism: demagoguery, race-baiting, the dogma of white supremacy, threats of defiance directed at outside intervention, the assertion of state rights, and the ineffectuality of southern liberals. But two new elements were evident in the Little Rock school crisis: the larger role of local blacks in demanding their legal rights and the federal intervention, however haltingly, to enforce the law of the land. In short, the Little Rock confrontation provides a significant case study of one aspect of the Second Reconstruction.

This previously unpublished essay was written in 1973 for a symposium entitled *Conflict in America: A History of Domestic Confrontations*. This collection, planned and coordinated by Professor Allen Weinstein, became the basis for a series of radio interviews broadcast in 1974–75 by the Voice of America. Other accounts of the Little Rock school crisis are Numan V. Bartley, "Looking Back at Little Rock," *Arkansas Historical Quarterly* 25 (Summer 1966): 101–16, and Corinne Silverman,

The Little Rock Story, rev. ed. (1959). Southern resistance politics and organized white opposition in the 1950s are analyzed in Numan V. Bartley's *The Rise of Massive Resistance: Race and Politics in the South during the 1950's* (1969) and Neil R. McMillen's *The Citizens' Council: Organized Resistance to the Second Reconstruction, 1954–64* (1971).

I N the late summer of 1957 public attention in the United States suddenly focused upon Little Rock, Arkansas, where a momentous constitutional crisis in federal-state relations was dramatically precipitated. The crisis grew out of the efforts in Little Rock to begin the implementation of the Supreme Court's famous school desegregation decisions of 1954 and 1955, and it was brought to a head by the state governor's defiance of federal court orders and apparent connivance in the development of mob resistance. This bold action prevented the admission of nine black students to Central High School, but it also forced the hand of a reluctant President Dwight D. Eisenhower, who finally dispatched a thousand army troops to stop further interference in the desegregation of the Arkansas school. The Little Rock encounter was charged with contending points of view and conflicting values; it reflected what C. Vann Woodward has described as "the old four-handed American game between the South, the courts, the Negro, and the Constitution."

In some respects Little Rock was an unlikely setting for the tense drama that unfolded in September 1957. The Arkansas capital had no record of extreme racial antagonism. Its buses had been desegregated and its police force contained some Negroes; it had a moderate mayor and an enlightened newspaper. Governor Orval E. Faubus was known as a moderate on the "race question," and Arkansas, having admitted Negroes to its institutions of higher learning, made a start in the desegregation of its public schools, and brought blacks into the committee structure of the Democratic party, appeared to reflect the milder racial attitudes and practices of the upper South. Immediately after the United States Supreme Court handed down its epochal desegregation decision of May 17, 1954, the Little Rock school board had announced its intention to comply with the ruling.

The plan that the board eventually approved, in May 1955, provided for a three-phase desegregation scheme, beginning with the token integration of one high school in September 1957. Although this very gradual plan was challenged by Negro parents, it was approved by the federal courts. Meanwhile, Superintendent Virgil T. Blossom had tried to enlist public support for the board's integration program by explaining it to scores of civic clubs and other groups.

There were some troublesome signs. Arkansas politics in the mid-1950s manifested widespread white hostility toward the idea of racial integration. Despite the moderate stance assumed by Governor Faubus in racial matters, he was too much a politician not to adjust his sails to the prevailing winds. In early 1956, for example, he endorsed two segregation proposals that became law by initiative petition: a pupil assignment act and a protest interposition resolution. During his campaign for renomination in the Democratic primary of 1956, when he faced an opponent who relied upon racial demagoguery, Faubus seemed to become more forthright in defending segregation. He promised that "no school board will be forced to mix the races in schools while I am governor." When the legislature passed four anti-integration measures early in 1957, Faubus signed them all into law.

With the passage of time, opposition to school desegregation in Arkansas also emerged in the form of a private and potentially extralegal resistance movement. The spearhead of this movement was the Capital Citizens' Council of Little Rock. Originally organized in 1955, the Citizens' Council became the largest and most vocal segregation group in the state. It worked throughout the summer of 1957 to defeat the school board's plan, putting pressure on school authorities, demanding that the governor intervene, conducting an intensive propaganda campaign, and playing upon the racial fears of white citizens in newspaper advertisements and other publicity. A band of kindred spirits existed in the recently organized Mothers' League of Central High School. On August 22 two prominent segregationist spokesmen from Georgia—Governor Marvin Griffin and political boss Roy V. Harris—spoke at a Citizens' Council dinner in Little Rock. Their appearance had a galvanizing effect upon the resistance forces in the Arkansas capital. "People are coming to me," Governor Faubus reported, "and saying if Georgia doesn't have integration, why does Arkansas have it?"

Having become disturbed over the mounting resistance to his desegregation plan, Superintendent Blossom repeatedly appealed to the governor for a public statement of support. Faubus had generally sought to avoid direct involvement in school desegregation, declaring it to be a local problem that should be dealt with at the community level. While giving some support to state segregation schemes, he had consistently rejected nullification theories. But the governor now found himself under pressure from both sides to act in the Central High School case, and he maneuvered desperately to avoid being drawn into the controversy. When Faubus contacted the Department of Justice in Washington and conferred with the head of its civil rights division, he learned that the Eisenhower administration did not wish to become involved in the Little Rock case and would assume no responsibility for maintaining order. This discovery, plus the rising clamor of the organized opponents, no doubt encouraged the governor to frustrate the school board's desegregation plan. In any case, he appeared in chancery court on August 29 to support an effort by a member of the Mothers' League to secure a temporary injunction to halt the desegregation of Central High. The state court granted the injunction, but on the following day it was nullified by the federal court.

Two days later Governor Faubus ordered the Arkansas National Guard into Little Rock, and on the night of September 2 some two hundred guardsmen surrounded Central High School. In a television address to the people of Arkansas that same evening, the governor explained that he had received many indications of impending violence at Central High. The mission of the militia, he said, was "to maintain or restore order and to protect the lives and property of citizens," not to act "as segregationists or integrationists." The nine Negro students, complying with the request of the school board, did not appear when classes began at Central High on September 3. The school board filed a petition with the federal court requesting instructions, and Judge Ronald N. Davies quickly issued an order affirming his previous directive to integrate the high school on schedule.

What happened on the following day was later described by Virgil Blossom:

On Wednesday morning at about eight o'clock, a slight, dusky girl wearing sunglasses and a freshly-ironed white dress and carrying school books under her arm approached the intersection of Fourteenth Street and Park Avenue, adjacent to Central High School. At the corner, Arkansas National Guardsmen wearing helmets and carrying rifles drew together, forming a solid line that blocked the girl's progress. The soldiers stared straight ahead and said nothing.

Looking neither to the right nor left, the girl turned and crossed to the opposite side of the street in front of the school building. She walked a few steps and then recrossed toward the main school entrance. Again, guardsmen lining the sidewalk pressed closely together to block her path. She swerved and walked steadily down the line of troops seeking an opening to the school grounds. She found none.

Suddenly, as the newspapers reported it later, about two hundred white adults further down the street saw her, and broke into a run to interrupt her line of march, shouting: "Don't let her in our school—that nigger!" "Why don't you go to your own school?"

A woman lunged at the girl, crying: "Go back where you came from!" but a guardsman pushed her back.

Trembling, but never losing her dignity, the Negro girl made a third vain effort to walk through the line of soldiers. Then she went back across the street and sat down on a bus stop bench at the corner. Tears were in her eyes. Some of the crowd followed, shouting abuse. A newspaper reporter learned only that her name was Elizabeth Eckford, that she was fifteen years old and legally enrolled in Central High School. A white woman who spoke to her kindly was jeered by the crowd. A bus came along and the girl climbed aboard.

During the following three weeks Little Rock was the center of a series of legal and political moves by the various parties represented in the conflict over school desegregation. At his weekly press conference, on the day after Governor Faubus dispatched the National Guard to Central High School, President Eisenhower remarked, as he had on earlier occasions, that "you cannot change people's hearts merely by laws" and that desegregation must be "executed gradually." In Little Rock Mayor Woodrow Wilson Mann was sharply critical of Governor Faubus' use of troops to block the admission of the nine black students to Central High. Soon afterward Faubus sent a telegram to President Eisenhower in which he referred to federal plans to take him "into custody, by force" and voiced a suspicion that the telephone lines to his executive mansion were being tapped. Eisenhower answered Faubus on September 5, assuring the governor that there were no plans to arrest him and that his telephone was not being tapped by any federal agency. "The only assurance I can give you," Eisenhower informed Faubus, "is that the federal Constitution will be upheld by me by every legal means at my command."

The Little Rock school board was in a quandary. It could not comply with the orders of the federal court without resisting the state authority being exercised through the National Guard. Municipal officials were of little help to the beleaguered school board, and most of the city aldermen quickly announced their approval of the governor's action in using the state militia. The board sought a way out of its predicament by petitioning the federal district court on September 4 for a temporary suspension of the integration order because of the rising tension in the community. Attorneys for the Negro parents objected, and following an open hearing on September 7, Judge Davies denied the request for a delay. Soon afterward Davies asked Attorney General Herbert Brownell and Osro Cobb, United States attorney for the eastern district of Arkansas, to enter the case as "friends of the court." The Justice Department responded swiftly, entering a petition to enjoin Governor Faubus from interfering further with the execution of the court's orders. Judge Davies then set a hearing for September 20. Faubus immediately filed a motion to dismiss the Justice Department's petition, but the judge rejected his plea.

While this legal maneuvering was taking place, the nation watched with bated breath. The White House felt the force of opinion at home and abroad favoring an end to the deadlock. Governor Faubus was under heavy pressure to maintain his position, although he received some moderate advice from U.S. Representative Brooks Hays, the longtime congressman from the Little Rock district. Hays, a widely respected southern liberal, managed with the help of presidential assistant Sherman Adams to arrange a personal meeting between Faubus and President Eisenhower on September 14. The meeting was held in Newport, Rhode Island, where Eisenhower was vacationing. The results were disappointing, since Faubus did not revoke his orders to the National Guard when he got back to Little Rock.

The next major development in the case came on September 20 at the hearing in the federal district court on the Justice Department's petition to enjoin Governor Faubus from continuing his obstruction. Judge Davies, noting that none of the witnesses had given evidence to indicate that violence might be imminent, granted a temporary injuction prohibiting Faubus from interfering with the school desegregation process at Central High School. Three hours later the governor withdrew the National Guard, thereby bowing to the court decree but leaving a dangerous law-enforcement vacuum in Little Rock and a tense weekend before the schools reopened on Monday, September 23.

By the time classes began at Central High on Monday morning, a crowd of about a thousand people had gathered around the school. Although the black students were slipped into the school through a side entrance, the protesting crowd remained, while many white children left the building or were taken out of class by their parents. Worried school authorities soon decided to take the Negro students home. In Washington that afternoon the president denounced the "disgraceful occurrences" at Little Rock and threatened to use "whatever force may be necessary" to enforce the law. He also issued a proclamation ordering "all persons" obstructing federal authority to cease and desist and disperse. Nevertheless, another milling throng congregated at Central High School on the following morning. Mayor Mann, who had been in telephone contact with the White House since the previous afternoon, sent a telegram to the president requesting federal troops. By this time Eisenhower was prepared to act; the only question was what form his intervention would take. At 10:22 A.M he issued Executive Order 10730, "Providing Assistance for the Removal of an Obstruction of Justice Within the State of Arkansas." The president federalized the Arkansas National Guard and sent in approximately a thousand paratroopers from the 101st Airborne Division. "We are now occupied territory," Governor Faubus lamented. On the morning of the following day, September 25, the nine black students attended Central High under troop escort, and the crisis slowly subsided.

Although the most dramatic part of the Little Rock crisis took place in the early fall of 1957, the struggle over desegregation in that city continued for another two years. White resistance rapidly solidified in the aftermath of President Eisenhower's intervention. The federal troops were not withdrawn until late May 1958, but federal authority was not used to protect the black students at Central High from provocative and abusive treatment or to prosecute the participants in the mob action of September. In June 1958 the school board secured from the federal district court a two-and-a-half-year "tactical delay" in the operation of its integration program, thus precipitating a second constitutional crisis at Little Rock. Meanwhile, Faubus easily won another term as governor, obtained legislative approval of a new series of school segregation laws, and after the Supreme Court ruled against a delay of desegregation at Central High, closed all of the high schools in Little Rock. During the 1958–59 academic year, a continuing struggle was fought between extremists and moderates for control of the Little Rock school board, with the moderates finally gaining the ascendancy. In June 1959 the federal courts struck down Arkansas' school closure laws and ordered the school board to proceed with its original desegregation plan. Central High was again desegregated in August 1959, amid some disorder but without any major mishap. The battle of Little Rock was finally over.

In searching for an explanation of the conflict over school desegregation in Little Rock, it is best to begin with the local situation. The desegregation plan itself was flawed. It called for a delay in integration until 1957, by which time a new high school would be completed. The new school, unlike Central High, would largely serve the needs of suburban upper- and middle-class families, and thus, as Numan V. Bartley has noted, the arrangement "added an element of class conflict to the racial controversy and allowed segregationist spokesmen to charge that integrationists were sacrificing the common citizen while protecting the wealthy." Superintendent Blossom and the school board, relying on a legalistic approach, failed to build a solid foundation of public support for their desegregation scheme or to make use of many potentially helpful people and institutions in Little Rock. The superintendent's numerous speeches to service clubs and business organizations were directed to people whose children, in may cases, would not be attending Central High School. Another local problem stemmed from the lame-duck character of Mayor Woodrow W. Mann's government, which would shortly be replaced by a city manager type of administration. The city police, as events soon demonstrated, were unprepared to cope with a large-scale disturbance.

The Capital Citizens' Council, which rallied the resistance forces against the desegregation of Central High School, did a good deal to provoke the Little Rock conflict. The council did not draw its controlling element or its main support from the traditional civic leadership or "substantial" middle class, as was often true in other parts of the South. But whatever its character, the CCC exacerbated the fears of the local populace and brought pressure to bear on public men. Equally telling was the "official lawlessness" of state authorities, including legislators, and their willingness to resort to all manner of chicanery to subvert federal court decisions. As a young lawyer said in discussing the frenzied opposition to desegregation in Clinton, Tennessee, "What the hell do you expect these people to do when they have 90 some odd congressmen from the South signing a piece of paper [the Southern Manifesto] that says you're a southern hero if you defy the Supreme Court?"

In the final analysis it was Orval E. Faubus who assumed the key role in the Little Rock confrontation. Faubus did not have the ingrained obsession with the race question that black belt and delta

Southerners customarily exhibited, but he was both a practical and an ambitious politician. Some observers have suggested that he had begun to calculate his chances of overcoming Arkansas' two-term tradition for its governors and that he hoped to be elected a third time by appealing to the racial prejudices of whites in the eastern lowlands. Faubus also had a more immediate reason for coming to terms with politicians from eastern Arkansas. Early in 1957 he was sponsoring a comprehensive tax program which may have encouraged him to engage in some horse trading. In any case, he signed several segregation measures in late February, and he got his tax program through the legislature. Even so, the governor did not immediately become identified with the resistance forces in the state, and in fact he was vilified by some segregationists until the very eve of the Little Rock crisis. Superintendent Blossom, who had several meetings with Faubus in the late summer of 1957, got the impression that the governor wanted the federal government to act in the Central High case and thus relieve him of responsibility for enforcing desegregation.

Yet why did the governor stand for eighteen days on the brink of armed rebellion? He was obviously encouraged in his defiance by southern resistance leaders who were eager for a conflict over integration that would mobilize regional opinion. He seems to have fallen prey to an extreme group of segregationists at Little Rock who convinced him that he must serve as the "preservator of the peace." Faubus probably believed that he could work out a favorable settlement with federal authorities, for he was well aware of Eisenhower's timidity in the field of civil rights. He had seen how federally ordered desegregation had succumbed to local white hostility in two Texas towns in September 1956 and how Governor Allan Shivers used Texas Rangers in one of those cases—at Mansfield—to defy a federal court order and prevent school desegregation. Having chosen a segregationist course in early September 1957, Faubus found his political options greatly reduced. He grew increasingly demagogic, egged on by Dixie extremists, and he savored his swelling popularity among white Arkansans and his new image as a heroic southern leader.

Once the Arkansas governor brazenly defied federal authority in Little Rock, President Eisenhower had to act to meet the challenge, regardless of his personal predilections. The Eisenhower administration had not developed a policy or program for use in dealing with official resistance to judicially ordered desegregation. The president's reluctance to formulate a more systematic and energetic approach reflected his political and philosophical views as well as his emotional reactions. Legally, in the early years following the *Brown* decision, there was probably not much that the president or his administration could have done to facilitate school desegregation. Eisenhower did complete the desegregation of the armed forces; he encouraged desegregation in Veterans Administration hospitals and military post schools; and he worked to eliminate racial discrimination in the District of Columbia. Eisenhower also agreed, at the persistent urging of Attorney General Brownell, to recommend the enactment of a civil rights bill in 1956, and during the presidential campaign of that year he strongly endorsed its passage. Yet he secured only a watered-down version of Brownell's proposed legislation, and in the preceding congressional struggle he readily abandoned a provision that would have permitted the Justice Department to initiate entry suits to force school desegregation.

President Eisenhower could have used his great personal popularity and prestige to mobilize public opinion in support of greater racial equality and to encourage liberals and moderates, particularly in the South. But he resisted such a role. He would not even say publicly whether he approved or disapproved of *Brown* v. *Board of Education*, although he admitted to one of his assistants, in the fall of 1957, that "as a matter of fact, I personally think the decision was wrong." One inhibiting factor in Eisenhower's mind was his concept of the presidency and his deep respect for the separation of governmental powers. He also seemed to think that national responsibility for resolving the segregation controversy was primarily a judicial matter and that the presidential role began and ended with the enforcement of specific court orders. The president frequently voiced his conviction that law was not an efficacious means of social control in race relations. He placed more emphasis on "understanding" than on "laws" in the implementation of desegregation decisions, and he said several times that he could envisage no circumstance in which he would use force to execute federal court decrees. Many of Eisenhower's statements concerning school desegregation and civil rights were impromptu comments at his press conferences, hardly the best forum for the enunciation of national policy.

The Little Rock crisis was, to some extent, the product of the anomaly and ambiguity of the American federal system. Thus many different officials and governmental bodies could rightly claim jurisdiction and responsibility in the Central High School case. Leslie W.

Dunbar has observed that while the majority in a democracy can require a minority to accept its procedurally correct decisions as to the public interest, it is extremely difficult in a large and complex society to ascertain and verify the majority opinion on any question. The imposition of the ultimate majoritarian power, moreover, is likely to be moderated by the practical as well as moral desirability of a minimal use of coercive power over fellow citizens. Dunbar noted that minority coercion is especially inexpedient when the minority is approximately identical with a territorial area, and even more so, in a federal state, when the minority is roughly identical with one or more of the federal units. In the case of the civil rights controversy in contemporary America, the minority itself was the predominant power within a large and compact part of the country, its power was enhanced and legitimized by the constitutional status of the federal units, and much of the controversy was between competing notions of right and morality.

The minority in the school desegregation cases—the southern whites—was defending what many Southerners regarded as a right or morality, rather than merely a notion of interest. School desegregation among white Southerners was almost universally unpopular. Segregationists, Anthony Lewis wrote in 1964, "have invested their cause with a searing emotional impact. It has been made to appeal to the most susceptible tribal impulses: patriotism, racial purity, religious dogma, group solidarity, status and personal pride." At the top, remarked Lewis, it "has been given an intellectual and political gloss by introducing questions of constitutionality and states' rights." Governor Faubus based his stand on "the will of the people," and he argued that in using the militia he was acting under the clear authority of the state constitution and the Tenth Amendment to the federal Constitution.

Finally, one may ask, what is the meaning of the Little Rock conflict and what is its place in the long struggle for racial equality in America? It was, for one thing, a test of the South's resistance to racial integration. Its immediate effect was to embarrass or silence southern moderates and to strengthen extremist elements. Yet thoughtful segregationists understood that the power of the national government could now be expected to enforce the decrees of the federal courts. "Remember Little Rock!" might be a red flag in the eyes of southern recalcitrants, but it was also a warning they were not likely to miss. After Little Rock it was no longer possible to use violence to nullify decisions of the federal courts. Eventually, with the reopening of integrated high schools in Little Rock in August 1959 and increasing compliance in other southern states in 1960, massive resistance collapsed in the region. Southern white leaders discovered the attractions of token school desegregation, since they had become convinced that "another Little Rock" must be avoided.

Little Rock was second only to Sputnik as the biggest news story of the year, and its impact on opinion in the United States and abroad was immense. The crisis aroused Americans to the dangers of the racial issue and crystallized opinion outside the South in support of federal intervention, despite some uneasiness over the use of army troops against civilians. It unified and encouraged American Negroes, partly because of their own involvement and the courageous behavior of the black students at Central High and partly because of the evidence it produced that the power of the national government would be employed to uphold the decisions of the courts. The Little Rock struggle was one of the early episodes in the Second Reconstruction, made memorable for blacks because it was a spectacular fight waged largely by Negroes for the validation of their civil and political rights.

The impact of the Little Rock crisis was also felt outside the United States. On the larger stage of the world, Emmet John Hughes recalled, "The tale carried faster than drum signals across black Africa. It summoned cold gleams of recognition to the eyes of Asians, quick to see the signs, in the heartland of America, of the racial enmities that had helped to make colonialism, through the generations, so odious to them." The response of the outside world to Little Rock had special meaning for black Americans, and particularly for the embattled Negro students at Central High, who received unexpected support from far-distant places. After the Little Rock crisis, Harold R. Isaacs has written, "hardly anyone could fail to know that American racism had become part of the world's business and was therefore now part of America's business with the world."

The 1957 crisis broadened the commitment of the federal government to the cause of civil rights and set the stage for more determined chief executives in later years to mobilize power and opinion in suppressing defiance and asserting the constitutional supremacy of national law. The Little Rock intervention set a modern pattern in the federal use of the militia "to execute the laws of the union," though later presidents, learning from Eisenhower's experience, relied on federal marshals instead of soldiers at Montgomery, Oxford, and Selma. Congress was also influenced by Little Rock, for in the

Civil Rights Act of 1960 it was made a federal crime for any person to obstruct or interfere with a federal court order or to attempt to do so by threats of force.

Perhaps the most compelling lessons of Little Rock were negative. The crisis provided a stark illustration of inadequate leadership, especially at the state and federal levels, and it revealed some of the difficulties of implementing a controversial policy in the American system. Orval Faubus demonstrated how mischievous and far-reaching the influence of a stubborn and irresponsible leader could be. Dwight Eisenhower failed to assume the leadership in preparing the country for the new era in race relations that was struggling to emerge, and his administration neglected even to develop a long-range policy on school desegregation. Eisenhower, through decisive leadership, might have averted the Little Rock crisis and made the course of school desegregation easier throughout the South. Strong leadership would have helped—in Washington and in Little Rock. But given the nature of American society, the long-standing racist attitudes of most white Southerners, and the conflicting values of Americans in the 1950s, a major social crisis over school desegregation was probably unavoidable.

12

The South and the Reconstruction of American Politics

⮑ This essay and the first one in this volume—"The South and the Politics of Sectionalism"—were written at about the same time and were meant to complement each other. They represent, in a sense, reverse sides of the same coin: one emphasizing distinctiveness and continuity in southern politics, the other stressing the increasing nationalization of the region's politics and the political possibilities inherent in drastic change in the South. Focusing on developments since the launching of the New Deal, the second essay examines some of the conspicuous manifestations of change in southern politics and argues that these alterations are likely to have a profound effect both on the nature of political affairs in the South and on the character of the national party system. The paper was first presented at the annual meeting of the American Historical Association in 1965 and subsequently published in the *Journal of American History* (September 1966).

The essay was conceived and written when the so-called Second Reconstruction was at flood tide and when Lyndon Johnson's Great Society was in full bloom. That may account for a note of expectancy in the discussion and some exaggeration of the prospects for the South's political metamorphosis. Yet it is clear that southern politics has undergone a great transformation during the last three decades. The Solid South has been disrupted, the Republican party offers a growing challenge to Democratic dominance in the southern states, the enfranchisement and political involvement of blacks have changed the dynamics of the region's politics, and the South has become a strategic consideration of genuine importance in national politics. Two large-scale studies of southern politics since the publication of Key's famous work in 1949 provide fuller treatments of the region's political experience since mid-century: Numan V. Bartley and Hugh Davis Graham, *Southern Politics and the Second Reconstruction* (1975), and Jack Bass and Walter DeVries, *The Transformation of Southern Politics: Social Change and Political Consequence since 1945* (1976).

T H E conflict between change and continuity in the southern part of the United States today is strikingly apparent in the region's politics. Although economic and social changes have contributed most notably to the South's recent transformation, it is clear that political affairs below the Potomac have been significantly altered during the last decade and a half. It appears not only that political practices within the region will be vastly different in the future but also that the changes now taking place will be profoundly important for American politics as a whole.

The elements responsible for change in the recent South are numerous and complex, but three factors should be emphasized in considering the evolution of southern politics since World War II. In the first place, federal intervention and the pressure of the national party system have steadily eroded the foundations of the South's political solidarity. Secondly, the industrialization, urbanization, and diversification of the regional economy have had a significant impact upon the course of southern politics. Finally, the movement for civil rights, encompassing as it does the emergence of a compelling national issue, the Negro's political activation, and his own remarkable leadership, is having a far-reaching effect.

In some respects, of course, the emerging South is the product of developments that antedate the Great Depression and the New Deal. Early in the twentieth century a strong bifactionalism emerged along liberal-conservative lines, an important middle-of-the-road progressivism appeared with an urban leadership and philosophy, and a significant farm movement greatly influenced the making of public policy. The Wilson administration brought the region its first real involvement in the control of the national government since the Civil War. During the progressive era and the decade following World War

I, state and municipal governments in the South began to adopt long-needed social reforms and introduced numerous public services. Meanwhile, the region was being differentiated in its economy and society by industrialization and urbanization, the rapid growth of Texas and Oklahoma, and the economic diversification of the upper South.[1] Some of these tendencies were evident in the disruption of the South in the election of 1928, although they provided only a momentary threat to the continued solidarity of the section in national politics.

Franklin D. Roosevelt's leadership and the New Deal precipitated an extraordinary popular agitation over political and economic issues in the South, forced national issues into state and local political contests, and introduced codes and standards that did much to undermine the old faith in freedom of contract and state rights. The New Deal also provided southern congressmen with an opportunity to contribute to the enactment of a momentous program of national reform and stimulated the liberalism of many southern leaders. But if the New Deal tended to nationalize southern politics and if it gave southern leaders a conspicuous place on the national stage, it also diminished the section's importance in the Democratic party. The repeal of the historic two-thirds rule for nominations in the national convention of 1936 and the consolidation of Roosevelt's national coalition in the election of that year made it impossible for the South to maintain as influential a role in the party's councils as had been true in the past. The revolution Alfred E. Smith began had been consummated.

Many things encouraged Southerners to respond favorably to Roosevelt's leadership during the early 1930s. The manner in which the movement for his nomination in 1932 challenged the eastern domination of the Democratic party, the understanding he showed of the agrarian traditions of the South and West, his espousal of Jeffersonian principles, his enormous personal charm, and the way in which he identified himself with the southern region all struck a responsive chord among Southerners. But somehow, as Frank Freidel has noted, Roosevelt's "states' rights and individualistic generalities seemed to lead him again and again to specifics involving positive government action." In time the unanimity of his southern support was destroyed and "the reservoir emptied—but only slowly." As men who felt strong personal ties of loyalty to each

1. Dewey W. Grantham, *The Democratic South* (Athens, Ga., 1963), pp. 42–68.

other and to the Democratic party, and as men who enjoyed the power provided by the party's majority position, southern congressional leaders were inclined, even after many of them had come to have doubts about the president's program, to give him what he wanted. For a time, moreover, some of them assumed that the New Deal was no more than a revival of the New Freedom—and would offer no greater threat to southern independence than had Wilson's administration. In addition, writes Freidel, the Roosevelt measures "represented a giant, nation-wide cornucopia from which federal aid poured into the desperately Depression-ridden South."[2]

This is a point of transcendent importance. It goes far to explain the ambivalent response of the South to the New Deal as well as the increasing integration of the region into the framework of national politics in later years. The sudden infusion of money through the agricultural price-support system, federal credit agencies, and public works programs reanimated the old dream of a New South. The rescue of the agricultural economy and the rejuvenating effects of land reform, river development, reforestation, and new public buildings, roads, and schools can scarcely be overemphasized. But if this New Deal largess met with the approval of almost all Southerners, many of them soon began to question such consequences of federal intervention as the growth of organized labor and the threat to regional wage differentials.

The New Deal also contained an implicit threat to the most vital element in the structure of southern solidarity—the dogma of white supremacy. The various New Deal expenditures designed to help the underprivileged inevitably went in considerable part to Negroes. Although the sharp opposition to Roosevelt's program provoked from Southerners in the late 1930s stemmed largely from economic considerations, some southern congressmen expressed their racial concern from time to time, and a few of them foresaw how "the tiny shoots of civil rights controversy would burgeon in later years."[3] The Supreme Court soon began to whittle away at the "separate but equal" doctrine, wartime innovations like the Fair Employment Practices Committee made their appearance, and racial tensions and dark rumors—of "Eleanor Clubs" and worse—swept the South in the

2. Frank Freidel, *F.D.R. and the South* (Baton Rouge, 1965), pp. 22, 47–48. See also James T. Patterson, "The Failure of Party Realignment in the South, 1937–1939," *Journal of Politics* 27 (August 1965): 602–17.
3. Freidel, *F.D.R. and the South*, p. 73.

wake of the Negro's economic advances and growing independence. By the end of the war it was easy for white Southerners to speak of the New Deal's "coddling" of the Negro.

The New Deal's transformation of the Democratic party at the national level, its extensive involvement in the economy, and its modest contribution to the incipient movement for Negro rights represent aspects of governmental centralization in the United States which have been greatly accelerated during the last quarter century. And these developments have left their marks on recent southern politics.

If southern leaders expected Roosevelt's successor to turn aside from the path charted by the New Deal, they were quickly disillusioned. The reform program Harry S. Truman sponsored would not only expand the economic measures of the 1930s but would also enter boldly into the field of federal civil rights legislation. The revolt of the Deep South that resulted in 1948 carried South Carolina, Alabama, Mississippi, and Louisiana into the columns of the States' Righters, precipitating a bitter and continuing debate over the nature of the Democratic party as a national organization.

The most recalcitrant southern politicians argued that the Democratic party in the United States was confederate in nature, with the state parties being virtually autonomous. But this contention made little headway outside of the Dixiecrat states, and the dictates of the national party became more and more controlling in the years that followed. Even in the states they carried in 1948, the States' Righters appropriated the official Democratic label on the ballot. Following the election the question of party loyalty became an issue in several southern states, and in 1952 most state party organizations did not openly desert the national ticket. New party rules adopted in 1955–56 involved the state parties and delegations to the national convention in good-faith commitments to work for the listing of the national ticket on the state ballot as the official Democratic party.[4] Pressure for a more specific "loyalty pledge" mounted during the next eight years, and at the 1964 convention a plan was adopted to guarantee a broader base for the party's organizational politics. A majority of the state and congressional leaders in the South actively supported the

---

4. See Allan P. Sindler, "The Unsolid South: A Challenge to the Democratic National Party," in *The Uses of Power: 7 Cases in American Politics*, ed. Alan F. Westin (New York, 1962), pp. 229–83.

national ticket in 1960, and this pattern was even more pronounced in 1964.[5]

Many Southerners had long assumed that, no matter how reform minded a national administration might be, the South's essential position, particularly in the area of race relations, could always be protected because of its powerful voice in Congress. But this assumption has been greatly weakened as a result of liberal Democratic leadership in Washington and the force it has exerted through the party for the implementation of its platform. This situation reflects the strength of the Democratic party in other regions. Meanwhile, the rigidity and negativism of southern politicians weakened their effectiveness as sectional spokesmen.[6] Southern congressmen were unable to prevent the passage of civil rights legislation in 1957 and 1960, and when the full resources of a Democratic administration were brought into play for the first time in 1963 and 1964, the Southerners found it impossible to prevent the enactment of a comprehensive civil rights law. Although the much-discussed conservative coalition of southern Democrats and nonsouthern Republicans continues to be effective after more than a quarter century of collaboration, it is significant that in 1964 most Republicans joined with the northern and western Democrats to pass the civil rights legislation, while the southern Democrats, especially in the House, did not combine with the Republicans in opposing the administration's antipoverty bill.[7] The power of the Lyndon B. Johnson administration, the growth of southern Republicanism, and the eventual decline of the

---

5. The discipline of the national party was also demonstrated when two notorious congressional defectors in the campaign of 1964, Representatives John Bell Williams of Mississippi and Albert Watson of South Carolina, were stripped of their seniority as Democrats. Watson then resigned his seat and, running as a Republican in a special election held in mid-June 1965, was overwhelmingly reelected. Nashville *Tennessean,* June 16, 1965.

6. Frank E. Smith, *Congressman from Mississippi* (New York, 1964), pp. 111, 117–19, 122.

7. The "conservative coalition," a voting alliance of Republicans and southern Democrats against nonsouthern Democrats, appeared on 15 percent of the roll-call votes in the 1964 session of Congress. In 1964 the Johnson administration won two-thirds of the votes on which the administration and the coalition took opposing stands, a great improvement over the record of the Kennedy administration. See "How Big Is the North-South Democratic Split?" *Congressional Quarterly Almanac* 13 (1957): 813–17; "'Conservative Coalition' Appeared on 15% of Roll Calls," *Congressional Quarterly Weekly Report* 22 (November 27, 1964): 2741–50; "Democrats from North and South Split on 24% of Votes," ibid. (December 25, 1964): 2835–40.

civil rights issue as the most compelling question confronting southern politicians may well lessen the significance of the interparty coalition in future years.

Since the mid-1930s the South's political defenses have crumbled one by one: the repeal of the two-thirds rule and the diminishing importance of the region in the Democratic national convention, the invalidation of the white primary and the liberalization of suffrage requirements, and the gradual weakening of the congressional seniority system.[8] Nevertheless, it would be a mistake to overemphasize the element of coercion in the process of integrating the South into the Democratic party as a national organization. Southern leaders in Congress and in the various states have frequently been eager to respond in a positive way to some if not all of the progressivism inherent in a dynamic reform party in control of the national government. This was evident in the contribution of the more constructive southern congressmen to the enactment of the major New Deal measures,[9] in the first presidential bid by a Southerner in modern times on the basis of a genuine national appeal,[10] and in the governorships of such men as Ellis G. Arnall of Georgia, Kerr Scott of North Carolina, and LeRoy Collins of Florida. A notable minority of congressmen from the South have not been true "southern coalitionists," and such men as Estes Kefauver, Albert Gore, Lister Hill, J. William Fulbright, and Russell B. Long have found opportunities in national Democratic administrations for service that goes beyond regional commitments.

Such considerations have contributed to the legislative successes of the Johnson administration, and they played an important part in the presidential election of 1964 in the South, despite the unique factors in that campaign. In Arkansas, to take one example from the 1964 contest, the continued desire for federal assistance conspired with the pressure from national party leaders and the challenge of the Republicans at the state level to produce the best organized and most

---

8. William Buchanan, "Cracks in Southern Solidarity," *Antioch Review* 16 (September 1956): 351–64; Frank Munger and James Blackhurst, "Factionalism in the National Conventions, 1940–1964: An Analysis of Ideological Consistency in State Delegation Voting," *Journal of Politics* 27 (May 1965): 375–94.

9. "It was Southern leadership in Congress," points out Freidel, "that enacted the New Deal program and subsequently supplied to the President the requisite margin of votes to pass defense measures in the late thirties and early forties." Freidel, *F.D.R. and the South*, p. 2.

10. Senator Estes Kefauver of Tennessee in 1952.

unified Democratic campaign in a generation. Governor Orval E. Faubus, while not outspoken in his support of the national ticket, discovered the merits of a Democratic campaign based on the "precinct to presidency" concept.[11] One is reminded, in pondering the nationalizing effects of our new federalism, of the story told to James A. Michener by a newspaperman who traveled with Johnson through the South during the campaign of 1960. The vice-presidential nominee would invade a state capital, convene the two senators and the governor, and commence a lengthy political confab enlivened with plenty of liquid refreshments. After expressing his sympathy with the state leaders' repugnance for parts of the national platform, their doubts about John F. Kennedy's religion, and their fears growing out of the civil rights movement, "Good Ol' Lyndon" would remind his fellow Democrats that if the national campaign were lost both he and Kennedy would remain in the Senate.

. . . and, Senator Buford and Senator Baxby, I just don't see how, if your defection is the cause of our defeat, you're ever going to get one little old bill through that Senate. Governor Beauregard, you say you have to have that new airport and you want to keep the Army base down here. How do you think you're going to get such bills through the Senate if Mr. Kennedy and I are sitting there solely because you didn't produce the vote that would have elected us?[12]

If federal assistance in its myriad forms explains why many Southerners approve and even welcome a dynamic government in Washington and are willing to come to terms with the centralizing tendencies of the party structure that accompany it, the economic development of the South, resulting in part from the aid of the national government, has strongly affected the region's politics. The South's relative position among the major regions has improved in almost every category of wealth since 1930. Factories and assembly plants have sprung up from Richmond to San Antonio; agriculture has been increasingly mechanized and diversified; sharecroppers and agricultural workers in large numbers have left the farms for the cities of the South and North, while a growing stream of technicians, managers, and businessmen has flowed into the region. The old agrarian South fell before the onslaught. The traditional staples in the

---

11. George C. Roberts, "The 1964 Presidential Election in Arkansas" (manuscript provided through the courtesy of its author).

12. James A. Michener, *Report of the County Chairman* (New York, 1961), pp. 183–86.

southern economy steadily declined in relative importance, and the proportion of the labor force employed in agriculture dropped in the 1960s to less than 10 percent (it had been more than 50 percent in 1920). The region's relative urban population increased in the single decade of the 1950s almost as much as during the preceding thirty years. The migration that contributed to the urbanization of the South and other sections has accounted for a decline in the southern farm population of some eight million people since 1940. It has also reduced the black-white population ratio in the South to 1 in 5, and today less than 50 percent of all American Negroes live in southern states.[13]

Much of this change was painful, and many depressed farmers and unskilled inhabitants of towns and cities knew little of the region's new prosperity. Yet the prosperity was real and there was firm support for the buoyant economic outlook that lifted southern hopes. Southerners became healthier and better educated; the face of the land was remodeled as a result of improved agricultural methods, river development, and recreational programs; and modern roads and mass communication media destroyed the old isolation of the more remote areas. Changes in the social mobility and the class structure of the South are clearly diluting the homogeneity of the section and creating a society that will likely become more impervious to the debilitating effects of white-supremacy politics. Greater general prosperity and new modes of urban life will almost certainly have an impact upon a political system in which great numbers of people have been too poor and apathetic to play any part. These developments may be expected to sharpen social and economic issues in such a way as to cut into the traditional domination of the black belts. Some states, particularly the so-called rim states, have moved much farther from the old regional patterns than have others, and their politics reflect this progressive shattering of the South.

In the long run the emergence of an urban politics may be among the most significant consequences of the new patterns of economic and social life in the region. The city makes it possible to mobilize

13. Thomas D. Clark, *The Emerging South* (New York, 1961); John M. Maclachlan and Joe S. Floyd, Jr., *This Changing South* (Gainesville, Fla., 1956); Rudolf Heberle, "The Changing Social Stratification of the South," *Social Forces* 38 (October 1959): 42–50; William H. Nicholls, "The South as a Developing Area," in *The American South in the 1960's*, ed. Avery Leiserson (New York, 1964), pp. 22–40; Walter Prescott Webb, "The South's Future Prospect," in *The Idea of the South: Pursuit of a Central Theme*, ed. Frank E. Vandiver (Chicago, 1964), pp. 67–78; William M. Gabard, "Georgia in the Dynamic '60's," *Atlanta Economic Review* 15 (May 1965): 3–5.

group sentiment and to organize coalition campaigns. In the urban South workers have a better opportunity to join labor unions and blacks have a better chance to vote. There is some evidence that the percentage of strict segregationists is smaller in urban than in rural areas of the South, that legislative contests are more competitive in metropolitan districts than elsewhere, and that congressmen from the urban South are less inclined to be influenced by sectional considerations in voting on foreign policy issues than are their rural colleagues.[14] The pressure for municipal reform, for expanded public services at all levels, and for legislative reapportionment reflects the new urban politics in the region.[15] In effect the city increasingly is providing the South's traditional underprivileged elements with a more democratic political setting.

But the process of economic growth and urbanization has proceeded at different rates of speed within the South as a whole and within each of the southern states. Ninety-eight of Georgia's 159 counties lost population in the 1940s, for example, and only 45 percent of the region's counties experienced any population growth at all during the 1950s.[16] The declining economic and social status of many rural and small-town Southerners coupled with their disproportionate political power and reactionary policies have made them the great conservators of the South's traditions.[17] It is this situation that accounts for much of the bitterness in the school desegregation controversy and the reapportionment struggle and that partially explains the upsurge of isolationism in the region.[18]

The civil rights movement as a national issue and the growing

14. See, for example, Malcolm E. Jewell, "State Legislatures in Southern Politics," in *The American South in the 1960's*, pp. 180–81; Murray Clark Havens, "Metropolitan Areas and Congress: Foreign Policy and National Security," *Journal of Politics* 26 (November 1964): 758–74.

15. See Robert H. Connery and Richard H. Leach, "Southern Metropolis: Challenge to Government," in *The American South in the 1960's*, pp. 60–81; Malcolm E. Jewell, ed., *The Politics of Reapportionment* (New York, 1962).

16. Joseph J. Spengler, "Demographic and Economic Change in the South, 1940–1960," in *Change in the Contemporary South*, ed. Allan P. Sindler (Durham, 1963), p. 28; Grantham, *The Democratic South*, p. 88.

17. For a suggestive analysis of the relationship between the political orientation of the various congressional districts in the South during the 1950s and such phenomena as per capita income, rate and kind of industrialization, urbanization, and rural decline, see Charles O. Lerche, Jr., *The Uncertain South: Its Changing Patterns of Politics in Foreign Policy* (Chicago, 1964).

18. The sharp increase in the tendency of southern congressmen, particularly from the lower South, to abandon the region's historic low-tariff position is shown in Richard A. Watson, "The Tariff Revolution: A Study of Shifting Party Attitudes," *Journal of Politics* 18 (November 1956): 678–701.

importance of the black voter in the South have also helped to re-shape the contours of southern politics. These developments are in considerable part the product of the great centralizing thrust in recent American politics and the vast changes in the southern economy. Long before federal intervention, the collapse of the old agricultural economy in the South sent a broadening stream of Negroes northward, where their urban concentration and political power made them a significant factor in calling the civil rights movement into being. Meanwhile, the South's rapid urbanization and the economic advances of its black citizens combined with the opening of the primaries and the gradual removal of suffrage restrictions to give Southerners of darker skin a new voice in political affairs. The political activation of the Negro and the broader movement for racial equality have become a mighty force in their own right and a major vehicle for the reconstruction of American politics. As a keen student of southern affairs points out, "Today, the Negro grip on the levers of social change is secure, and much more firm than the remnants of white direction."[19]

The first significant increase of black voters in the modern South came in the wake of the Supreme Court decision in the case of *Smith v. Allwright* (1944), which opened the primaries to Negroes.[20] By 1952 about 20 percent of the Negro adults in the former Confederate states were registered to vote, and this percentage has slowly climbed since that time, reaching about 44 percent (more than 2,174,000) early in 1965 as compared with a white registration of approximately 73 percent.[21] But Negro registration varies widely within the South (and within the individual southern states), ranging from a low of 6.7 percent in Mississippi to a high of 69.4 percent in Tennessee at the end of 1964.[22] Intimidation, subterfuge, and various kinds of pres-

19. Leslie W. Dunbar, "The Changing Mind of the South: The Exposed Nerve," in *The American South in the 1960's*, p. 9.

20. Other factors that encouraged blacks to take a more active interest in politics included the democratic slogans of World War II, Negro economic gains, the growth of a black intellectual class, the repeal of the poll tax as a registration requirement in Georgia and Tennessee, and the success of Negro registration drives.

21. Much of this increase resulted from the establishment in 1962 of the Southern Regional Council's Voter Education Project, a foundation-backed enterprise that cooperated with civil rights organizations and local groups in a nonpartisan campaign to train Negroes to register and vote. Mounting pressure from the Department of Justice was also important in some areas. See the Southern Regional Council's mimeographed analysis, "What Happened in the South?" November 15, 1964.

22. Margaret Price, *The Negro Voter in the South* (Atlanta, 1957); table "Southern Negro Voter Statistics," corrected to January 1, 1965, furnished the author by the Southern Regional Council; *Congressional Record*, 89 Cong., 1 Sess., Appendix, A1389.

sure applied by whites, as well as tradition, poverty, and illiteracy, have inhibited the political activation of Negroes in many parts of the region.[23] Nevertheless, hundreds of registration drives and the new note of militancy among black leaders suggest that the ballot has become one of the most cherished symbols in the Negro's long quest for equality. The commitment of the Kennedy and Johnson administrations to the realization of this goal and the drive for federal legislation culminating in the voting rights law of 1965 will have a profound effect upon future southern politics. They foretell the emergence of a "new breed" of southern politicians.

Although the Negro vote in the South has not become the balance of power the demagogue perennially warned against, it has become too important to ignore. A student of Louisiana politics has pointed out, for instance, that black votes were "a crucial element in Adlai Stevenson's narrow victory in Louisiana in 1952; in Earl Long's first primary triumph in the 1956 Democratic gubernatorial primary; and in Eisenhower's precedent-shattering conquest of Louisiana's electoral vote in 1956."[24] In 1960 Negro voters provided an indispensable contribution to Kennedy's narrow victory over Richard M. Nixon.[25] The overwhelming Negro support (something like 95 per-

23. The studies of Donald R. Matthews and James W. Prothro reveal a correlation between the level of Negro registration and certain attributes of the white population and of the total community, including the extent of Negro concentration and the relative dominance of the agrarian economy. The nature of a state's voter qualifications and their administration, the structure of its factional politics, and the existence of black voter leagues and white racist organizations are also important in encouraging or restraining the political participation of Negroes. See the four articles by Matthews and Prothro: "Southern Racial Attitudes: Conflict, Awareness, and Political Change," *Annals of the American Academy of Political and Social Science* 344 (November 1962): 108–21; "Political Factors and Negro Voter Registration in the South," *American Political Science Review* 57 (June 1963): 355–67; "Negro Voter Registration in the South," in *Change in the Contemporary South*, pp. 120–47; "Southern Images of Political Parties: An Analysis of White and Negro Attitudes," in *The American South in the 1960's*, pp. 82–111.

24. John H. Fenton, "The Negro Voter in Louisiana," *Journal of Negro Education* 26 (Summer 1957): 327. See also Hugh D. Price, *The Negro and Southern Politics: A Chapter of Florida History* (New York, 1957); J. Morgan Kousser, "Tennessee Politics and the Negro: 1948–1964" (Senior thesis, Princeton University, 1965).

25. There was a marked falling off of Negro support in the South for the Democrats in the election of 1956, stemming in some measure from the notoriety of southern congressmen like James O. Eastland and the region's mounting resistance to school desegregation. In 1960 southern blacks returned in large numbers to the Democratic column.

cent) Johnson received in 1964 made it possible for him to win just over half of the southern vote, and black votes made the difference in at least four of the southern states he carried.[26]

Not only are Negroes becoming a vital consideration in presidential and statewide elections in the South, but they are also emerging as a major force in the liberalization of congressional districts and metropolitan areas.[27] Negroes are now being elected to city councils and state legislatures, and they have suddenly begun to acquire an unaccustomed leverage in obtaining a fairer share of municipal services. Southern politicians are increasingly taking black voters into account. "Perhaps the most impressive new fact of Texas politics," commented the *Texas Observer* immediately after the election of 1964, ". . . is the politically coercive influence of Negro and Latin-American voters. It has become dangerous to the career of a statewide candidate to be known as an opponent of civil rights."[28] The growing increment of Negro voters and the passage of the Civil Rights Act of 1964 and the voting rights legislation of 1965 will free many southern politicians from their long subservience to race and encourage economic liberals to adopt a more constructive approach to civil rights and related issues. The campaign for Negro enfranchisement will bring the ballot to many neglected whites in the section, reversing one of the side effects of Negro disfranchisement half a century ago. The possibility of a durable coalition between a por-

26. These states were Virginia, Tennessee, Florida, Arkansas, and probably North Carolina. The five Deep South states carried by Goldwater had the lowest Negro registration in the region, in no case more than 45 percent of the black adults. One must be cautious in attributing Johnson's successes in the five southern states mentioned above solely to the Negro vote, as important as it was. Other factors may have been equally vital. In Arkansas, for instance, the decision by Governor Faubus and other state leaders to endorse the national ticket was probably of great significance in the election result in that state.

27. Negro support was extremely important in 1964 in the Senate victories of Ross Bass and Albert Gore in Tennessee, and in the election of such urban representatives as George W. Grider and Richard Fulton of Tennessee, Charles L. Weltner and James A. Mackay of Georgia, and Hale Boggs of Louisiana. In some cases, it should be noted, Negro support helped carry Democratic conservatives into office.

28. *Texas Observer*, November 13, 1964. See also Virginius Dabney, "Richmond's Quiet Revolution," *Saturday Review* 47 (February 29, 1964): 18–19, 28. Southern Negroes are by no means a bloc in voting for Democratic candidates, although the "lily-white" strategy on the part of Goldwater Republicans in 1964 will perhaps encourage such voting in the Deep South. In 1962, 70 percent of the blacks voting in the congressional election in Richmond supported the Republican candidate against a veteran Democrat.

tion of the white electorate and a substantial number of black voters below the Potomac is much more promising in the present situation than were the Reconstruction and Populist experiments.

No aspect of recent southern politics is more significant in its promise for the reconstruction of American politics than the rehabilitation of the Republican party and the arrival of genuine two-party competition in presidential elections in the South. This development, in its early stages at least, was related more to economic than to racial considerations, and it would seem that over a long period of time economic and social changes will provide the most lasting foundation for the growth of Republicanism in the region. But in the short run, and particularly in the Deep South, racial alienation has been an important factor in the erosion of traditional Democratic loyalties. There was, for example, a noticeable "Dixiecrat to Ike" trend in the states carried by J. Strom Thurmond, and in some cases the States' Rights ticket became a halfway house along the road to Republicanism. There was some evidence of this in the election of 1960 and it was massively demonstrated in the lower South in 1964. Mississippi, which was captured by a slate of unpledged electors in 1960, gave Barry M. Goldwater a stunning 87 percent of its votes four years later. One wag was moved to remark that "we now have two parties in Mississippi but we're getting them one at a time."[29]

Although the number of "Presidential Republicans" in the South increased during the 1940s, the election of 1952 was the event that set off the explosive forces long building up in the region.[30] The basic explanation of the Republican party's southern victories in the 1950s lies in deep-seated economic and social forces, and in the growing dissatisfaction on the part of many southen Democrats with New Deal and Fair Deal economic policies. The Republicans retained their traditional strength in the upland regions of the South, but their most spectacular gains came in the urban areas. In city after city in the southern states Dwight D. Eisenhower carried the upper-income precincts by handsome majorities (and many of the middle-income

29. Gordon G. Henderson, "The GOP in Mississippi" (mimeographed paper prepared for the 1964 meeting of the Southern Political Science Association, Durham, N.C., November 1964). The Republican tide in Alabama not only swept five Democratic congressmen out of office but also resulted in the capture of ten county governments.

30. For evidence of growing southern interest in Republicanism during the early 1950s, see Paul T. David, Malcolm Moos, and Ralph M. Goldman, eds., *Presidential Nominating Politics in 1952* (Baltimore, 1954), vol. 3, *The South.*

precincts by less generous majorities), while Stevenson carried the lower-income districts by equally substantial margins.[31] In 1956 the Republicans won no less than 60 of the approximately 100 urban counties in the 11 ex-Confederate states. While their percentages declined somewhat in 1960, the same pattern is evident in the returns from that election. In the 68 metropolitan counties and independent cities (those with an urban population of 50,000 or more) in the former Confederate states, Nixon received 49.3 percent of the total vote as compared with 47.8 percent for Kennedy.[32] The Republican candidate undoubtedly benefited from the fact that Kennedy was a Catholic, and it should be noted that he ran better than Eisenhower in the black belts of 6 southern states.[33]

This southern Republicanism reflected a strong liking for Republican conservatism and an intense dislike of Democratic liberalism. Southerners who had grown wealthy in the 1940s and 1950s often proved to be inordinately sensitive about threats to free enterprise, while many professional people and small businessmen were suspicious of big government and heavy public expenditures which they associated with Democratic control in Washington. Individualism remained strong in the flush industrial areas, many farmers and ordinary workers continued to respond to the incantation of state rights, and large numbers of Southerners agreed philosophically with conservative Republicanism. The process of siphoning off conservative Democrats was clearly under way. In Texas during the early 1960s there were reports of "Resignation Rallies"![34] Republicans benefited from the white migration into the region, the increase in the number of professional people and college

31. See, for example, James W. Prothro, Ernest Q. Campbell, and Charles M. Grigg, "Two-Party Voting in the South: Class Vs. Party Identification," *American Political Science Review* 52 (March 1958): 131–39.

32. Donald S. Strong, "The Presidential Election in the South, 1952," *Journal of Politics* 17 (August 1955): 343–89; Strong, *Urban Republicanism in the South* (University, Ala., 1960); Bernard Cosman, "Presidential Republicanism in the South, 1960," *Journal of Politics* 24 (May 1962): 303–22.

33. Philip E. Converse, Angus Campbell, Warren E. Miller, and Donald E. Stokes estimate that Kennedy suffered a net loss from Protestant Democrats and Independents of 16.5 percent of the two-party vote in the South, compared with a net gain of 1.6 percent outside the South resulting from Catholic gains over Protestant losses. "Stability and Change in 1960: A Reinstating Election," *American Political Science Review* 55 (June 1961): 269–80.

34. William L. Rivers, "The Gonzalez Victory," *Reporter* 25 (November 23, 1961): 34.

graduates, the expanding middle class, and the rapid urbanization. As class and group differentials emerge in a two-party context, urban Republicanism in the South will probably level off, but the cities and suburban areas appear to provide the best hope for continued Republican gains in the southern states.[35]

One scholar recently observed that

the GOP is discovering the wonders and infinite possibilities of leadership, organization, grass-roots contact, research, primaries, permanent headquarters, attractive candidates, contested elections on every level, the exploitation of dissatisfaction with Democratic one-party politics, issues, all-out, all-weather and all-year efforts, and grasping the impact of vast changes on traditional habits, loyalties, and images of the South.[36]

The party's activity at the state and congressional levels did increase noticeably during the late 1950s and early 1960s. By 1964, according to party reports, all but 138 of 1,140 counties in the eleven Old South states were "organized."[37] In 1958 Republican candidates for the United States House of Representatives from southern states polled only 609,108 votes; four years later the party's candidates obtained 2,083,971 votes.[38] In 1964 Republican candidates ran in 84 of 119 congressional districts in the thirteen southern states, winning eighteen seats (as compared with fourteen in the previous Congress).[39]

35. Carl N. Degler, "American Political Parties and the Rise of the City: An Interpretation," *Journal of American History* 51 (June 1964): 58–59, thinks that the large cities in the United States will likely remain Democratic for some time to come, but he concedes that this may not be true in the case of the South.

36. Samuel DuBois Cook, "Political Movements and Organizations," in *The American South in the 1960's*, p. 146. In the South as well as other parts of the country, remarks Paul T. David, it is no longer necessary for people to join the dominant party: "The situation has changed to the point where many of the greatest political opportunities of the future are probably now available in minority party situations where the smaller of the two parties is still greatly outnumbered." David, "The Changing Political Parties," in *Continuing Crisis in American Politics*, ed. Marian D. Irish (Englewood Cliffs, N.J., 1963), p. 65.

37. George L. Grassmuck, "Emerging Republicanism in the South" (mimeographed paper prepared for the annual meeting of the American Political Science Association, Chicago, September 1964); Virginius Dabney, "What the GOP Is Doing in the South," *Harper's Magazine* 226 (May 1963): 86–94.

38. See Milton C. Cummings, Jr., "Southern Congressional Elections" (mimeographed paper prepared for the annual meeting of the American Political Science Association, Chicago, September 1964); Gerald Pomper, "Future Southern Congressional Politics," *Southwestern Social Science Quarterly* 64 (June 1963): 14–24.

39. Bernard Cosman, "An Overview of Southern Republicanism" (mimeographed paper delivered at the annual meeting of the Southern Political Science Association, Durham, N.C., November 1964).

Republicans have also become more active on the local scene, particularly in urban places, and they have won a scattering of offices.[40] Although Republican victories in the South's local politics have scarcely rippled the waters of the long one-party calm, the grass-roots effects of economic change, urbanization, and reapportionment are becoming evident.[41]

The forces of tradition, the vested interests making up the one-party structure, the obsession with race as a political issue, the conservative Democratic control of state and local government, and the prestige and influence of southern congressmen will all no doubt inhibit the emergence of a more thoroughgoing two-party system in the southern states. Nevertheless, millions of Southerners in recent years have voted Republican for the first time, and that party has acquired a respectability—and even glamor—in some southern quarters that greatly enhances its competitive position. The shift from "postoffice Republicanism" to competitive Republicanism, the accelerating pace of GOP campaigning, and the increasing southern turnouts in presidential elections also augur well for the Republicans.[42]

The deviant character of the national election of 1964 may have interrupted the emergence of a competitive Republican party in the rim states of the South, and the future of a Republicanism in the

40. Following the elections of 1964, Republicans held some 44 senate seats and 137 house seats in southern legislatures. See *Congressional Quarterly Weekly Report* 22 (November 6, 1964): 2629–31, 2635–58; ibid. (November 20, 1964): 2709; New York *Times*, June 18, 1965.

41. In the north Louisiana city of Shreveport rapid industrial and business growth fostered a political conservatism among the city's new economic and social leaders that found an outlet in a local Republican movement. Stimulated by the national Republican successes of the 1950s, this movement brought a two-party system to Caddo Parish for the first time in the twentieth century. In 1963 Shreveport Republicans succeeded, with some assistance from the racial issue, in electing the first two Republican legislators in Louisiana in modern times. For an account of the early development of this movement, see Kenneth N. Vines, *Two Parties for Shreveport* (New York, 1959).

42. The increase in total presidential votes cast in the South in 1960 relative to those cast in 1956 was 25 percent; outside the region the increase was 7 percent. Converse, Campbell, Miller, and Stokes, "Stability and Change in 1960," pp. 269–70. The removal of the poll tax and the vigorous organizational efforts to get out the vote in Virginia resulted in an increase of more than 35 percent in the number of presidential ballots in 1964 over the number cast in 1960. See Ralph Eisenberg, "Virginia Votes for President: Patterns and Prospects," *University of Virginia News Letter* 41 (September 15, 1964): 1–4; Eisenberg, "The 1964 Presidential Election in Virginia: A Political Omen?" ibid. (April 15, 1965): 29–32.

Deep South keyed to racism is clouded with uncertainty.[43] But in some respects the election of 1964 may prove to be extraordinarily significant in its impact upon southern politics. A great many Southerners supported the Republican party for the first time in their lives, and never before had the full implications of a national campaign reached into so many parts of the region. In states like Virginia and Florida the concept of party loyalty assumed new meaning and importance for Democratic leaders. And a majority of the southern states demonstrated their unwillingness to be dominated by racial or economic extremism.

Genuine two-partyism will probably develop in the inner South—the five states carried by Goldwater—more slowly than in the outer South. But the historical pattern of the border states may be duplicated by more and more southern states as they undergo social and economic changes. Following the Civil War, Democrats captured control in all of the border states. But in each of them Republicans were strong enough to pose a constant threat and occasionally to defeat the Democrats when the latter's factionalism flared up in bitter controversies. In time a party realignment, reflecting economic and demographic trends as well as New Deal politics, brought most of the Negroes, many of the upland inhabitants, and the laboring classes in the industrial region into the Democratic party, while the business interests and the old Democratic Bourbon element, originally Whig, increasingly went over to the Republican party.[44]

The dynamic elements in the southern economy and the new wealth have heightened the conservative tendencies of southern politics, but the new society is also producing other groups that will eventually serve to counteract the dominant ones and to fragment and liberalize state and local politics. Such factors as socio-economic status, migration patterns, and issue orientation are not altogether absent even in the racially dominated politics of the Deep South, and

43. In general the growth of Republicanism in the South fits V. O. Key's definition of a "secular realignment," by which he meant "a movement of the members of a population category from party to party that extends over several presidential elections and appears to be independent of the peculiar factors influencing the vote at individual elections." Key, "Secular Realignment and the Party System," *Journal of Politics* 21 (May 1959): 198–210.

44. John H. Fenton, *Politics in the Border States: A Study of the Patterns of Political Organization, and Political Change, Common to the Border States—Maryland, West Virginia, Kentucky and Missouri* (New Orleans, 1957). See also William G. Carleton, "Two-Party South?" *Virginia Quarterly Review* 41 (Autumn 1965): 481–98.

the recurrent cleavages within the Democratic party in some areas are being translated into a Democratic-Republican division in national elections. The division of the electorate in the senatorial contest of 1962 between Lister Hill and James D. Martin may foreshadow a restructuring of the state's politics in a way that will align upland whites and enfranchised blacks in partisan opposition to black-belt Bourbons and urban middle-class conservatives.[45] In Texas, to take an even more promising case, the changing economic and social developments of the last quarter century and the impact of New Deal policies are clearly producing a system based on class and group politics.[46]

As the urban populations come to exert greater weight in the political process through reapportionment and the political activation of the less affluent social elements, it is reasonable to expect southern politicians at all levels of government to broaden their programs. In Florida the governor increasingly speaks for the booming urban areas, and one result of reapportionment may well be a shift from the old struggle between the governor and the legislature to a conflict within the legislature, with the governor supporting one side or the other.[47] In Virginia the rapidly growing urban corridor extending from the northern part of the state to the Tidewater cities has already diluted the power of the rural-based Byrd machine and the traditional Democratic dependence upon the Southside.[48] The cities may provide much Republican support in future Virginia elections, but they are also likely to bring the Democrats recruits in the form of Negroes, organized labor, and the middle-class "swing vote."

45. Walter Dean Burnham, "The Alabama Senatorial Election of 1962: Return of Inter-Party Competition," *Journal of Politics* 26 (November 1964): 798–829.

46. In their study, *Party and Factional Division in Texas* (Austin, 1964), James R. Soukup, Clifton McCleskey, and Harry Holloway found strong evidence that the most consistently liberal counties in the 1950s were significantly influenced by Populism and, more recently, a clear-cut identification with the national Democratic party. The sharpened competition of an ideological nature in recent Texas politics reflects such developments as the ardent conservatism associated with new wealth, rapidly growing cities and suburbs, new and vigorous voluntary organizations, and the liberal tendencies of Latin Americans, blacks, and organized labor.

47. Jewell, "State Legislatures in Southern Politics," p. 195; Malcolm B. Parsons, "Quasi-Partisan Conflict in a One-Party Legislative System: The Florida Senate, 1947–1961," *American Political Science Review* 56 (September 1962): 605–14; William C. Havard and Loren P. Beth, *The Politics of Mis-Representation: Rural-Urban Conflict in the Florida Legislature* (Baton Rouge, 1962).

48. See James Reichley et al., *States in Crisis: Politics in Ten American States, 1950–1962* (Chapel Hill, 1964), pp. 3–23.

The adjustment of state government to the demands of the modern era, halting and inadequate though it is, has proven nevertheless to be an innovating factor in southern politics. Responding to new social problems produced by economic and population shifts, and also to the pressure of numerous federal programs that assimilated state and local governments into their machinery of operation, the states have greatly expanded their functions during the last two decades. One of the most notable features of state government in this period has been the emergence of the governor as a political and legislative leader, in part because of the lack of leadership in most legislatures. "With very few exceptions," says one student of state government, "the governor of a southern state is a program-oriented individual who sees the accomplishments of his administration in the light of program goals."[49] In the future, as the effects of reapportionment and a broadened franchise become more obvious, governors in the South, as in other regions, are likely to prove increasingly responsive to the urban masses, including blacks. The same will be true of a majority of southern legislators.

It is not too much to say that a political revolution, the end of which is not yet in sight, has swept the South since the 1930s. That revolution is intimately related to America's swiftly changing federalism and the Democratic dominance in our party system during the past generation. The federal government has probably had a greater impact upon the South than upon any other section—whether in the form of TVA, military and space installations, or court decisions and legislation in the field of civil rights. After conducting an intensive study of federal expenditures in Mississippi, the general counsel of the Civil Rights Commission observed in 1963, "We approached Mississippi as if it were pitted against the Federal government, but the most striking thing we found was the *presence* of the Federal government, in its aid programs and other activities, throughout the state."[50] The national government has been the principal instrument in the broadening of the southern electorate, in making Southerners more politically conscious, and in orienting them toward substantive issues. The growth of federal power since

49. Coleman B. Ransone, Jr., "Political Leadership in the Governor's Office," in *The American South in the 1960's*, p. 198.

50. Barbara Carter, "The Role of the Civil Rights Commission," *Reporter* 29 (July 4, 1963): 13. In 1962 federal tax collections in Mississippi were $270,793,000, while federal expenditures during the same period amounted to $644,617,217.

1932 has served to liberate the states in important ways and to stimulate their administrative functions.[51] The national parties have
gradually extended their discipline into the South and have involved
state and local units more completely in presidential campaigns.
Democratic administrations in Washington have facilitated the appearance of "integrated liberals" in Congress from some southern
metropolises and encouraged a selective liberalism on the part of
more moderate leaders interested in public power, health, education,
and other economic assistance from the federal government. National policies and issues, along with economic change and moderate
leadership, have also contributed to the recession of racist politics in
the outer states of the South. On the other hand, southern disaffection in and out of Congress with New Deal and Fair Deal reforms has
been compounded by new currents in foreign affairs which
weakened strong ties that once existed between many Democrats in
the region and the national party on international questions.
Economic and social changes have also had their effect. The South no
longer possesses a distinct economic interest, and its well-to-do and
rising middle classes find much in common with conservatives in
other regions.

One of the consequences of the New Deal revolution was the
assault on one-partyism through the resurgence of the Democratic
party in many nonsouthern states. The erosion of sectionalism in
other parts of the country deprived the Republican party of many
safe congressional seats, and this situation encourages the GOP to
compete with the Democrats in the South today.[52] A slow convergence has taken place between "critical facets of mass electoral
behavior" as they appear in the South and elsewhere in the United
States.[53] Meanwhile, the geographical center of the race issue is shifting from South to North as a process of "de-regionalization of the
problem" takes place.[54]

51. See Leonard D. White, *The States and the Nation* (Baton Rouge, 1953); V. O.
Key, Jr., *American State Politics: An Introduction* (New York, 1956).

52. As the Republican party becomes more competitive in the South, southern
Democrats in Congress will become more vulnerable. The result may be that they will
turn more frequently to the national party organization for help and that the party will
achieve greater cohesion and stronger support for its national policies.

53. See Philip E. Converse, "A Major Political Realignment in the South?" in.
Change in the Contemporary South, pp. 195–222.

54. Norman Cousins, "The De-Regionalization of a Problem," *Saturday Review* 46
(October 19, 1963): 28.

Whether or not the "Negro problem" accelerates the process of party realignment in the region, it has surely been the most incendiary issue in recent southern politics and a major factor in the revolutionary character of political affairs in the contemporary South. The Second Reconstruction of the South has in fact come within sight of accomplishing what the First Reconstruction promised but failed to achieve: the full guarantee to the American Negro of his rights as a citizen. The Second Reconstruction, writes C. Vann Woodward, has "turned a corner."[55] It is instructive to note how it differs from the first attempt at Reconstruction. In the current Reconstruction the Negro himself is a decisive participant, his voting power is more strategically located, the movement is sparked by black leaders and organizations, it is supported by white allies in the South as well as the North, and it is inspired by the pervasive awareness among Negroes of the enormous moral and political power of their cause.

The South has served in some measure as the nation's political conscience or, to use Leslie W. Dunbar's phrase, "America's exposed nerve."[56] The region has provided the best example of the flouting of America's most hallowed political traditions: the two-party system, the expression of minority and dissenting views, and responsible and broadly representative political leadership. Yet, fundamentally, what happened in the South was the perversion of the democratic process in American writ large. The recurrent dialogue that other parts of the country have carried on with the South suggests that Americans outside the region have long recognized their own image in the mirror held up by that wayward section. But the South has changed in our time, changed enormously, and so has the rest of the United States. To understand the real meaning of the revolution the South is now experiencing, it is necessary to remember that the country as a whole has undergone a momentous change since 1929—a change grounded in the Great Depression, the New Deal, and the Second World War. The Second Reconstruction of the South, in its broadest dimensions, is only a part of that profound transformation in our national life.

55. C. Vann Woodward, "From the First Reconstruction to the Second," *Harper's Magazine* 230 (April 1965), 132–33.
56. Dunbar, "The Changing Mind of the South," pp. 3–21.

13

Jimmy Carter and the Americanization of Southern Politics

Have the forces of change finally transformed southern politics? The election of Jimmy Carter to the highest office in the land seemed to some observers, including the writer, to mark the continuing evolution if not the climactic transmutation of the region's political affairs, including a significant shift in the role of the South in national politics. Since this essay was written soon after Carter's inauguration, its attempt to assimilate the election of 1976 into the broader pattern of recent southern politics is necessarily tentative and impressionistic. There may be a moral here: historians should perhaps recall the old Chinese proverb to the effect that it is always hazardous to make predictions, especially about the future!

Nevertheless, one can say with some confidence that no other part of the country has experienced more drastic changes in its political life during the period since World War II than the American South. The extent of these modifications—the disruption of the Solid South, the emergence of a competitive Republicanism, the entry of blacks into the mainstream of southern politics, and now the election of a Deep South politician as president—can be appreciated most fully if one views them against the backdrop of V. O. Key's vivid analysis thirty years ago. Whether or not the Carter presidency accelerates the process of the South's political transformation, the Georgian's election was unquestionably an event of great significance in the evolution of modern southern politics. The election was extraordinary in that most Negro voters and a substantial number of whites in the South came together to help make possible the election of a native Southerner who conducted a truly national campaign. The result was widely interpreted as a milestone that would enhance southern prospects for national leadership. It appeared to symbolize the South's more complete integration into national politics. It also seemed to demonstrate a change in the way many Americans from other regions perceived the South. Some observers even suggested the ironic possibility that Carter's appeal outside his native region mirrored a yearning for a more stable, traditional, and self-assured society like that of the South! Of course, it is not necessary to embrace the idea of a redemptive South to find in Carter's election compelling evidence of the increasing Americanization of southern politics.

T HE election of Jimmy Carter as the thirty-ninth president of the United States has given renewed impetus to the idea of an isolated and wayward South finally entering the mainstream of American life. This theme was widely sounded during and after the campaign of 1976. According to the poet and novelist James Dickey, the South has finally won out "after all these years" and is now the "political pivot" of the country. In a recent book on southern politics Jack Bass and Walter DeVries express the opinion that as "the region adjusts to the changes brought by industrialization, urbanization, and development of a pluralistic social structure, the South is emerging into an era of consolidation in which its destiny blends with that of the rest of the United States and that should add vitality rather than disruption to the nation's political process." One of the records of the southern rock musician Charlie Daniels simply proclaims: "The South's Gonna Do It Again."

Carter's electoral victory may represent a climactic point in the process that the writer John Egerton has called the "Americanization" of Dixie and the "Southernization" of the North. Humbled, isolated, and bereft of a positive role in national affairs, the South continued long after the Civil War as a kind of political pariah in America. Southern influence in national politics increased in the twentieth century, but the region's political institutions, like other significant aspects of its culture, remained distinctive even in the post-World War II period. Although Woodrow Wilson and Lyndon B. Johnson were "southern" in many respects, Jimmy Carter is the first full-fledged president from the South in more than a hundred years. Carter's election coincided with and probably resulted from kaleidoscopic changes that have swept over the southern section and the entire country since the Great Depression of the 1930s. The manifestations of these changes, while filled with paradox and ambiguity, are increasingly evident in politics. The question is what effect Carter's presidency will have on the evolving political structure of the South. Will it encourage the political activation of southern blacks and other disadvantaged elements? Will it promote the development of a more genuine two-party system in the southern states? Will it bring the region's politics more directly into the operation of the national party machinery? Will it enhance the influence and recognition of southern politicians and voters in the conduct of the nation's public affairs?

While it is clear that southern politics has undergone a remarkable transformation since the end of the Second World War, only time will tell what impact the election of a president from the Deep South will have on the political attitudes and behavior of Americans, both in and out of the southern region. The history of the modern South should make one wary of predicting the early disappearance of the nation's most distinctive geographical area and its ultimate integration into our national political life. After all, the theme of impending political change, like the periodic announcement of the emergence of the New South, has marked the course of the region's history for more than a century. As the historian George B. Tindall has recently remarked, "somebody will always be staging a symposium on the changing South." "It is," Tindall wryly notes, "one of the flourishing minor industries of the region, one in which countless professional southerners have build up a vested interest."

Nevertheless, it is easy to minimize the extent of the South's political alteration during the last quarter century. Indeed, it can be argued that no other section of the country has experienced so drastic a period of political crisis and change. When V. O. Key was writing his classic interpretation of the Solid South, *Southern Politics in State and Nation* (1949), he stressed four institutional supports for the region's political isolation and peculiarity: disfranchisement, the one-party system, the structure of Jim Crow and racial proscription, and the malapportionment of legislative districts. The regional politics Key illuminated so brilliantly tended to suppress issues, to subordinate economic interests to the appeal of racial solidarity, to limit the political influence of Negroes and of poor whites, to encourage racial demagoguery, and to concentrate political power in the hands of economic elites and rural conservatives.

During the last three decades all of the institutional props for the traditional politics of the Solid South have crumbled under the impact of rapid economic and technological change, the civil rights revolution, and the nation's continuing political centralization and social homogenization. "It used to be," Congressman Andrew Young told an interviewer a year or two ago, "[that] Southern politics was just 'nigger' politics, who could 'outnigger' the other—then you registered 10 to 15 percent in the community and folk would start saying 'Nigra,' and then you get 35 to 40 percent registered and it's amazing how quick they learned how to say 'Nee-grow,' and now that we've got 50, 60, 70 percent of the black votes registered in the South, everybody's proud to be associated with their black brothers and sisters."

Despite its hyperbole, Young's comment epitomizes the radical transition in the place of Negroes in southern politics. Racism remains pervasive, in the South as in other sections, but the politics of race seems to have ended almost everywhere. The legal structure of Jim Crow has virtually disappeared, and the resurgence of blacks into politics has already had a profound effect upon public affairs in every southern state. Not only are blacks registering and voting at percentage levels that are approaching those of white Southerners, but their leaders and organizations are developing coalition strategies in municipal, state, and national campaigns that make them an increasingly potent force in southern politics. Just as Negro voters in northern cities became a vital element in the Roosevelt coalition during the 1930s and 1940s, so blacks in the 1970s have become a major part of the Democratic coalition in the South as well as the rest of the country. There is more than a little irony in the fact that the first United States president from the Deep South should have been elected with the support of 90 percent of the black vote! It is no less ironic that the "race question," which served as the main bulwark of the Solid South for almost a century, should eventually have become a key factor in the disruption of the region's political solidarity, the revitalization of its party politics, and the nationalization of its public affairs.

Jimmy Carter's election and administration promise to accelerate the emergence of a two-party South. Although the presidential election of 1928, in which five southern states supported the Republican candidate Herbert Hoover, gave some premonitory signs of the ultimate breakup of the Solid South, the region's solidarity in national politics was not shattered until after World War II. The first notable manifestation of this regional rupture came with the Dixiecrat revolt of 1948, when southern opposition to Harry S. Truman's civil rights proposals and Fair Deal reforms led to the organization of a third party which carried four states in the lower South and denied the Democratic ticket 39 electoral votes. The process continued in 1952 and 1956, when Dwight D. Eisenhower captured several southern states and won almost half of the South's popular votes. The rise of massive resistance and widespread opposition in the southern states to the Second Reconstruction contributed to the collapse of the Democratic South in presidential elections, as did the region's economic growth, technological advances, and demographic changes. The fragmentation became even more evident in the 1960s with additional Republican gains and the third-party movement led by Governor George C. Wallace. In 1972 Richard M. Nixon, whose "southern strategy" was calculated to appeal to white racial sensibilities, law and order sentiment, and economic conservatism, carried every one of the former Confederate states. Momentarily, at least, the South had come full circle. It was a far cry from the old days when, as Senator Carter Glass of Virginia once explained, "a Democrat in the South would as soon think of deserting his church as deserting his party."

The South's strong swing back to the Democratic ticket in 1976 suggests not only the regional loyalty felt for a native son, but also the volatile nature of southern politics in the 1970s. Although the old one-party South is obviously a thing of the past, the character of the new political order is not yet apparent. Southern politics is in flux. It is one thing to have party competition in presidential elections but quite another to have real two-party contests at the state and local levels. Still, Democratic ascendancy in every southern state has been shaken during the last decade or so. The Republican party has experienced noteworthy growth and reorganization throughout the South. It has begun to compete for offices which in earlier years were habitually conceded to the Democrats without a struggle. During the sixties and early seventies the GOP gradually increased its share of the South's congressional delegations, and Republican candidates have been elected to the governorships and U.S. Senate seats in more than half the southern states. Republican successes in legislative and local contests have been less frequent, and only in Tennessee is there yet a viable two-party politics. But all of the southern states have developed greater party competition in recent years.

The revitalized Republicans have had a decided influence upon the Democratic party in most southern states, forcing it to reorganize and to broaden its appeal to the electorate. One result has been the emergence of a group of moderate southern governors such as Jimmy Carter, Dale Bumpers, and Reubin Askew. Carter's presidency will probably strengthen this type of moderate and broad-based governorship. The Carter administration may also become a catalyst for the assimilation of white Southerners into the emerging two-party politics throughout the region. Circumstances in the South now appear to be singularly conducive not only to freer and more vigorous competition at the ballot box but also to the sorting out of party preferences in the wake of the last generation's dislocations and on the basis of a national program proclaimed by a Southerner in the White House.

The tangible benefits the South may reap from the Carter administration are no doubt substantial. But it is quite possible that a southern president will prove even more significant in a symbolic sense. For the symbolic uses of the presidency are very great, and Carter's leadership may serve to legitimize southern power in national affairs as well as to facilitate the more complete integration of the region into national politics. The geography of power does not entirely explain the South's political sectionalism and isolation. Indeed, in some respects southern politicians have wielded extraordinary influence in national affairs ever since the 1890s.

Yet the South's role on the national political stage has almost always been a peculiarly truncated and constrained one. The region's power in Washington more often than not has been negative in character. This is true in part because southern leaders were united in protecting and perpetuating, through the Democratic party and with other means, certain regional interests, including white supremacy. This task was furthered by the great party realignment of the 1890s, which made the Republicans dominant in national politics while enabling southern Democrats to exert great weight in the national councils of their own party. Until 1936 the rule requiring a two-thirds majority for presidential nominations also gave Southerners a powerful voice in the selection of the Democratic party's national standard-bearers. In Congress southern Democrats usually outnumbered their party counterparts from other regions, and in periods of Democratic control their long seniority made it possible for them to control the committee system.

The party realignment of the 1930s, which transformed the Democrats into the normal majority party, changed the situation drastically. With the emergence of the New Deal coalition the southern Democrats had become a minority in a majority party. But even after the South could no longer control one of the two major parties, southern congressmen used their powerful committee positions, parliamentary skills, and informal coalitions with Republicans to safeguard their sectional interests. These devices of obstruction and strategic control were employed so effectively by southern Democrats that it almost seemed that John C. Calhoun's "concurrent majority" was finally being realized. While protecting the fundamental position of the South, moreover, the Dixie congressmen contributed to the long legislative deadlock in Washington that began in 1939. "All in all," V. O. Key wrote in 1949, "their strategy of obstruction provides an instructive illustration of the great power—at least negative power—of cohesive and determined minorities."

On occasion the South responded positively to the challenges and opportunities of national politics. The southern states played an essential role in the nomination and election of Woodrow Wilson, an expatriated Southerner whose administration struck a southern tone and evoked many expressions of regional pride. Franklin D. Roosevelt, only the second Democratic president in the twentieth century, also enjoyed a large southern following. Wilson and Roosevelt appointed numerous Southerners to high office, and their administrations brought many southern leaders into the orbit of national and international affairs. Wilson and Roosevelt also relied on the legislative support of southern congressmen in the enactment of their principal reforms. The same was true of later presidents. Even so, southern congressional leaders tended to be parochial in outlook; they were apt to judge national issues, particularly in the realm of domestic reform, by the standard of how well they fit the special requirements of a caste-bound society and a one-party politics.

Lyndon B. Johnson, a Texan and something of a blend of Southerner and Westerner, may have helped to change the region's political orientation. He certainly wanted to reconcile regional differences in the United States. As Eric F. Goldman has written, "the fact that it was a Southern President who put through the tough civil rights laws made an enormous amount of difference. So too did Lyndon Johnson's skillful exploitation of this fact, the general thrust of his domestic policies, and his persistent, patient message to the South—delivered publicly and still more often privately—to let up on 'nigro, nigro' and concentrate on economic and social advancement."

President Carter faces fewer odds than did Woodrow Wilson, Franklin D. Roosevelt, and Lyndon B. Johnson in giving the South a more integral part in our national political life. He speaks in the idiom of his native region, but he invokes ideals and aspirations that are as broadly American as those expressed by any of his predecessors. Although not a latter-day Populist, Carter reflects a strain of economic liberalism in southern politics that goes back to the New Deal and to Populism. His emphasis on moderation, social harmony, economic development, and governmental modernization is reminiscent of the southern progressives early in the twentieth century. The political coalition that made Carter's election possible is based on strength in the South but also on his considerable appeal to other parts of the country and to the traditional components of the Democratic majority. It reflects an ethnic politics approach and an assumption that blacks and whites can work together for mutual political benefit. The Georgian's efforts to subordinate racial differences and his appeals to economic and personal concerns shared by many ordinary white and black Southerners will almost certainly pull the South more fully into the milieu of national political competition.

The Carter administration will also have an opportunity to weaken and perhaps destroy some of the remaining sectional antipathies and stereotypes. North and South, C. Vann Woodward has written, historically served each other as inexhaustible scapegoats in the old game of regional polemics. "Back and forth the dialogue has gone, sometimes at shrill pitch and sometimes in low key, depending on the temper of the times and the moods and needs of the participants." Northern censure of the South's "peculiar" institutions was matched by southern suspicion and condemnation of outside meddling and coercion. But the very fact that a one-term governor of Georgia could be elected president suggests that sectional acrimony in national politics has lost much of its onetime potency. If Carter's presidency inaugurates a new and more constructive role for the South in American life, the result may well contribute to a further reduction of prejudice in the North-South dialogue.

Recent American history has tended to put the long sectional conflict between North and South into a new and subtly different perspective. The increasing convergence in the objective conditions of the southern region and the rest of the country has contributed to this revision of historical vistas. But the political divisiveness and social upheaval of the 1960s have also had a profound effect on this alteration of historical view, the dimensions of which encompass much more than sectional prejudices and differences. In any case, the predominant attitudes and values of Americans have begun to assume a notably novel aspect. The racial attitudes of white Americans from all parts of the country appear to be more alike than dissimilar, and the fundamental outlook of Southerners on a whole range of central questions—economic growth, political ideology, nationalist sentiment—does not seem very different from that of other Americans. Professor Woodward has pointed out, moreover, that recently "the balance of trade in cultural determinants seems to be swinging the other way, with the South the growing exporter, the North the main importer." This has now reached the point where one of the region's exports resides at 1600 Pennsylvania Avenue!

Nevertheless, the South remains the most distinctive region in the United States, and it provides the most clearly defined and enduring example of sectional particularity in the American experience. White Southerners still constitute a distinguishable ethnic group. Despite the seemingly inexorable pressures of political nationalization and cultural homogenization, the South is not likely to vanish in the foreseeable future as a unique element in the nation's political and social character. Evidence to support this conjecture can be found in a fascinating study of the regional subculture by John Sheldon Reed. He argues, in *The Enduring South: Subcultural Persistence in Mass Society* (1972), that Southerners remain "distinctively Southern" and that "two institutions, the family and the church, are more powerful in the South" than in any other region. The Southerner's strong sense of place also remains distinctive. President Carter, who grew up in a part of Georgia where his family had farmed for generations, seems to embody this identification with the land and consciousness of community. History also explains why the concept of regional difference is still important. For regional distinctions in our time have tended to become primarily ones of historical experience and consciousness. This is evident in the brilliant interpretations of such historians as C. Vann Woodward, David M. Potter, T. Harry Williams, and George B. Tindall, who have reconstructed a southern past that is markedly different from, and quite un-American as compared with, the history of other parts of the United States.

Southerners, perhaps more than other Americans, have been acutely aware of change. Their tragic encounter with history during

the Civil War and its aftermath, as well as their long rearguard struggle to protect their regional way of life, conditioned them to the
notion that change itself was a threat to be resisted. Yet many Southerners yearned for a larger role in national affairs and kept hoping
that a new day for the South would arrive. Walter Hines Page, an
ardent advocate of a New South, wistfully remarked in 1911 that
"Every year of our lives the new era was just about to begin." Such
yearnings, however, clashed with the reality of the widespread
commitment to white supremacy and the Solid South. The consequence was a kind of political schizophrenia among many thoughtful
white Southerners.

Much of this painful ambivalence has been dissipated in recent
years, and the "new era" Page so eagerly sought may have arrived,
though not in a form that he ever imagined. Southerners today, one
suspects, have more reason to equate change with progress than
most other Americans. Political dissent in the region is no longer
widely regarded as racial disloyalty. The South no longer makes a
cult of the Democratic party, and the region shows signs of becoming
less willing to follow extremists in an effort to preserve the status
quo. State governments are more open and more responsive to the
public than was ever true of the old one-party system. Blacks have
become a significant force in politics, and voter registration among
all groups has shown an upward surge. Women are entering politics
in greater numbers. The sources of two-party competition have increased rapidly during the last two decades, and the southern states
are no longer isolated from national politics.

It is possible, of course, that the Carter administration will in-
tensify rather than diminish the sectional basis of American politics.
Southern conservatism runs deep, and many vestiges of the old politics persist. Enormous economic and demographic changes have not
yet undermined the exaggerated influence of rural forces in the region's politics. Labor unions are still weak in most southern states,
and vested interests, especially business groups appealing to the
cherished idea of economic growth and development, exert immense
power in legislatures and other decision-making bodies. Many of
these conditions, of course, characterize all sections of the United
States today.

There is little doubt that Jimmy Carter has an unprecedented
opportunity to move the South toward a more rational and constructive role in our national politics. "Whatever else he may do," Tom
Wicker has written, "Jimmy Carter has removed the last great cause

for Southern isolation; and even in the remote little farm towns that dot the Southern countryside, it is already possible to sense that Southerners are coming to believe that they finally belong to something larger than the South." If that is true, and if non-Southerners come to share that perception, Carter's election may indeed complete the Americanization of southern politics. The South will then perhaps be able to participate more confidently and more fruitfully in the nation's public affairs.

14

Contemporary American History

The following discussion of dominant themes in American life since World War II may provide a national context for several of the preceding essays. Although the war is interpreted as a watershed in modern American history and the postwar period is viewed as a new and distinct epoch in the national experience, my intent is to show how consensus and conflict are intertwined in our recent history. The essay is concerned with the interaction of social change and politics, and it gives some consideration to the nature of contemporary history. It is reprinted from *Contemporary American History: The United States since 1945* (1975), a pamphlet published by the American Historical Association.

F R O M the vantage point of the 1970s, the years since 1945 constitute a new and in many respects revolutionary age in American history. "The gulf separating 1965 from 1943," the cultural anthropologist Margaret Mead has written, "is as deep as the gulf that separated the men who became builders of cities from Stone Age men."[1] The new era was ushered in by the Second World War, which dramatized the apocalyptic nature of modern society and pointed up the general cultural crisis of the twentieth century. The

1. Margaret Mead, *And Keep Your Powder Dry: An Anthropologist Looks at America*, 2d ed. (New York, 1965), p. xxx.

war led to the creation of a mighty military force, brought about a great mobilization of industry and other resources, banished unemployment and freed the economy from the grip of the depression, helped redefine the role of government, invoked new international policies, and changed the nation's social structure. The most compelling of all the contrasts with former times was the bomb. The explosion of the first atomic bomb in July 1945, in a remote New Mexico desert, cast its shadow over the entire postwar period.

Yet much of the past persisted in the years after 1945. Established institutions remained strong, and older attitudes and values demonstrated remarkable vitality. Although events after World War II overtook Americans with breathtaking speed, they were far less revolutionary than were developments in many other parts of the world. It was ironic that the United States, itself the product of a revolution, should have come, in a new age of national revolutions, to be viewed by many people in other countries as a conservative society, dedicated to the maintenance of the status quo. Nevertheless the postwar period in the United States, as elsewhere, was essentially an era of historical change, disruption, and discontinuity.

The problem of periodization inevitably concerns all students of history, for the element of time is a fundamental determinant of any identifiable pattern of social change. Obviously the last three decades are not all of a piece. The uniformities apparent from a bird's-eye view become, upon closer inspection, much more diversified by time and circumstance. For example, the 1950s witnessed a general revival of religion, while the next decade brought a massive assault on the structure of American religious institutionalism. Indeed, the second half of the 1960s may represent a sharp turning point in our recent history, for the United States during those years experienced what appeared to be a pronounced shift in moral, religious, and esthetic attitudes. But however broken and incoherent the shape of their overall development may have been, the postwar years had much in common. They also share a distinctive historiography, since virtually all historical accounts of the period have necessarily been written by persons alive at the time of the events they describe.

The growing recognition of contemporary history as a legitimate field is no doubt rooted in the acceleration of the rate of change—in the increase in the velocity of history. Despite the limitations that surround it, contemporary history offers an invaluable perspective. As John Lukacs has noted, "The person who, in one way or another, participated in the period which he is describing, who had some kind of a living contact with the people and the events he deals with, has a potentially . . . inestimable advantage over other observers." The contemporary historian is in a position to appreciate the popular inclinations of the time, to detect the real tendencies in the opinions and sentiments of the people, and to be conscious of the passions that move the participants in his account. He can also contribute to what Lukacs calls "the deepening of the personal consciousness of history."[2]

The task of the historian of the recent past is to place contemporary events in historical perspective or, one might say, to treat the present as history. This is no easy matter. It is still hard to see the broad shape of the postwar period, to understand how it is related to the prewar epoch, and to perceive the pattern of its evolution through time. One's view is inevitably affected by a large amount of present-mindedness. Yet, by attempting to organize and interpret the tumultuous years since 1945, we can engage in the process Felix Gilbert describes as "reconstructing a historical consciousness that integrates the present with the past."[3] And without some awareness of the complexity, ambiguity, and burden of the past, we will surely be ill prepared to deal with the kaleidoscopic present and the onrushing future.

The Economic and Social Context

Emerging from the depression that racked the nation in the prewar years, the United States entered the greatest and most sustained period of prosperity in its history. The passage from war to peace was difficult, but the economy did not revert to the hard times of the 1930s. Instead Americans enjoyed an almost uninterrupted boom that raised production figures, incomes, and standards of living to heights which would have been unbelievable a short time earlier. Despite several recessions the gross national product, in constant dollars, increased more than twice the rate of population growth. By 1960 the GNP had reached $500 billion, and within little more than another decade it had climbed to the trillion-dollar level. "It became clear to all the world," the economist Harold G. Vatter writes, "that the United States economy after mid-century was capable of producing enough to provide every man, woman, and child with a

2. John Lukacs, *Historical Consciousness; Or, The Remembered Past* (New York, 1968), pp. 93, 97.

3. John Higham, with Leonard Krieger and Felix Gilbert, *History: The Development of Historical Studies in the United States* (Englewood Cliffs, N.J., 1965), p. 387.

minimum-comfort level of living."[4] Although the postwar years were not a time of affluence for all Americans, the economy seemed to have reached a new maturity on the basis of the transforming effects of the New Deal, the Second World War, and several novel ingredients introduced after 1945.

The unaccustomed prosperity brought good jobs, business opportunities, and social mobility. Postwar America, in Eric F. Goldman's colorful phrase, "was not so much settling down as it was settling upward."[5] Visual and statistical evidence alike confirmed the boast that the United States had created the highest standard of living in the history of mankind. Foreign visitors remarked that Americans seemed more prosperous each time they visited the United States. In the new "affluent society" the business world was drawn as if by a magnet to the needs and desires of the consumer. The consumer market not only spread into all manner of personal services but also came to encompass an endless array of durable goods. Americans spent increasing amounts of money for entertainment, recreation, and travel, and the far-flung consumer culture spawned a variety of new institutions such as gourmet food stores, art centers, record stores, and pet shops.

All levels of American society increased their incomes during and after the war, but the relative positions of the various income segments did not change a great deal. The top 5 percent of the recipients got a little over 20 percent of the national income in 1970, as compared to about 33 percent in 1929. On the other hand, the poorest fifth of the population consistently obtained 5 percent or less of the national income during the 1940s and after. In the late 1950s social critics began to point out the persistence of poverty in the United States. One of the writers who publicized its existence was Michael Harrington, who argued in *The Other America* that too much had been made of the country's affluence, since, by his count, something like one-fourth of all Americans were living in poverty. "The millions who are poor in the United States," he wrote, "tend to become increasingly invisible." Yet they were actually all around, not only in the back country of the Appalachian Mountains, but in the Negro slums of the big cities, among migrant workers in the West, among

4. Harold G. Vatter, *The U.S. Economy in the 1950's: An Economic History* (New York, 1963), p. 1.

5. Eric F. Goldman, *The Crucial Decade—And After: America, 1945–1960* (New York, 1960), p. 47.

those everywhere who lacked a high school education, and among the millions of people over sixty-five who were trying to live on incredibly small incomes. As Harrington said, poverty in America "is a culture, an institution, a way of life."[6]

No aspect of the American economy was more prominent than the continuing trend toward large-scale corporate enterprise. By mid-century giant corporations dominated almost every area of the nation's business. The emerging supercorporations were national and even international in operation, bureaucratic in organization, and increasingly diversified in the range of their products and services. Economic concentration clearly led to a decline in traditional competition, increased the incidence of "administered prices," and made for instability in the economy. According to John Kenneth Galbraith in *The New Industrial State* (1967), the huge corporation had achieved such dominance of American industry that it could control its environment and immunize itself from the discipline of the competitive market and all mechanisms of external control. Nevertheless, a good deal of competition continued to exist in certain sectors of the economy, and some economists contended that a system of checks and balances operated to ensure a maximum of efficiency and justice in economic life. Small business enterprise did not disappear, though its role seemed to become less significant. In 1958 there were some five million individually owned businesses outside of farming, mining, and fishing in the United States, but 85 percent of all employed persons were working for someone else—as compared with 36 percent in 1900.

During the New Deal an interplay of powerful public and private groups had come to regulate the economy. The emergence of an industrial labor force into public recognition and organized strength constituted an important part of the changing character of American capitalism. Organized labor continued to grow in the postwar years, but by the fifties the movement had lost its momentum and the unions' share of the total labor force began to decline slightly. A change in public opinion and several legislative acts withdrew some of labor's key advantages. Organized labor's loss of vitality was also related to the changing structure of employment. Increasingly after mid-century new jobs in the labor market were being created in such tertiary areas as government and services rather than manufacturing,

6. Michael Harrington, *The Other America: Poverty in the United States* (New York, 1962), pp. 2, 16.

where some older industries were declining and automation was taking its toll of workers. The white-collar worker was difficult to organize, though the unions eventually began to make gains among such groups as retail clerks, teachers, and government employees. In addition to its loss of militancy, organized labor had become a central institution in the American economy.

Farmers also composed an important element in the political economy of the postwar era. While agriculture in general did not fare as well as most other parts of the economy, the political influence of farm associations and agrarian spokesmen remained strong. Basic agricultural policies adopted during the period of the New Deal were perpetuated year after year, even though much controversy surrounded acreage controls and price supports. Although millions of farmers and agricultural workers fled the farms and the number of farms dropped precipitously, the "farm problem" remained, the paradoxical offspring of a technological revolution in agriculture and great numbers of small and inefficient farm units whose position in the farm economy was steadily made more untenable by that revolution.

Government, too, had come to play a vital role in the operation of American capitalism. Government aided business in many ways, and businessmen more and more looked upon public agencies as allies rather than adversaries. During World War II the federal government began to assume the financial risks of innovation in many areas of scientific research, and this support was expanded after 1945. A community of interests developed between the Pentagon and the corporations that received the bulk of the military procurement funds, and the defense contractors were frequently able to avoid competition or to secure payments for billion-dollar cost overruns, as in the case of Lockheed's C–5 transport plane. Although federal administrators made recurrent attempts through antitrust suits to halt the trend toward ever-greater economic concentration, their successes were limited. As a matter of fact, the public showed little interest in the concentration of control in the economy and could be stirred out of its apathy only by some dramatic evidence of corporate abuse, as in the disclosure to the Kefauver committee in the late 1950s of fantastic profits in the drug industry. Nevertheless, the national government now played an indispensable part in the nation's mixed economy, not so much through stringent regulation as through fiscal and monetary policies, administrative procedures, and assistance to business enterprise by means of a wide range of programs and activities.

So expansive was the United States economy that the output of goods and services doubled and then redoubled during the postwar period. Although the prosperous years after 1961 brought the longest unbroken peacetime economic growth in American history, those years were followed by a time of economic troubles and mounting concern over future prospects. The rate of growth slowed, unemployment reached a relatively high level, and in the 1970s inflation became acute. Meanwhile the administrations in Washington attempted one curative procedure after another without noticeable effect. Faced with fuel crises, worried by pollution and threats to the environment, and frustrated by the problem of uncontrolled inflation, Americans in the seventies were more deeply worried about their economy than at any time since the depression-ridden thirties. It appeared likely in the mid-1970s that the United States, whose economy had become far more interdependent than ever before, was entering an era of painful readjustment.

The enormous growth of the economy and the pervasive influence of technology quickened the pace of social change at midcentury. The population proved to be extraordinarily expansive, increasing from 139.9 million in 1945 to more than 211 million in 1974. The great increase in population and other demographic shifts were basic factors in the evolution of American society after the war. By the mid-1950s, W. W. Rostow observed in 1957, America had become "a suburbanizing nation, increasingly at work in large bureaucracies, with a new security of employment, rising levels of welfare, rising standards of education and of intellectual sophistication, and an increased social and political homogeneity." In certain respects the nation's society had become more homogeneous, more stable, more conservative, and less divided by geography and national origin. As Irene and Conrad Taeuber wrote in 1971, "Ours has been an assimilative society, with geographic migrations and social and economic mobilities contributing to, if not creating, a plural society rather than a fragmented population."[7] Even so, the United States retained much of its ethnic and "racial" heterogeneity.

Americans had always been a people on the move, and in the postwar years the open road beckoned them as never before. Millions of Negroes and poor whites left the South for northern cities during the 1940s and 1950s, and the sunshine and warm climate of

7. W. W. Rostow, "The National Style," in *The American Style: Essays in Value and Performance*, ed. Elting E. Morison (New York, 1958), p. 291; Irene B. Taeuber and Conrad Taeuber, "People of the United States in the Twentieth Century: Continuity, Diversity, and Change," *Items* 25 (1971): 18.

California, Florida, and the Southwest attracted a host of new residents to those regions. In the age of the automobile, the jet airliner, and the expense account, people traveled constantly for business and pleasure. One out of every five Americans changed his place of residence each year. This constant movement, coupled with increasing social mobility, contributed to the erosion of regional, class, and ethnic distinctions and to the nation's growing cultural homogeneity. But the consequences of these movements were also manifested in such social problems as the swelling ghettos of large cities, the disintegrated, uprooted families, and the mounting volume of crime.

Among the most notable features of this geographical mobility was the continued shift from farm to city, bringing with it a decline in rural population and the triumph of the city over the country in customs, manners, and habits of thought. The cities grew so rapidly that, as Constance McLaughlin Green pointed out several years ago, "all American social history had become in essence urban history."[8] The most remarkable characteristic of postwar urbanization was the suburban explosion. By mid-century the suburbs had begun to shape and increasingly to dominate American society. The suburban trend reflected the great increase that was simultaneously taking place in social mobility. Much of the young, active, and better-educated population left the older parts of the metropolis for suburbia. The growth of the suburbs encouraged the decay and disorganization of the great cities and tended to lock millions of nonwhite and other poor people in the urban ghettos.

Social mobility in the United States during the 1940s and 1950s was almost as conspicuous as the movement of people across the face of the land. While there was substantial working-class social mobility in this period, the most impressive economic and social leveling was the broadening of the middle class. The steady increase in per capita income, the vast changes in the structure of employment, and the great expansion in the number of college graduates all helped to swell the ranks of the middle class. A new popular culture was emerging, promoted, as Daniel Bell has written, by "the cultural absorption into American life of the children of the immigrant generation; the *embourgeoisement* of the working class; the spread of suburbia; the increase of income—involving, in turn, a growing desire on the part of the lower middle class to live conspicuously well."

8. Constance McLaughlin Green, *The Rise of Urban America* (New York, 1965), p. 178.

One aspect of this mass culture, as Daniel J. Boorstin has suggested, was the part played by technological developments that have changed the "meaning of the moment" by "democratizing the repeatable experience."[9]

The extent to which political and economic power was monopolized in the postwar period has been a matter of considerable disagreement among social commentators and scholars. It was argued by many political scientists and other social analysts that a "pluralist" system had emerged in the United States, despite the trend toward economic concentration, bureaucracy, and centralized administration. Power in this system was dispersed among numerous voluntary associations or "veto groups," which balanced each other in a rough equilibrium. Other analysts contended that power was concentrated in the hands of economic and social elites. In *The Power Elite* (1956) the sociologist C. Wright Mills asserted that most people in the American political system were powerless and that a complex elite of political, business, and military leaders ruled the country. Mills stressed elite domination rather than class control, but in the 1960s several other writers began to emphasize class differentials and tensions in explaining the concentration of wealth and power in the United States.

If the middle register of the American social order was expanding, it also appeared to be increasingly homogenized. Americans, especially the white-collar employee and the suburban dweller, seemed to conform not only in dress, food, and housing, but even in their ideas. Novels such as Sloan Wilson's *The Man in the Gray Flannel Suit* (1956) and sociological studies like C. Wright Mills's *White Collar: The American Middle Classes* (1951) called attention to the loss of individuality, the stuffiness, and the mindless materialism that characterized much contemporary middle-class living. Machine industry and mass production, some observers noted in the 1950s, were leading to a cultural standardization on a fairly low level and to a loss of individual initiative. The psychologist Erich Fromm, for instance, wrote of the prevalence of individuals with a "marketing orientation," individuals who wanted to avoid having to make choices and eagerly accepted values imposed by the group. David Riesman pointed to the way in which the consumer-oriented

---

9. Daniel Bell, "Modernity and Mass Society: On the Varieties of Cultural Experience," in *Paths of American Thought*, ed. Arthur M. Schlesinger, Jr., and Morton White (Boston, 1963), p. 415; Daniel J. Boorstin, *The Americans: The Democratic Experience* (New York, 1973), pp. 359, 371.

economy reinforced the old American tendency to conform to the tastes and attitudes of one's neighbors. Riesman suggested, in *The Lonely Crowd: A Study of the Changing American Character* (1950), that the national character had changed from an "inner-directed" type, responding to a sort of internal gyroscope, to an "other-directed" personality, basically attuned to the mass values of one's neighbors.

The social conformity that Riesman and other writers described—and probably exaggerated—was related to a widespread nostalgia for older values and a quest for security in the assumed certainty and stability of the old America. An extreme manifestation of this mood was McCarthyism, which, in part at least, was a product of new social anxieties. The so-called radical right of the fifties and sixties seemed to fear not only communism but "modernity" as well, and thus to be alienated from contemporary society. The search for identity among the pressures of a plural but conformist society was a principal theme in the sociological studies of the postwar era. Thus Will Herberg, in *Protestant—Catholic—Jew: An Essay in American Religious Sociology* (1955), interpreted the increased religious activity of contemporary America as a way of maintaining group identity in a democratic society that frowned upon the maintenance of sharply differentiated national groups. Meanwhile, after a period of rising birth rates and preoccupation with domesticity that lasted through the 1950s, the American family began to show unprecedented signs of strain and instability. This was not the case with the voluntary association. In fact, the voluntary group had become more than ever before the primary institution for maintaining American society or reforming it. People were likely to belong to voluntary associations of many types, and in a sense the family, the church, and the community were reduced to virtual subspecies of such organizations.

Political Patterns

The political scene was turbulent and uncertain during Harry S. Truman's presidency. Congress wanted to reassert its authority after the long years of executive dominance under Franklin D. Roosevelt. The Republicans, repeatedly frustrated by Roosevelt's party leadership, were impatiently waiting to resume control of the national government. Every interest group identified with the Democratic party, moreover, came out of the war with high hopes and expectations for the future, and the Truman administration quickly discovered that it was unable to move far in any direction without seeming to jeopardize the gains made by some important group of constituents. Postwar prosperity also weakened the force of economic liberalism. There was a certain ambiguity in the outlook of the new middle class, which was steadily absorbing portions of the "have-not" groups and urban masses attracted to the New Deal in the 1930s. While loyal to New Deal liberalism, on the one hand, these groups were, on the other, becoming more politically conservative. Although Truman won broad support for his foreign policies, his administration's preoccupation with the cold war inhibited domestic reforms and endangered civil liberties.

The early postwar elections proved indecisive. The elections of 1946 returned the Republicans to control of Congress for the first time in sixteen years, but Truman's startling victory in 1948 apparently demonstrated, if not the continuing vitality of the Democratic coalition, at least the determination of its principal components to preserve the gains of the New Deal. In spite of all its vicissitudes, the New Deal constituency held together reasonably well during the Truman years. Still, the politics of stalemate, evident as early as 1939, persisted, sustained by the powerful conservative coalition in Congress, the internal conflict within the majority party, and the ambivalence of the public mood. The Truman administration failed to achieve a breakthrough on the domestic front comparable to the radical new departure it introduced in the international sphere. Truman secured, however, additions to many New Deal programs, and in the Fair Deal he formulated a long-range agenda for liberal action.

Dwight D. Eisenhower's huge majority in 1952 apparently indicated the breakup of the Roosevelt coalition. Coming to office at a time of confusion, division, and bitterness, the immensely popular "Ike" rendered the politics of the 1950s less acrimonious, eased the tensions after a generation of crisis, and helped restore a sense of national unity. Eisenhower's restrained approach to government and his moderate Republicanism blended comfortably into a national mood of complacency, well-being, and self-indulgence. Richard Rovere has suggested that, in part because he was a Republican, the thirty-fourth president was able to do "many of the things that needed doing and that could not have been done by a Democratic administration."[10] Thus he liquidated the Korean War without being called an appeaser and accepted the essential features of the Roosevelt "revolution," helping to consolidate it as the programma-

10. Richard H. Rovere, "Eisenhower over the Shoulder," *American Scholar* 31 (Spring 1962): 177.

tic base of American politics. Yet the general did little to alter the static quality of the nation's politics, and he interpreted his mandate in domestic affairs as one of conservatism and slowing the pace of change.

The yearning for repose and the conservative temper began to change in the late 1950s. The Democrats, who regained control of Congress in 1954 and greatly strengthened their majorities in 1958, became more aggressive. During the second Eisenhower administration they began to develop new programs, draft remedial measures, and secure party commitment to such reform proposals. These developments laid the basis for what would ultimately become the New Frontier and the Great Society. Taking advantage of a cultural shift that had begun to spread through American society and identifying himself with the growing desire for a renewed sense of national purpose and a more dynamic government in Washington, John F. Kennedy narrowly won the presidency in 1960. Kennedy was the first Catholic to become president, and his election seemed to signal a reorientation of American politics. But he was unable to end the executive-legislative deadlock in Washington, even though his style and personality had a remarkable impact upon his contemporaries, particularly young people. His tragic death produced its own mythology, including the legend of Camelot, whose gallant king gave the nation a moment of glory before dying for its sins.

Making the most of Kennedy's martyrdom and associating himself with the goals of the New Frontier, Lyndon B. Johnson completed the enactment of his predecessor's reform measures and proceeded to sponsor the most advanced program of social reform in American history. For the first time in more than a quarter century the hold of the southern Democratic-Republican coalition in Congress was broken. In the mid-1960s a spate of Great Society bills swept through the two houses on Capitol Hill. Johnson also created, momentarily, what he liked to consider a national political consensus. The consensus seemed to be evident in Johnson's landslide victory at the polls in 1964, a triumph produced by the president's record of accomplishments and the Republican party's venture into militant conservatism under the leadership of Senator Barry M. Goldwater. The senator's extremism alarmed and divided the Republican party, allowing Johnson to capture the political center.

Then, almost overnight it seemed, the Johnsonian consensus was disrupted and the Great Society lost its momentum. The dark forebodings aroused by John F. Kennedy's assassination in 1963 and the Watts riot of 1965 were realized with a vengeance in the social violence and conflict that characterized the following years. Johnson became increasingly preoccupied with the war in Vietnam, which provoked a far-reaching protest movement at home, tested the fundamental assumptions underlying American foreign policy, and encouraged a critical reappraisal of the nation's political institutions, culture, and values. The president's problems were complicated by what many Americans came to see as his duplicity—his "credibility gap." Frustrated and unable to govern effectively, Johnson suddenly announced, in March 1968, that he would not accept another nomination as his party's candidate for president. But by this time the Democratic party was riddled by schism. The ensuing struggle for the nomination, the murder of Robert F. Kennedy, and the bitter confrontations at the Democratic national convention in Chicago completed the party's disarray. The Democratic coalition was threatened both by the fragmentation of the political left and by the defection of southern whites and working-class Democrats, many of whom were attracted by the conservatism of Governor George C. Wallace.

Richard M. Nixon, the Republican nominee in 1968, took advantage of the divisions in the Democratic party and the spreading wave of reaction among millions of Americans. Like Eisenhower in 1952, Nixon promised to end the war in the Far East and to restore stability and unity to American society. Nixon's campaign was also designed to take advantage of the fact that race relations and crime and lawlessness, along with the Vietnam War, had become the major areas of public concern in the United States. Emphasizing what he called the "forgotten Americans," the Republican leader urged an end to violence and confrontations, the need for retrenchment and a reexamination of domestic welfare programs, and a commitment to the support of "law and order." His "southern strategy" enabled him to divide the South with Wallace's American Independent party. The public sought out the "defensive middle ground" in 1968, and as David S. Broder says, the central paradox of the election is that, in a year of almost unprecedented violence, turmoil, and political oscillations, the electorate gave "a terribly conventional result." [11] Nixon's popular plurality was nevertheless only slightly larger than Hubert H. Humphrey's vote, and the election was one of the closest in modern United States history.

11. David S. Broder, "Election of 1968," in *History of American Presidential Elections, 1789–1968,* ed. Arthur M. Schlesinger, Jr., and Fred L. Israel (New York, 1971), 4: 3705.

Although the Nixon administration catered to the fears and prejudices of the "silent majority," the Republicans lost the midterm congressional elections of 1970 and approached the presidential election of 1972 with great apprehension. But they benefited from the strife-torn Democratic party and from Senator George S. McGovern's image as a candidate of the left, as well as from the president's bold initiatives in foreign affairs. Despite the fact that Democrats continued to control Congress, Nixon's overwhelming electoral success in 1972 seemed to provide support for the idea of an emerging Republican majority. Republican hopes were quickly dashed, however, by the Watergate scandal, which dominated national politics in 1973 and 1974, forced President Nixon's resignation in the face of almost certain impeachment, and brought Gerald R. Ford to the White House in August 1974 as the nation's thirty-eighth president.

Several explosive issues came to the fore in the years after 1945, arousing deep emotions among the voters and cutting across the existing party structure. The Republican party, as the minority party, attempted to capitalize on these potentially realigning issues, while the majority Democrats, hoping to avoid realignment, usually emphasized the traditional economic and class-related issues that had served them well in the 1930s.

Communism was the first of these major issues to develop following the war. In the late 1940s and early 1950s an exaggerated fear of internal subversion swept over the United States. Frustrated by their loss of the presidency in 1948 and encouraged by a series of shocking developments in 1949 and 1950, including the fall of Nationalist China and the Korean War, Republican leaders eagerly seized upon anticommunism as a partisan issue. In addition the race question emerged as a powerful political issue in the 1950s. It lent a new urgency to the problem of racial injustice, contributed to the coalescence of a new wave of social reform, and became the most immediate factor in the defection of the South from the classic Democratic coalition.

In the 1960s two other issues had a profound impact upon the nation's politics: Vietnam and the question of "law and order." The bitter conflict engendered by Lyndon B. Johnson's policies in Vietnam fragmented the Democratic party, promoted the rise of a new social radicalism in America, and made it possible for the Republicans to recapture the White House in 1968. The issue of "law and order"—what Richard M. Scammon and Ben J. Wattenberg have labeled "the social issue" [12]—was also employed to good effect by Republicans. Closely related to the race issue, "law and order" became code words that summed up the growing middle-class fear of violence and opposition to crime, ghetto riots, student disorders, and the national welfare system.

Although Dwight Eisenhower and Richard Nixon shattered the Democratic majority coalition in presidential elections, no major party realignment has occurred since the 1930s. The election of 1952 proved to be a deviation, and despite the remarkable majority registered for the Republican presidential ticket in 1972, the Democrats retained control of Congress and more than held their own in state and local elections. None of the issues of the postwar period produced a decisive political realignment, mainly, it appears, because they were not issues on which the major parties took distinct and opposing policy positions. In other words, the two parties have not differed much on basic policy objectives, but rather, as James L. Sundquist observes in *Dynamics of the Party System* (1973), on the selection and administration of the means to agreed-upon ends. Only the race question, of the four disruptive issues cited here, still seems to offer some prospect as a realigning issue. Nevertheless, all of these issues had a disrupting effect upon the Democratic party, and while the Democrats continued to get a majority of the total votes in national elections, many of their supporters became less firmly attached to the party than in earlier years. Indeed, the movement of large numbers of voters from identification with either of the major parties to independence is one of the most pronounced trends in contemporary American politics. At least a third of the nation's voters now classify themselves as independents, and there is a great deal more ticket splitting than formerly.

Despite the fierce party battles and the polarizing effects of issues like communism in government and racial equality, a fundamental consensus prevailed in American political thought during the early postwar period. The relative success of the New Deal in creating a "balanced" society, along with the threat of totalitarianism before and after the war, promoted this consensus. The war itself, while weakening liberalism in some respects, encouraged a broad reaffirmation of American society and values. Liberals and conserva-

12. Richard M. Scammon and Ben J. Wattenberg, *The Real Majority* (New York, 1970), pp. 20–21, 35–44.

tives now seemed less distinct, less separated by ideological differences. Following the war the Republican party accepted the essentials of the New Deal as well as the cold-war assumptions and containment policies of the Truman administration. Liberals assumed a militantly anti-Communist position and stressed what Arthur M. Schlesinger, Jr., called "the vital center" in his book of that name (1949), a central doctrine midway between the totalitarian poles of fascism and communism. President Truman and other American liberals also stressed a new approach to economics—the notion of a continually expanding capitalist economy undergirded by Keynesian fiscal policies and an extensive social welfare program.

The widespread satisfaction with the American system was reflected in the work of the consensualist social scientists and historians who influenced the intellectual currents of the 1950s. Emphasizing the positive and functional side of existing institutions in the United States, they tended to assign a normative role to America's pluralistic, democratic capitalism. Some social theorists such as Daniel Bell even proclaimed "the end of ideology" in the economically mature democracies of the West, whose "open" and pluralistic societies had apparently avoided the dangers of philosophical absolutism and monolithic social structures.[13]

Momentarily, at the height of Johnson's Great Society, liberalism seemed on the verge of realizing its most cherished goals. But a time of crisis quickly followed, precipitated by the struggle in Vietnam but also reflecting the criticisms of earlier dissenters. "Something in the experience of many young men and women at the end of the 1950s," writes Irwin Unger, "had produced an altered consciousness that made for a critical, disapproving, and hostile view of American—and Western European—life and created a desire to change it in drastic ways."[14] By the mid-1960s the intellectual-political consensus was under sharp attack, and much of the criticism came from within the political left. The growing awareness of poverty and racism in America, the sharpening perception of a military-industrial complex, and the endless and destructive war in Southeast Asia created mounting disillusionment, protest, and radical social critiques. A "New Left" took shape, calling attention to the shortcomings of the nation's pluralistic economy and challenging the

13. Daniel Bell, *The End of Ideology: On the Exhaustion of Political Ideas in the Fifties,* rev. ed. (New York, 1962).

14. Irwin Unger, *The Movement: A History of the American New Left, 1959–1972* (New York, 1974), p. 29.

accuracy of "pluralism" as a description of American society. By the early 1970s the New Left as a phenomenon of social relevance had gone into eclipse, its demise hastened by Nixon's foreign policy initiatives, Watergate, and daily concern over a runaway inflation. Perhaps cultural dissent will be the New Left's most lasting contribution. But in any case, the radical criticism of the late sixties was part of a broader reevaluation of American life, part of a moral and esthetic revolution that may constitute a watershed in our recent experience.

Revolutionary Themes

One avenue to an understanding of postwar America is to identify and evaluate the complex social changes that have swept through our society during the past three decades. The revolutionary spirit in this period has had many facets—technological, social and economic, political, and cultural. But among the multiple revolutions in American life since the end of the Second World War none was more portentous than the involvement of the United States with the rest of the world. Americans soon discovered that in the cold war it was virtually impossible to discuss domestic questions without referring to foreign affairs; almost every political issue was affected with a global interest. Geographically the nation's diplomatic concerns became far broader than ever before, and many new agencies and instruments were soon involved in the conduct of foreign relations.

Americans had begun to forsake their traditional isolationism in the late thirties. The Japanese attack on Pearl Harbor destroyed the old myth of American impregnability, and during the war the United States became the organizer and leader of the United Nations in destroying the Axis powers and establishing an international organization for peace. Most Americans thought that it was both possible and desirable for the United States to use its immense power to help reshape the world along the lines of its own democratic capitalism. A national consensus soon developed to support Washington's opposition to the Soviet Union in the cold war, which Americans viewed in terms of mortal combat between their own traditional ideals and moral judgments and a "totalitarian" system and an "evil" ideology. They were prepared to tolerate a long period of twilight between total war and total peace, a generation of almost unrelieved tension, repeated crises, and prolonged stalemate.

The revolution in American foreign policy was directly related, of course, to certain changes in the rest of the world. One such change was the decline of Europe's preeminence in world affairs, a development associated with the collapse of Western imperialism, the revolt of the peoples of Asia and Africa, the rise of Eastern nationalism, and the polarization of power between the United States and the Soviet Union. A second impetus to America's changing foreign policy was the end of what C. Vann Woodward has described as "the era of free security"—the physical security from hostile attack and invasion the country enjoyed through most of its history. The end of this era came so suddenly and swiftly that Americans could hardly bring themselves to face its practical implications.[15] A third factor in transforming the nation's foreign policy was the revolution in weapons technology that began during World War II. Historic changes in weapons, tactics, and strategy were insignificant when contrasted with the distance separating the preatomic and the nuclear ages.

The bulwark of American foreign policy in the cold war was the doctrine of containment. First applied in 1947 when the Truman Doctrine was devised to counter the Russian attempt to make a major breakthrough in the eastern Mediterranean and the Marshall Plan was worked out to deal with the postwar crisis in Europe, containment was later extended to Asia and the Middle East. Tension between the two superpowers waxed and waned, but the United States steadily adhered to the containment rationale. The policy of deterrence was a companion of containment. In order to block Communist expansion, U.S. leaders insisted that the country must possess military power of such formidable proportions as to discourage or prevent any attempt by its adversaries to take territory by force. It is not surprising that the Russians made the same assumptions. A third American policy in the postwar period was aid to underdeveloped areas. It was assumed in the Marshall Plan and other programs that one way to fight communism was to use United States wealth to provide succor to the poor, the hungry, and the hopeless in non-Communist lands. Humanitarian considerations and an awareness of long-range economic benefits also motivated American policy makers. The most popular addition to foreign-aid programs in the 1960s was the Peace Corps, which effectively combined youthful idealism and many forms of technical assistance.

President Truman's decisive action in sending American troops

---

15. C. Vann Woodward, *The Age of Reinterpretation*, Service Center for Teachers of History Series, no. 35 (Washington, 1961), pp. 2–7.

into battle in support of South Korea demonstrated that the United States would enforce its containment policy in the Far East as well as in Europe. But the Korean War put many aspects of the new foreign policy to the test, and after the Eisenhower administration ended the struggle with a compromise settlement in 1953, the focus of American concern in East Asia shifted to Indochina. The large-scale United States involvement in the Vietnam War that began in 1965 eventually brought about a partial repudiation of the containment doctrine. The rapprochement with Communist China and the détente with the Soviet Union arranged by President Nixon and Henry A. Kissinger attested to the fact that international affairs were no longer dominated by the East-West conflict and the old cold-war suppositions. By the 1970s there were at least five great power centers—the United States, Russia, Western Europe, China, and Japan—and American leaders were searching for viable arrangements that would recognize the new realities. Opinion surveys in the early 1970s indicated that a growing percentage of Americans wanted their country to assume a more modest role in international affairs and that many people no longer considered it important for the United States to be "the world's most powerful nation." Vietnam also stimulated an attempt to curb presidential power in foreign policy, especially the power to commit troops to battle. The military establishment remained powerful, however, and "national security" continued to evoke broad public support.

Another revolutionary change in postwar America occurred in the position of the nation's largest minority group. Stimulated by the political ferment of the New Deal and by the economic advances and democratic slogans of the Second World War, Negro leaders and organizations in the late 1940s and early 1950s began more vigorously to assert their claim to equality and to protest their race's second-class status. The Truman administration committed itself to a broad civil rights program, and in 1954 the United States Supreme Court, in *Brown* v. *Board of Education of Topeka,* handed down an epochal decision that served to mobilize the energies of the black community and to give impetus to a great national reform movement. The role of the Supreme Court as an agent of change in race relations was the most conspicuous part of a far-reaching judicial revolution in the fifties and sixties embracing democratic and libertarian goals.

The civil rights movement soon entered into a more active phase in which new leaders, new organizations, and new tactics came to the fore. Having found a great symbolic leader in Martin Luther

King, Jr., and a powerful tactic in the doctrine of nonviolent resistance, the equal rights movement gained still more impetus and achieved a new urgency. The federal government was drawn increasingly into the struggle, both by forcing compliance with desegregation court decisions, as at Little Rock, Arkansas, and Oxford, Mississippi, and in the passage of stronger laws. As public pressure mounted and the Kennedy and Johnson administrations mobilized their full resources in behalf of stronger legislation, Congress finally responded, in 1964, with the enactment of a comprehensive Civil Rights Act that outlawed segregation in places of public accommodation and struck at other types of racial discrimination. In 1965 a sweeping voting rights law was adopted, and during the following year still other federal restrictions against racial discrimination were written into law. By the mid-1960s the "Second Reconstruction" had achieved far more than had the first Reconstruction almost a century earlier, leading C. Vann Woodward to conclude, in a revised edition of *The Strange Career of Jim Crow*, that a "national consensus" on the race issue "was in the making and a peaceful solution was in sight."[16]

But even as state-imposed segregation was being struck down there were signs that the black American's long quest for equality was still far from being won. Ironically the legal and political progress of the early sixties served to heighten black expectations, which all too often were not realized. Nothing revealed the growing mood of frustration, bitterness, and anger in the black community more dramatically than the explosion of ghetto riots between 1964 and 1968. By the middle of the decade the transformation of black protest from its emphasis on civil rights to what came to be called "black power" had already begun. Nonviolence as the guiding philosophy of black protest was increasingly challenged by black power. White and black attitudes were rapidly polarized, a "white backlash" began to manifest itself throughout the country, and "law and order" emerged as a key political issue. A variety of militant black leaders and organizations appeared, emphasizing black nationalism, self-determination through economic and political power, and the development of black pride and Afro-American culture.

Although racial tensions subsided somewhat as the political climate became less volatile in the early 1970s, the reality of racial in-

16. C. Vann Woodward, *The Strange Career of Jim Crow*, 2d rev. ed. (New York, 1966), p. 189.

equality in America was still widely apparent. Yet a great social upheaval and a vast alteration had taken place in race relations in the United States in the postwar era. Equal rights for black Americans had become a momentous national issue, a new crisis in federalism had been precipitated, and the national government had mobilized its authority to destroy the legal structure of segregation and to combat racial discrimination in its many forms. The black revolution also served as a catalyst for other minority groups, which quickly began to emulate its organizations and tactics. The Chicano movement in the Mexican-American community, for instance, was based upon a deepening commitment to end discrimination against the members of that group and to uphold the values of cultural pluralism.

A third revolutionary theme in contemporary America is the "crisis of the cities." Somewhat paradoxically, the metropolis during the last three decades has been the dominating influence in American life while simultaneously sprawling far out into the surrounding countryside and being fragmented into scores of discrete population groupings. As the exodus from the central city to the mushrooming suburbs continued in the postwar years, most large cities were hard hit by the separation between the two regions. A whole range of social and human problems developed having to do with welfare, housing, education, transportation, crime, and the drug traffic. Much of the nation's social turmoil in the sixties and seventies was centered in its large cities, leading to talk of the "dying city." The urban crisis evoked extensive social analysis, and a great deal of energy and money was mobilized in reconstruction efforts, extending all the way from the activities of local governments and private organizations to federal programs like Johnson's Great Society.

Two other relatively new issues were related to the urban crisis. One of these was the sudden "discovery" of poverty in the midst of postwar affluence. Although millions of rural dwellers in contemporary America lived in poverty, the urban ghettos provided spectacular evidence of economically depressed elements. Thus the city slums were a major target of the federal government's war on poverty in the 1960s. The metropolitan areas were also a focal point of the growing environmental crisis. One reason for the rapid growth of the suburbs was the desire to escape from the congestion, noise, and pollution of the inner city and to find more space, clean air, and trees. Wherever they lived, Americans were increasingly aware of the fact that economic growth was accompanied by unwanted side effects, including a steady decline in the quality of the air and water, a series of man-made disasters of ecological imbalance, and widening alarm over the imminent destruction of the natural environment.

Still another manifestation of revolution in the postwar period was cultural in nature. An upheaval in American culture occurred in the late 1960s. This cultural revolution was evident in the emergence of a radical movement in politics, a counterculture led by young people, and a new morality that promoted a revolt against institutional unresponsiveness and hypocrisy, social inhumanity, and depersonalized life-styles. The protest against the Vietnam War triggered much of this dissent, but its roots reached down to more fundamental conditions such as the enormous strain placed on existing institutions by population growth and rapid technological change, the dominance of giant organizations in government, industry, labor, and education, and the pervasive feeling of impotence and powerlessness that overcame modern man. According to Theodore Roszak in *The Making of a Counter Culture* (1969), the cultural rebellion of youth was fundamentally a revolt against the dehumanizing effect of scientific and technological values and against an increasingly impersonal and bureaucratic society and in favor of the New Left's participatory democracy. The students who attacked the military-industrial complex in the late 1960s were rebelling against the anonymity of contemporary society and the impersonality and bureaucracy of the multiversities, the government, and virtually every important social institution. The student insurgence, the development of a counterculture, and the women's liberation movement all demonstrated in one way or another the search for new forms of community in a swiftly changing society.

The crisis of confidence that overtook Americans in the late sixties and early seventies mirrored a remarkable change in national outlook. A profound crisis of the spirit had settled over America, accompanied by a deep-seated pessimism unknown in the United States since the depths of the Great Depression. A series of enervating events contributed to this sense of foreboding. The energy crisis of the 1970s evoked the image of an economic "catastrophe," and the growing importance of ecological issues reflected the alarming realization that the quality of life itself might be worsening. The experience of the United States in Vietnam, more than any other aspect of the nation's recent history, demonstrated the limits of American power, destroyed a large part of the public's confidence in the country's capacity to deal with foreign and domestic problems, and bruised the national spirit as had no other development in the twentieth century. Then came Watergate, which made Americans acutely aware of the fragility of their political institutions and deepened the doubts that had already entered the public consciousness. But the malaise went deeper still, to fundamental questions like the sanctity of work, the stability of the family, and the threat to such "familiar totems" as premarital chastity, the postponement of gratification, and filial gratitude for parental sacrifice.

The years after 1945 also dealt harshly with some of our national myths—with such illusions as America's uniqueness, moral superiority, invincibility, and inevitable success. Americans had long thought of themselves as a chosen people, as what Paul Varg has described as "the model republican society that the rest of the world would emulate." [17] Such assumptions died hard, but in a new age of revolution they could no longer be sustained with widespread confidence. Still, few Americans were inclined to adopt a fatalistic outlook. Somehow they could not share the attitude of Daniel Patrick Moynihan, one of Kennedy's New Frontiersmen. When the young president was struck down in Dallas, Moynihan stood the shock better than most, remarking simply, "I don't think there's any point in being Irish if you don't know that the world is going to break your heart eventually." [18] Most Americans yearned for a happy ending, or at least for the promise of one. We Americans, observes Professor Woodward, have characteristically sought our identity in the future. Perhaps we still do, and like F. Scott Fitzgerald's Gatsby believe in the "future that year by year recedes before us." "It eluded us then," Fitzgerald wrote at the end of *The Great Gatsby*, "but that's no matter—tomorrow we will run faster, stretch out our arms farther. . . . And one fine morning—"

Historiographical Perspectives

Scholarly inquiry into United States history since 1945 is still in an early stage. The character of the Truman period has been marked out in our recent political history, the nature of postwar foreign policy has been probed, and the civil rights movement has been elucidated by historians and other scholars. Otherwise the history of the last three decades remains in large part *terra incognita*. There are as

17. Paul A. Varg, *Foreign Policies of the Founding Fathers* (East Lansing, 1963), p. 303.

18. Quoted in William L. O'Neill, *Coming Apart: An Informal History of America in the 1960's* (Chicago, 1971), p. 93.

yet relatively few historical monographs and virtually no large-scale syntheses for the postwar era. Much of the literature that exists is understandably impressionistic, lacking in historical depth, and weak in analytical techniques. Even though the new interest in black history and the history of other neglected minorities has stimulated and broadened historical research, the best of this work has tended to focus on earlier periods.

For much that has happened in the recent past one must rely on the explosion of "instant" social history, social commentary, and eyewitness accounts sparked by postwar events. Writings in this genre are rarely satisfactory as history, but they are often valuable not only for their reconstruction of what happened but also for their assessment of the impact of motivating forces and the role of public opinion. Theodore H. White's *The Making of the President, 1960* (1961) is an example of a vivid eyewitness account that is well worth reading by anyone interested in contemporary American history. Books by participants are sometimes essential. Thus Dean Acheson's sprightly *Present at the Creation: My Years in the State Department* (1969) throws light on the foreign policy of the Truman administration. The two volumes of George F. Kennan's *Memoirs, 1925–1963* (1967–72) are a contribution both to the historiography of the cold war and to an understanding of decision making in recent U.S. foreign policy.

Some of the work of social scientists is even more valuable in reconstructing contemporary American history. Sociologists and other social scientists have often written the first scholarly interpretations of the recent past, though their primary object has usually been to analyze the nature of modern society. These studies also frequently compare contemporary phenomena with those of earlier periods. Social science investigations into such areas as urban problems, race relations, and the environmental crisis illuminate recent history, as do analyses of contemporary voting behavior, legislative action, economic development, and demographic trends. Historians have also been influenced by the ideas, concepts, and methods of the social sciences, and developments in those disciplines have brought them closer to various public policy concerns and stimulated their interest in interdisciplinary research.

The exigencies of the Second World War and the onset of the cold war encouraged a broad sympathy for the American past among historians. The early historical accounts of the postwar period reflected this conservative view, leading in the 1950s to a "consensus" emphasis upon the uniformities in our national life. Historical writings on the recent past also mirrored a broader interest in a new institutional approach and an organizational synthesis that focused upon social systems which increasingly defined and gave meaning to the lives of Americans. Finally, the radical revisionism of the 1960s had a telling impact on the historiography of the postwar era. The historians of the New Left condemned the cold war, distrusted established groups, opposed the "old politics," and began to elaborate a critical analysis of traditional American liberalism. They were intent upon creating a "new" past that would lend support to their analysis of contemporary society and politics. Responding to the events of the 1960s, the revisionists helped promote historical inquiry into such fields as black history and the reinterpretation of the cold war.

As might be expected, the Truman administration has been the subject of more historical study than any other part of the postwar era. The Truman presidency attracted historians not only because of the availability of many of its sources but also because numerous social and political crises after mid-century first became visible during that period. The substantial extent of the historical scholarship on the Truman years was revealed in a book edited by Richard S. Kirkendall in 1967 entitled *The Truman Period as a Research Field*. A sequel to this volume—*The Truman Period as a Research Field: A Reappraisal, 1972* (1974)—consisted of a set of conflicting interpretations of the Truman administration. It showed, in addition to the continuing progress of historical research and writing on the period, the impact of revisionist scholarship on its historiography, including what one contributor described as the "demythologizing tone" of recent Truman literature. Most important, perhaps, was the evidence these two volumes provided of solid monographs and specialized studies in such areas as agriculture, labor, housing, veterans' affairs, congressional action, civil rights, internal security, and foreign policy.

Gaddis Smith has pointed out that the historian dealing with American foreign relations since the end of World War II confronts three special problems: the size and complexity of the subject; the diversity, immensity, and partial inaccessibility of sources; and the "distorting impact" of the Vietnam War on the perceptions of both the interpreter and his students.[19] But these handicaps have not deterred scholars from entering into the field of postwar American diplomacy, and in fact no other aspect of recent United States history

---

19. Gaddis Smith, "The United States in World Affairs since 1945," in *The Reinterpretation of American History and Culture*, ed. William H. Cartwright and Richard L. Watson, Jr. (Washington, 1973), p. 543.

has been quite so extensively investigated. Much of the early post-war work in diplomatic history was carried out by the so-called power realism school—historians and political scientists such as George F. Kennan, Hans Morgenthau, and Robert E. Osgood. They tended to be critical of United States policy on the grounds that it was too often moralistic, legalistic, and inflexible, and that it thereby sacrificed the national interest. A more thoroughgoing group of re-visionists began to emerge in the early 1960s.

One of the most influential members of this group was William Appleman Williams, who as early as 1959 published *The Tragedy of American Diplomacy*, a wide-ranging reinterpretation that explained United States foreign policy as largely the result of a conscious, ideological commitment to open-door expansion. Most of the New Left historians in later years stressed economic factors instead of ideology in explaining American expansion. But they were all in-clined to view the American past as discreditable and in need of revising. They have been primarily interested in the origins of the cold war and in the American involvement in Vietnam. The New Left analysis of Vietnam contrasts both with the official interpretation and with a liberal dissenting one that pictured the American entrap-ment as an honest but tragic mistake. Radical revisionist histories concentrated on American behavior to the neglect of what was hap-pening in other countries, were frequently present-minded in pro-jecting current fears and frustrations onto history, and exaggerated the impact of economic forces on decision making while slighting the interplay of domestic politics and public opinion in the formulation of U.S. foreign policies. Nevertheless, New Left interpretations pro-vided a useful antidote to the generally admiring view of American policy held by many diplomatic historians.

All of these interpretive emphases have enriched our percep-tions of the period since 1945. Although the great expanse of our contemporary history—from the 1950s on—is just beginning to be intensively studied by historians, the embryonic historiography of the postwar era is dynamic, controversial, and increasingly complex. It is clearly a part of the larger reinterpretation of American history that is now under way.

Index

Racial imperative, in the South, 77–106
(*See also* Racial attitudes; Racism)
Racism, xi; in the South, 5–6, 82–83,
88–90, 99, 104–106, 108, 216, 224
Radical Reconstruction (*see*
Reconstruction)
Railroad regulation: federal, 52; in the
South, 57
Raleigh *News and Observer*, 81, 137; on
Roosevelt-Washington dinner, 40, 42
Raleigh *Post*, 40
Raper, Arthur F., 169
Ratchford, Benjamin U., 176
Readjusters, in Virginia, 5
Reapportionment, in the South, 16, 217
Reconstruction, 5, 9n, 11, 25, 26, 31, 35,
149; First, 23, 79, 82, 87, 112; Second,
14–16, 18, 23, 151, 185–86, 192–97, 199,
220, 225, 252
Redeemers, southern, 6, 24, 29
Redemption, of the South, 4, 82
Reed, John Shelton, 53, 229
Reelfoot Lake, and night riders, 66, 74
Reelfoot Lake Fish Company, 74
Regional imagination, ix, xi, 153, 154,
168, 184
(*See also* Social sciences, in the South;
South, intellectual development of)
Regional Land Tenure Research Project,
177
Regionalism: as a concept, ix, 153, 169,
182-83; literature of in 1930s, 168–69;
in modern America, ix, 154, 159, 161,
165, 183; as a tool of analysis in the
South, 165–68, 176, 183
Religion, and racial orthodoxy in the
South, 105, 106
Religious fundamentalism, 9, 161
Religious issue: in Louisiana politics,
19n; in presidential election of 1960,
213
Republican party, 17, 34, 42, 51, 81,
242–48
in the South, 7, 12, 13n, 16, 92, 150,
199, 204, 205, 219, 221
in Kentucky, 56–57, 62
in mountain areas, 12
and Negro participation, 34–35
during 1930s, 10
obstacles to full development, 17
recent growth, 212–16, 225–26
after Reconstruction, 4, 6, 20
in southern legislatures, 17n
in Tennessee, 6n, 61
urban, 213–15, 217
victories in 1928, 9

Research commissions, in southern
states, 174
Research institutes, in southern
universities, 159, 163
Rhodes, James Ford, 48
Richmond *Planet*, 96
Richmond *Times*, 38
Riesman, David, 241–42
Ringold, May Spencer, 28
Robinson, Walter, 147
Robock, Stefan, 176
Rockefeller Foundation, 11, 164, 172
Roosevelt, Franklin D., 9, 152, 203, 224,
242; influence in the South, 10, 147,
201, 227, 228; and southern
congressmen, 10–11
Roosevelt, Theodore, 34, 60, 89, 93, 108,
113; and appointment policy in the
South, 33–37, 48–49, 51; and dinner
with Booker T. Washington, 33–34,
37–49, 52, 80; and Indianola
controversy, 49–50; on the Negro
question, 49n, 50; southern response
to, 34–35, 37–46, 48–50,52
Roosevelt, Mrs. Theodore, 39, 50
Roosevelt administration (1930s), 20, 202
Roosevelt-Washington dinner, 33–34,
37–49, 51–52, 80
Rosenwald Fund, 135, 160, 163
Rostow, W. W., 239
Roszak, Theodore, 254
Rovere, Richard, 243
Rubin, Morton, 178
Rural-urban cleavage, in southern
politics, 9, 208

Saloutos, Theodore, 66
Sartorises, 15n
Savage, Henry, Jr., 31
Scammon, Richard M., 246
Schlesinger, Arthur M., Jr., 248
Schomburg Collection, New York Public
Library, 135
School of Applied Sociology in New
Orleans, 93
School desegregation, in the South,
185-97
Scott, Emmett J., 44
Scott, Kerr, 205
Secession crisis, 3, 4
Sectional reconciliation, 25
Sectional rivalries (*see* Sectionalism)
Sectional solidarity (*see* Solid South)
Sectionalism, southern, x, 2–3, 6, 7, 8,
14, 16